The Crazy Life of Brendan Behan

The Rise and Fall
of Dublin's Laughing Boy

By Frank Gray

authorHOUSE®

AuthorHouse™ UK Ltd.
500 Avebury Boulevard
Central Milton Keynes, MK9 2BE
www.authorhouse.co.uk
Phone: 08001974150

© 2010 By Frank Gray. All rights reserved.

No part of this book may be reproduced, stored in a retrieval system, or transmitted by any means without the written permission of the author.

First published by AuthorHouse 8/23/2010

ISBN: 978-1-4490-6895-0 (sc)

This book is printed on acid-free paper.

Prologue

BRENDAN FRANCIS BEHAN, the Irish playwright known as much for his off-stage antics as his on-stage story-making skills, was born in Dublin's Holles street hospital on February 9 1923 and died in the Meath hospital, on March 20 1964. His wife, Beatrice ffrench-Salkeld, was born in south Dublin four years later and would go on to survive him by another twenty-nine years. She finally succumbed to what these days we would call depression. She died at the Anglesea Road house where she lived for five years with her husband and where she went on to live till her death in 1993. She was buried alongside Brendan's grave marker, a huge granite stone shaped like a fist with a hole in it. It bears the simple inscription in the Irish language *brendan o beachain.*

There is not much significance these days in being able to say which side of Dublin, north or south (the river runs west to east), marked one's place of birth. A lot of water has flowed along the banks of the Liffey since Behan's heyday and what was significant to one generation of people is less so for the next. But in Behan's youth, and up to recent times, account had to be taken of such matters. Ireland, with its concentrated population and still wearing the slow-healing wounds of an intense civil conflict with England, was a deeply political country. So it was for those reasons that southsiders were considered to be louche, a little too well fed and less politically acute than their northside bretheren who, to a man, were considered Republican-supporting sons of the soil. To be a southsider somehow made one a little less Irish. No wonder then that such rock-ribbed republican stock as Brendan Behan took care to draw a curtain on his south side origins. To have claimed to be a northsider while knowingly having been born south of the Liffey was seen as a near-traitorous act, at least in the country's pubs. It goes beyond the fact that the Holles and Meath hospitals were located on the south side. In political families it always helped a little to be able to claim a date of birth on or after January 1 1922 – day one of the establishment of the interim Irish Free State government and the commencement of Ireland's phased independence from England. To have been born even a single day earlier, and to have claimed otherwise, was tantamount to having missed the dawn of creation, or worse, to have been born 'English'. Behan, one of 20th century Ireland's most renowned nationalist personalities, was safe by a year but for the fact of his having been born south of the Liffey.For this reason, he took care to avoid any probing discussion of his birth details. Better to leave the lid shut on this most personal issue.

Brendan Behan lasted only to the age of 41 before succumbing to a variety of drink-related afflictions. Beatrice, better known among friends as 'Beatsie,' was, like her husband, 'partial to a drink,' but she was not an alcoholic. She knew the secret of his birth circumstances, but she would brook no discussion of it. In this and many other ways she was protective of her reckless husband. She eventually yielded to the rigours of a turbulent life. It would have been more accurate for her autopsy to have given as cause of death: Life with Brendan!

But 'life' – often in the extreme -- was what it was all about. In the space of a decade (1954-64), Brendan Behan rocketed to fame as a playwright, autobiographer, columnist, humorist, wit, roustabout, debauchee, charmer. He wrote, or assembled, perhaps a dozen works. Most are out of print now but for his three enduring works, *The Quare Fellow, The Hostage* and *Borstal Boy.* Some would, incorrectly, have called him, an icon, a term he would have detested. He liked the roar of the crowd and convinced himself he could cope with instant fame, the more reckless the better. He had had plenty of practice on his noisy perambulations around the streets of Dublin, Paris, London and finally New York, the scene of his greatest triumph.

Depending on how one is operating his moral compass, Behan can be said to have indulged himself in a full life; he liked the affections of women, he had male companions and there was at least one child born out of wedlock. Therefore, it was perhaps just as apt to refer to Behan as a 'magnificent rogue', a descriptive, which readily applies to many of Ireland's characters -- politicians and writers in particular -- whose effervescent personalities have added colour to the landscape like brush strokes on a Van Gogh canvas. He was an unlikely success, but by the late 1950s a few observers were comparing him with Sean O'Casey, the dean of those Irish playwrights who made their mark since The Troubles. He cheekily compared himself with Ernest Hemingway whom he nearly met in New York. Just as Hemingway was America's greatest living writer, so was he, Behan, Ireland's. The two nearly met which would have been a photo opportunity, bar none, for the world's paparazzi. In the end, it did not happen. Behan was Quixotic and, like Cervantes' hero, given to tilting at windmills, sometimes with honourable intent but with self-destructive results. He did not seek elective office, his biggest liability was his taste for alcohol, but many have considered what fun it might have been to be 'on the stump' with candidate Brendan.

At full stretch, Behan, was a stammering five feet, six inches tall. He was shaped like an inverted pyramid, his shoulders as broad as a rugby player's, his frame tapering down to two tiny feet. In moments of self-deprecation, he called himself 'tulip-shape'. Even he had to admit – sometimes -- that he looked funny. His pugnacity led him into many battles, some of them big fracas with the Irish and English police that resulted in him being put 'inside' for many years. There were lesser disputes, the kind that get resolved outside pubs. In any case, it was this background that helped forge the template under which he was to live part of his adult life. But forever self-righteous he fancied himself a David pitted against so many Goliaths.

Like any seasoned Irish Republican, his list of enemies went back centuries. No need to mention them all here, but two missed opportunities by the Government of the British Isles helped bring shape and substance to Ireland's attitude towards the so-called 'mother' country. Firstly there was the failure of the English parliament to scrap the Act of Union, a piece of intrusive legislation dating from 1801 which thereby ended the dream of a separate Irish parliament in Dublin. While the mood in Ireland was for the devolution of power so as to better share the economic wealth of 'these islands', the mood in Westminster was the opposite. And so began nearly a century of increasingly precipitous positioning of interests that would one day lead to the conflict known as The Troubles. For devotees of Behania, the theme is dealt with in his popular play, *The Hostage,* but is far from being a Republican rant, to the dismay of many of his associates. Said Rae Jeffs, his literary collaborator from London: "How was it that Brendan, who had so much cause for bitterness, had managed to write the play without a trace of it – instead a compassion that showed the futility of patriotic fervour when it led to hatred and violence."

Perhaps as profound were the consequences of the potato famine. It is not for nothing that the Irish have a reputation for being implacable bearers of ancient grudges. It was in 1845 that the calamity of the famine would strike Ireland, leaving in its wake the deaths and dislocation of up to one million people, starved off the land and left foundering and publicly wasting away by bureaucratic ineptitude back in Westminster. The famine and the way in which it was handled would change forever how the Irish regarded the English, There had been crop failures before but nothing like this. Given that some workmen and farmers were eating three kilos of potatoes per day – and nothing else – the impact was sudden and swift. It was accompanied by the dead hand of one Charles Trevelyan, a senior civil servant with great expertise in trade and exports, but with little capacity as to how to recognize a crisis when one was staring him in the face. The problem was this: Ireland, where poverty had long reigned, was now a land where said poverty co-existed with hunger. Jobs and food were equally scarce and the economy was too narrowly developed to quickly respond to the economic tinkering that then might have been put in place as part of a recovery programme. The fruits of the industrial revolution were spilling over to the benefit of Belfast in the north, and Glasgow. The Scottish city's population would grow to 900,000 by the end of the century from little more than 100,000 at the start. Tragically, there was not the imagination to hand to mobilize a recovery for Ireland.

The blight hit again, in 1846. The population of Ireland at the start of the famine was nearly 9 million people (150 years later, the effects of massive emigration would see this figure halved). Emigration began in earnest, first stop Liverpool, Glasgow, Manchester and eventually London; second stop the steerage class decks of any ship heading to Boston, New York, Quebec City and far-away Australia.

The famine "left hatred behind," wrote Cecil Woodham-Smith. "Between Ireland and England the memory of what was done and endured has lain like a sword. Other famines followed where other farmers had gone before, only it is the terrible years of *The Great Hunger* which are remembered and only just beginning to be forgiven," she wrote.

Throughout the famine, Trevelyan's policy had been to soldier on as normal. Keep meeting export targets and the problem of the famine would solve itself, he thought. Theoretically this was true but at what cost, not only to Ireland but to England and its beloved Act of Union with Ireland? As historian Robert Kee has written: "One eye witness described the eviction of 143 families (700 individuals) from an estate in Tipperary as "the chasing away of 700 human beings like crows out of a cornfield. Often they were too weak to be chased or had to be evicted dead. In either case, their corpses were found soon afterwards littering the hedgerows."

In stating the grim circumstances, Kee wrote that there was no specifically anti-Irish callousness in the government's outlook, but:

"The agricultural lower classes of Ireland were of no less theoretical concern to the government than the industrial working classes of England. The trouble simply was that in neither case was the concern great enough. Complex situations had developed within both patterns of lower class living with which the government had never contemplated having to deal."

Brendan Behan said only months before his death that the abolition of the Irish parliament "was a big loss to us because a colonial parliament would have evolved in the course of time into a national (Irish-based) parliament – without war and without the insolent business of killing people . . . We would not have had the famine and would have had our own government as far as we wanted it with a customs union with the rest of Britain."

This work is not a story about a flawed empire but about one of its children, a tenement-raised upstart who could write. He was many things, among them a convert from violence to humanity. He was an accomplished purveyor of blarney, a uniquely Irish commodity, particularly useful in the battle with Perfidious Albion. Behan's shortcoming was the tendency to bump into things and beings on his way through life, leaving confusion and whinnying horses in his wake. This did not diminish his personal bravery, but it did say a lot about his competence. Like many of his predecessors, he was an unlikely hero but a hero nonetheless.

Contents

Prologue	v
Acknowledgments	xv

BOOK ONE

1.	A Dubliner Is Born	1
2.	Growing Up	13
3.	Borstal's Boy	27
4.	Brendan Underground	41
5.	Halcyon Days	47
6.	A Quare One	54
7.	A Shock At The BBC	63
8.	'Beatsie'	71
9.	Sussex Lady	79
10.	The Littlewood Factor	90
11.	Hostage To Fortune	97

BOOK TWO

12.	A Taste Of The Apple	107
13.	The Behan Travelling Road Show	114
14.	The Hemingway Factor	122

15.	From Coast To Coast	131
16.	At The Precipice	141
17.	Help From Astor	152
18.	Chelsea Nights	159
19.	The End Of Something	173
20.	Cortege To Glasnevin	186

BOOK THREE

21.	Aftermath	197
	Epilogue	219
	INDEX	231
	Addenda	239
	Bibliography	249

Acknowledgments

I FIRST HEARD of Brendan Behan in 1961 when he emerged noisily from a just-landed jetliner at San Francisco International Airport to start an uproarious week-long visit to promote his recent play, *The Hostage.* The visit was aimed at using his box-office talents to launch his very Irish plays before North American audiences. There was no shortage of Irish in San Francisco, a city which, over the years, had gained a reputation as a kind of Dublin – West Coast. Visitations from 'sons of the soil' were always welcome On his arrival he unleashed a fusillade of one-line jokes for the delectation of the local press, VIPs and the public at large there to meet him.

The media hype was intense and revolved around anxieties as to what he might get up to during his stay. His reputation had been preceded by news reports from the eastern U.S. and before that from London and Dublin of his being a one-man wrecking crew, a Prometheus unchained. San Francisco was my home town and, as such, I and a coterie of friends, feigning sophistication far beyond our years, took a territorial interest in what fortune or misfortune lay ahead. Would his visit be a reprise of the 1906 earthquake, we wondered?

His play was duly presented at the Geary Theatre, parties took place and not unexpectedly he landed in hospital as a result of his debaucheries. The hospital was St Mary's, in which I was born 20 years earlier. It was all rollicking stuff. He played the wild Irish man both on stage and off, and his audience loved it. The reality was that he was rescued from near death (and not for the first time) by Beatrice, his wife, who, arrived by train a few days later, just in time to pick up the pieces. After some days, he recuperated, presented himself to the city's media, complete with pugnacious and toothless smiles, cracked jokes, and was soon off to Los Angeles, for more of the same.

To those who knew of him and had seen his plays, there was a feeling that he was in a one-man footrace – would he stay the course and significantly enhance his reputation as a leading modern playwright or would he flame out like a comet after only briefly lighting up the night. The dark secrets of his San Francisco visit would not emerge for many years, and for those of us following and enjoying his hi-jinks, he had, as they say in show business, 'delivered'.

Eighteen years later, I was in Dublin standing in the office of a short, portly man named Sean Macreamoinn, director, external affairs, *Radio Telefis Eireann (RTE),* sometimes known as the Pope of Dublin for his knowledge of practically everybody in the Irish capital. He had a renowned ability to fix contacts with all and sundry even, it was claimed, Karol Wojtila, the Pope himself. He exuded jollity, good humour and mischief, at least most of the time, while holding forth in Irish and English to various visitors availing themselves of the contents of his drinks cabinet at his office in the suburb of Montrose. I had finished researching a series of business stories on the Irish economy for my then-employers, *The Financial Times* of London, and he, having been notified in advance of my visit, was anxious to broaden my knowledge of cultural matters. What he had in mind was a reception at the Royal Dublin Society on behalf of the Allied Irish Bank to present a cash award to the octogenarian writer Liam O'Flaherty, famed author of many works, especially his 1930s novel *The Informer*.

Thus it began: a handshake and brief exchange with O'Flaherty (I was in awe); another with Brendan OhetHir (O'Hare), his writer- nephew; Garech Browne, folklorist, Behan enthusiast and Guinness heir; Desmond Mackie, friend of Brendan Behan; the Senator Monckton, whose knowledge of the arts was wide and deep. On it went. Apart from the honoured guest, the name of Behan was mentioned frequently that evening, usually followed by shouts and uproarious comment as the guests tried to best one another with their renderings of Behan stories. My interest yielded many invitations to talk about Ireland's much lamented laughing boy who, in the minds of many, was still very much alive.

With Sean Macreamoinn opening up his contact book, it soon became clear that there were many in Dublin and abroad who wanted to talk about Behan, not least his widow, Beatrice ffrench-Salkeld, whom I would meet for many rounds of drinks on a later visit to Dublin, again arranged by 'the pope.' There, too, was famed bartender Paddy O'Brien, linked forever with the McDaids public house, the centre of Dublin pub life; I was able to track down Brian Behan, the playwright's talented younger brother, at a west London pub. If there was a keeper of the Behan flame, it was Rae Jeffs, formerly ex-Hutchinson publishing company, who editorially nursed Behan through his later works and who was a generous fountain of Behania.

My researches led to *The Observer* newspaper in London and the office of Conor Cruise O'Brien, former Irish diplomat and then, heading into the 1980s, editor of the famous newspaper which, years before and under editor David Astor, provided backing to Behan during one of his bouts of ill-health. O'Brien was a man with whom Behan would seem to have had little in common, but this proved to be untrue, for despite their differences O'Brien knew an editorial craftsman when he read one.

The actor Niall Toibin, then appearing in the Dublin adaptation of *Borstal Boy* and soon to achieve fame in Evelyn Waugh's epic television production of *Brideshead Revisited,* turned on the charm and imparted many anecdotes about Behan. By extraordinarily good luck, I met Alan Simpson. It was Simpson who first put Behan on the English-speaking world's theatrical road map with the 1954 staging in Dublin of Behan's first play, *The Quare Fellow.* Our meeting took place initially at the Queen of England pub in west London one damp and windy day. This was followed by a head-to-head interview at the home nearby of his daughter. Simpson, a big man, was not in good health and was mourning the recent death of his daughter but insisted on talking about Behan, almost as a form of therapy. He died within six months of our interview. His widow, Carolyn Swift, and a co-equal in stage presentations, helped make possible the arrangements for the Simpson interview.

The demands of editing business copy asserted themselves and my Behan project went onto the back burner, only to be revived by contact with Desmond MacNamara, said to have been Behan's best and most understanding friend, and living in northwest London. Despite failing eyesight he was generous with his time and his reminiscences about Behan and was happily responsive to my numerous visitations and telephone calls.

Joan Littlewood, one of the giants of modern theatre, disappeared into retirement on the continent in the late 1970s after the death of her partner and collaborator Gerry Raffles, but thankfully she left behind a verbose autobiography from which one was able to corroborate many stories about working with Behan. Fortunately one key member of her stage troupe, Murray Melvin, the first person to play the lead role in *The Hostage* (at Littlewood's Stratford East Theatre in east London,) was alive and well, and as recently as 2006 proved to be an enthusiastic contributor to the Littlewood-Behan 'oeuvre'.

In New York as late as 2007, I met with Stanley Bard, just before his ouster as long-time manager of the Chelsea hotel. He acutely remembered Behan's prolonged stay in 1963 and Brendan's enforced (by his wife) return to Dublin. On that same visit to New York, I learned that J. P. Donleavy, the creator of *The Ginger Man* (whose main character, Gaynor Crist), happened to bear a striking resemblance to the young Behan), was in town. We met at the Grammercy Park Arts Club. It was as if time had stood still as he carefully conjured a peek into some, but not all, aspects of Behan's life. Other things, he told me, were better left in the dark.

On many occasions, I met individuals, both male and female, who claimed to have known Behan and whose stories about him lent credence to these claims. If they didn't know him, they knew people who did and, in this way, I was able to substantially underpin and balance the foundations of the Behan story and develop and follow new leads. Among these were colleagues and journalists Kevin D'Arcy, David Lennon, Tim Cheatle and Christopher Cragg who had long and well-informed views on the labyrinthine subject of Anglo-Irish relations. A great morale booster on the Behan project, not to mention a supplier of self-described C.A.R.E. packages of incidental Behania that blew refreshing wind into my sails when the going got slow was John McCaughey, a man of Tyrone who was taken from us far too early at the age of 61 in 2008. A timely and always available point of reference was Ros Scanlon, then of the Irish Institute in London. There is special thanks too to Frances Bailey, who was knowledgeable on Anglo-Irish matters, and thanks also to Toronto-based wine writer Tony Aspler, who decades earlier had organised one of Behan's visits to Canada, the details of which he vividly recounted. His recollection recalled Job: '. . . and I only am escaped alone to tell thee.'

Closer to home, there was the invaluable production, proofreading and editorial support provided by my son Nicholas and the keen editorial eye exhibited by my wife Carole. One is grateful for the chastening remarks offered by San Francisco school friend Terrence Ryan.

Perhaps most significant of my contacts was that of a poised lady named Valerie Hemingway, formerly Valerie Danby-Smith, who in 2004 published her autobiography, *Running With the Bulls*. It told much about her relationship with and marriage into the Hemingway family dating back to 1959. It told rather less about the birth of her son Brendan and more about her time as an aspiring reporter just out of her teens who met and worked for Ernest and Mary Hemingway. In 1961, she took up *ad hoc* employment in New York for a Dublin acquaintance, one Brendan Behan, whom she would one day join in San Francisco for a brief but life-changing encounter. If she was protective at first about her memories of Behan, she later grew more discursive, and our meeting in London and subsequent communiques all provided valuable foundation stones for the Behan story.

BOOK ONE

Chapter One

A Dubliner is born

"Da used to read for me for I had poor eyesight. Indeed, he read for us all Dickens, Thackeray, all the greats. He would read for hours with the children listening to him. It is something every mother and father should do, encourage reading. There is nothing better for a child's imagination"... Kathleen Behan, The Mother of All the Behans

SOME TIME IN the 1950s, when playwright Brendan Behan was first hitting his stride as a creative writer and as an attention-getter around town, a young man burst excitedly into his house in Dublin and took a seat at the kitchen. He paused a moment or two to catch his breath. His parents, seeing his excited state, asked what he had been doing.

"I was just at the bank, and he talked to me!"

"Who talked to you?" asked one of the old folks.

"Brendan Behan," said the lad.

"What did he say?"

"Hey, fooker, where's the bank manager's office?"

"Mind your tongue!" said the young man's father

"But don't you see? He talked to me. Brendan Behan talked to me."

Behan was perhaps 25 years of age when the above incident is said to have occurred. He was already the stuff of 'urban legend', the welcoming recipient of the accusingly pointed finger when something outrageous happened, the type of personality about whom an eavesdropper would have said: 'well, it sounds like Brendan, doesn't it.' By the time he was in his mid-20s, Brendan Behan was well on his way to making his life a work-in-progress, a fact which could be attested to by the experiences of countless Dubliners who had encountered the colourful, tousle-haired house painter and monologist in and around the Irish capital.

Even at a young age, he was the scourge of pubs. He was a natural raconteur and fearless at 'taking over' drinking premises on the spur of the moment while regaling the patrons with Republican folk songs or he simply launched into vigorous commentaries on current affairs. He was always keenly up to date and not one to easily yield the floor to a more glib debater. He prompted J. P. Donleavy, the Irish-American author of *The Ginger Man*, to observe: "There is a great deal of room made in Ireland for anybody behaving in an outrageous way." Donleavy added that Behan had no peer in getting even with people.

"He was a hearty fellow and was showing promise as a new, thrusting playwright and contributor to the London and Dublin stage", said Alan Simpson who, in 1954, had presented Behan's first stage work, *The Quare Fellow,* an early form of modern prison drama. This one was singular in that the protagonist never makes an appearance in the play but casts a giant shadow across the stage and into the balcony seats.

A Dubliner is born

The late Sean Macreamoinn, one of broadcast journalism's pioneers at Irish radio and television (RTE), remembered the writer's instinctive generosity, especially when times were tough. "I met him walking along the street and sensed that he was going to try to cadge some money from me. When I told him I had none to be cadged -- for that was the way it was in those days -- he said that that would not do, and immediately set about raising some spending money for us both from passers- by. He could be very generous."

Rae Jeffs, whose grandfather had started *Hutchinson Publishing Company* in London in the 19th century, said she had never met anybody like him. It made no difference that they were such opposites – she the aloof and sophisticated Englishwoman, he the streetwise Irish pub-rowdy. She put it simply: "When he came into a room, he lit the place up like a 599 watt light bulb." Note her emphasis on the figure of five-nine-nine, much more emphatic than six hundred.

We have noted Brendan Behan's date and place of birth. It is assumed that he was like any other new-born, given to howling and being generally disruptive, since he had strong pulsations of rebel blood in his veins. It is an accurate enough supposition, for it would take only 16 years from his birth before he would begin to extend his noisy reputation from the shores of Dublin's Fair City across the Irish Sea to England, in his mind's eye a distant and dangerous land, where there resided a people who bore malice to the Irish. That early prejudgment, reinforced by many a Hollywood low budget picture in the 1930s such as those of John Ford, would shape the young Behan's life and, by the narrowest of margins, catapult him to international notoriety. A few slip-ups and it might have turned out differently. But his robust personality ensured that the unmuzzled boy was surely to grow up into an unmuzzled adult.

But Brendan did not have exclusive domain over the name of the Behan family – there was too much talent in the tenement-hardened family for any single person to claim such dominion. Firstly, the fires on which Brendan Behan's personality was forged began not with a Behan but with the union of John Kearney (1854-97) and Kathleen McGuinness (1861-1907). Their lives were short, reflecting the low health standards of the time, particularly tuberculosis and consumption, but were long enough for them to produce five children, two of whom showed signs of the precocity which was to mark the family's wide reputation. John, the eldest, was followed by Peadar; a rebel who teamed with a friend, Paddy Heaney, to write *The Soldier's Song*. In the fullness of time (1949), it would officially become Ireland's national anthem, though in practice it had been wearing this mantle for decades.

The third born to the Kearney family was Kathleen. She was born in Dublin in 1889 and was to live till 1985, her life filled with events, music, friends, exuberance and a quiver of Republican barbs. Hers was a name to conjure with. Thanks to the alacrity of Brian, one of her writing sons, she became known as *The Mother of All the Behan's* and is still remembered years after her death as one of the popular characters of daily Dublin life. Just as Rhett Butler had been drawn to Scarlett O'Hara out of the novel *Gone With the Wind* because of her 'zest for life', so it was that Kathleen found herself with one of life's greatest assets, the gift of friendship and the ability to induce laughter in others. This is not to suggest that life was not tough for her and the family in general, confined as it was to the gentle but asphyxiating grip of genteel poverty in the less-than-salubrious urban neighbourhoods of Dublin.

Tough times notwithstanding, they were not poorer than their neighbours; there was said to have been plenty of mattress money about. Two more children followed onto the Kearney family tree, they were two daughters, Maggie and Maura.

A Dubliner is born

Kathleen recollected to son Brian that the family was derived mainly from farming stock. Her grandparents had owned farmland in County Meath, and her great grandmother was hard hit by the potato famine of 1845. It was this adversity that tended to heat up the family's political anger and stoke the embers of feisty Republicanism that had been building since the The Act of Union of 1801. But at some point they became city folk, Brendan's urban street credentials were beyond reproach. His robust use of Dublinese and his natural skills at folk music and tub thumping rebel songs derived as much from his mother's influence as from what he picked up from his day-to-day trekking through the city.

Brendan, when it pleased him, would play the country-boy card but, like an elusive high-C on a trumpet, it was not a note he could sustain. There was too much of the Dublin street fighter in him, the city urchin scuttling along a wet, cobbled street as often as not in search of a drink, a laugh or a fight in any order in which they came. Sometimes, he would firmly disown any suggestion, of agri-origins, preferring to call Ireland's rural classes 'kulchie bastards.'

"My family's land in Dublin was all in window boxes," he often said, "and the only time I ever dug a field was with my father at the time of the strike when the Dublin Corporation gave the men plots of one-eighth of an acre."

"It is the working classes that have bound me to Dublin," he told Peter Arthurs, an Irish-born US merchant seaman whom Behan befriended in Los Angeles in the early 1960s. Arthurs elaborated: "Brendan showed no genuine love for and desired no intimacy with the peasantry. . . . He rarely associated himself with Dublin's working class. . . He found the company of Ballsbridge's upwardly mobile middle class and their exclusivity and gentility more suitable."

While Brendan abandoned formal education at the age of 14, he satisfied his precocity by reading hungrily. He knew the history of his country well. If he happened to be in a discursive mood, he could tell entertaining stories about life in Ireland past and present, north and south, urban and rural, Protestant and Catholic. For a man with short arms, he had a long reach on matters Irish as is shown in his various travel and fiction 'entertainments' such as *The Scarperer* and his witty oeuvres on Ireland, Paris and New York and a small but skilfully rendered array of short stories betraying a maturity far beyond their author's years. Among these was *A Woman of No Standing*, suggesting Oscar Wilde's deep understanding of the opposite sex.

Those things and people that interested him were plucked out of the air. He had an ear for contradiction, and his ability to sponge up disparate pieces of information helped create and enrich his personality and make him a formidable combatant across the publican's bar or the kitchen table. The downside was that one often did not know what he was talking about. He would break into song at the slightest provocation, and no wonder given that one of his great influences was Peadar Kearney, Kathleen's elder brother by John Kearney and Kathleen McGuinness. Peadar was born at 68, Lower Dorset Street in Dublin in 1883. He grew up in the Dolphin's Barn area, was educated by the Irish Christian Brothers (it was difficult on those days not to have a religious education), joined the Gaelic league in 1901, and was sworn into the Irish Republican Brotherhood in 1903. He was Republican stock all the way, as were the Behans, and he took part in the Easter Rising in 1916. Kathleen Behan, in her memoirs, remembered the frequency with which The Soldier's Song, was sung. Kearney was arrested by the British authorities and jailed in 1920 and was released on the signing of the Home Rule Treaty at the end of 1921 creating the oddly named Irish Free State. A Republican in his soul, Kearney nevertheless served on the Free State side in the ensuing civil war. Unpretentious and unmaterialistic, he returned to casual labour after the civil war. He died at his home in Inchicore, Dublin, in November 1947.

The words to the anthem form a musical cornerstone for a modern Ireland and go like this:

THE SOLDIER'S SONG

I'll sing you a song, a soldier's song,

With a cheering rising chorus

As round our blazing camp-fires we throng

The starry heavens o'er us.

Impatient for the coming fight

And as we watch the dawning light

Here in the silence of the night.

We'll chant the soldier's song.

Soldiers are we, whose lives are pledged to Ireland,

Some have come from the land across the sea. . . ."

Kathleen would become the third-born of the Kearneys and McGuinnesses, and several decades later, on the void created by the death of The Grannie, the wife of James Behan and the mother of Stephan Behan (who would become the Father of All the Behans), she would emerge as a kind of cultural anchor for the family. But those developments lay in the future. It was in 1916, she met and married Jack Furlong and in two years bore him two sons, Rory and Sean. But it was the deadly worldwide influenza epidemic in those pre-penicillin days that was to take Jack Furlong's life. He died in 1918. In 1922, she married Stephan Behan, whose trade was house painting. Also an active trade unionist, Behan knew the ways of tenement life. He brought his wife into a rent free dwelling on Russell Street, and from 1922 to 1935 it became home to the fast-growing Behan tribe. Crowded though it was -- sleeping two and three abed was commonplace -- it had the advantage of being near the centre of urban Dublin. The rent-free arrangement was thanks to Stephan's mother, the Grannie English, who in fact owned the property and who would prove herself to be as clever at handling money as her son was at house painting. It was a marginally satisfactory arrangement, even though Kathleen was desperate for more room. Room or not, it was there, on Russell Street in the heart of north of the Liffey Dublin in 1923, that the family established its base. Brendan was the first born, in 1923, Seamus, 1925, Brian, 1927, Dominic, 1929 and Carmel 1932. Given the claustrophobic environment, Kathleen, beholden to her husband's mother, kept a low profile as she managed her family. Her turn would come in 1933 when with the Grannie's death.

The Grainnie's passing – and her control of the family purse-strings – meant time for a change. This time the Behans would take their chances on a street named Kildare Road in a neighbourhood called The Crumlin in the far western suburb adjoining Phoenix Park. Here is how younger brother Dominic described it in his bittersweet remembrance of those days.

"Seventy Kildare Road is part of a two-house block both of which houses together would hardly make the sweating room for a second-class Turkish baths, and yet it was supposed to be one of the more superior dwellings for which the (Dublin) Corporation charged an extra two and sixpence per week. It had, of course, a separate two bathrooms, that is not to say that it was apart from the toilet, it merely meant that it was a seven-shillings-and-sixpenny model; the bathroom was combined with the kitchen; and an added feature in the cheaper house had the novelty of passing through the kitchen/bathroom to get to the toilet."

Today the Crumlin's main historic feature is a small commemorative plaque over the door where Brendan Behan spent some of his teenage years; otherwise it looks much as it did when the Behans moved in, a monument to the lack of imagination in the design of public housing by Anglo-Irish (and Scottish) urban planners in those days. Dubliners today say little has changed, miles of dreary dwellings, providing basic necessities but little in the way of pubs and urban social centres. The dwellings themselves project resignation, their pebble-dash and stucco exteriors presenting an image of urban exhaustion to the unsuspecting visitor.

Kathleen Behan hated it at first and didn't mind saying so to her biographer-son Brian. But she moderated her tone given that the Crumlin's few amenities were still more than existed on Russell Street "Crumlin was a desperate place when first we went there, no schools, no shops, nothing except plenty of desolation, but I was glad enough in a way to go there – a house to you is better than rooms. It is good to have a clean home even if it is in the middle of nowhere."

The move went ahead because, as far as public housing went, it beat the going commercial rate of 15 shillings a week. Little Behan also hated it. He was 14 and might as well have been forced to move across the Atlantic Ocean, so far -- two miles -- was he from his north side and Southside friends. In his primary school years, he had made friends at St. Canisus School (torn down in recent years). For anyone who has grown up in a concentrated urban environment, such a disruption can have profound effects on the young, like a bowling ball among the tenpins, but the colourful street life provided the outlet, not to mention the action that goes with living close to a city centre.

Just after their marriage, Stephen Behan was rounded up in a raid by Free Staters and put in Kilmainham jail, outside Dublin. For two years, just after little Brendan was born. Kathleen carted their son to the jail and lifted him high enough to get a glimpse of his father. It would be the first of many dozens of times that Brendan Behan would be looking through bars at a relative or friend, though for the most part it would be from the inside looking out. The country had rid itself of the British Black and Tans and now was embroiled in a civil war – Years later when Brendan was able to understand the events of 1922, he quipped: "If that was what a civil war was like, what must an un-civil war be like?"

Kathleen recalled in her memoirs: "So we weren't among the very poorest of the poor. In fact, if Stephen had been a bit more careful, we would have been on the pig's back. My sister used to say that he (Stephan) drank a couple of houses in the pubs. You might have bought one from the dregs."

Nevertheless, the Behans were to provide a fine example of how creativity can flourish in the most unpromising soil. In later years, after several dangerous detours that led to a series of stays in jails in Ireland and England, Brendan Behan would become one of Ireland's most famous writers. He would not be alone for Brian would make his own contributions to the art of playwriting and biography as would Dominic, who brought several successful stage productions to London's west end and to Irish television.

A tough rivalry built up between Brendan and Dominic. The relationship, at its most concessionary, could be described as sarcastic and was at its best only when they avoided each other's company. Dominic told of a time when Brendan was commanding the floor before both him and half-brother Rory. After a lull in the conversation, he shook his head in reference to Dominic. "I shouldn't have said that in front of that skinny bastard because he'll write it down."

It may be indicative of Behan's need to be in the driving seat that he sometimes picked a row over some matter of no great import – such as that old chestnut of what constitutes a true Dubliner, or what otherwise might be called the 'north of the Liffey t'ing'. A close look at his rather erratic living habits shows that he spent about as much time in north Dublin as on the south side of the Liffey, to which must be factored in a further five years in jail, some of it in connection with an Irish Republican Army (IRA) attempt to plant an explosive device in Liverpool.

There was really one arbitrator of the issue and that was Paddy O'Brien, one of Ireland's most famous bartenders and for 34 years a puller of pints at McDaids on Harry Street. He said in an interview in 1984 before his death that it was his view that the unifying characteristic of northsiders and southsiders was that they "were good chatter-uppers with the gift of the gab." Nevertheless, he said, there were fundamental differences:

"Northsiders are inclined to be settled, more community-minded. All live in terraced houses. You have examples of generations living in the same community. Southsiders are from the country, from somewhere else, they are people who migrated to Dublin for a job and they tend to live in flats because all the flats and big houses are in south Dublin. They are less settled and come and go a lot. They are just a different race of people, but once inside the pubs there's no difference."

Desmond MacNamara, Behan's most enduring friend, put a different spin on the argument. In an interview after his 85th birthday he explained:

"A lot of the north-south thing had to do with the schools. Up to the middle 1930s, the remaining Georgian slums, buildings, boulevards, streets had sunk into tenements. Multiple tenement occupation was mainly in north Dublin. South Dublin had not gone through this in the same way. Merrion Square remained Merrion Square, more or less, and Stephens Green still had its Stephens Green Club. Today, film crews, capitalising on Ireland's tourism boom and urban gentrification developments, gather outside south Dublin Georgian structures and facades which serve as reminders for how the rich lived in the heyday of the Ascendancy.

"The convent and the university were just off one corner of the square," O'Brien said. "So this remained; it kept its side up whereas North Dublin slipped down and became the centre of working class resistance. Now I think the two Dublins are growing together and they are spreading further and further out. I have no idea where Dublin ends; perhaps it is in the mountains by now."

If the north-south issue was not enough to get Brendan's goat, there were other ways. One, in later years, was to tease him about his similarity to that of welsh poet Dylan Thomas, who died in New York from alcoholic excesses in 1953. When Behan's attained literary success a few years later, the critics put him under intense scrutiny and found remarkable parallels.

CHAPTER TWO

GROWING UP

"There was no mistaking our author, a good-looking Irishman with a coxcomb of black wavy hair, a Roman nose, a few teeth missing and a pronounced stutter. He seemed incredibly shy – as did his friend Joe (McGill) for that matter, and Behan had brought him along because the thought of meeting a crowd of strange English on his own would be too much for him . . . ." – Joan Littlewood

DESMOND MACNAMARA SAID that in Ireland's hard times, there was always the comfort of the hearth for tenement youngsters. But hard times there were indeed. The country was exhausted and near bankruptcy – a result of the long struggle with England, then followed by its own civil conflict. The Irish struggle war never truly over despite the elevation of Eamon de Valera to the post of prime minister after the 1932 poll victory for the Fianna Fail party. His big challenge was that of nation-building, the making of a multi-party political entity that would accommodate the interests of the various political wings, ranging from the anti-democratic IRA committed to national unity on any terms and by any means, to the powerful Catholic Church. Although the Irish Republican Army had been neutralised, it was still a going concern and not above a little spontaneous mischief as were other legitimate and illegal political organisations, all nibbling for a share of the meagre fruits of victory. Imports of manufactures were up, and exports of manufactures were off, Had it not been for the Bank of England, still Ireland's banker of last resort, the value of Irish goods and services would be off the graph .They were bad enough anyway – the British pound was well overvalued, thus damaging the pound in Ireland which was tied to sterling.

Until The Troubles (the euphemism for the period of the Civil War), Irish whiskey, had been the preferred whiskey of the empire and was an important Irish export. By the end of the 1920s, its overseas markets had been lost, the region's some 70 distilleries began to close rapidly, not helped by Prohibition in the United States and the domination of the U.S. black market by such Irish-American entrepreneurs as Joseph Kennedy who chose to export Scotch rather than Irish spirits. Sales of Irish whiskey in the U. K also plummeted as unofficial trade barriers were thrown up in the UK. Although prohibition was ended in 1933, the problems persisted thanks now to the onset of the Great Depression which affected all forms of trade. The decline was inevitable and it was only in 1985 that the Irish distilleries saw their market share finally hit bottom with just five principle brands of whiskey left to call their own – Bushmills, Jamesons, John Power, Paddy and Tullamore Dew. The industry was saved in the 1980s by a white knight rescue by French distiller Pernod-Ricard which provided timely marketing and sales support.

By 1932, de Valera threw up import barriers of his own in hopes of boosting internal investment in the undercapitalized farming and manufacturing sectors. Boosting inward investment was

Growing Up

not going to prove easy in the face of an unstable population still exporting more people than products.

If people were not leaving the country in search of jobs overseas, they were migrating from the countryside into Ireland's few sizeable cities in search of jobs that were not there. In Dublin; its population stood at 167,000 in 1804. This grew to 232,000 in 1845, the year of the Famine. In 1901, the capital, now a city of shattered dreams and unsupported by a meaningful economic underpinning, had clawed its way to 290,000, then 316,000 in 1926. In 1951, the population of Dublin was 537,000. In the half century since then, Dublin has experienced big population growth for the first time in its history – and this time accompanied by sporadic surges in job creation. By the millennium it was not unusual to find taverns and restaurants being staffed by Ukrainians and Poles or Chinese news agents with thick Dublin accent, a far cry from the Dublin of Behan's youth.

MacNamara was aware just how tight spending money was when he was just starting school. But for a youngster, developing a political awareness of the institutions around you was not a problem. He has recalled that "the politics of the time were simple; you belonged to one side or the other. You belonged to the Free Staters – that is, those in favour of the Collins agreement to the partition of Ireland and eventual independence for the south or you favoured unity of all of Ireland, including the six counties of Ulster. Not many people thought much about the Six Counties when I was small.

"In the early 1930s, my mother had a shop in the middle of Grafton Street, a couturier shop with a work room with seven or eight girls. The girls were divided sharply between Republicans and nothings. There was a fascist threat, a real threat, represented by something called the 'Blue Shirts' similar to the Brown Shirts and the Black Shirts in Germany and Italy."

The Blue Shirts were officially known as the National Guard and were headed by General Eoin O'Duffy. There were parades, marches and salutes in the style of the times, all intended to wrong-foot the IRA which was watching its members drift away into other less ominous organisations. Street clashes between the Blues and the IRA were brought to a halt after the invocation of national emergency laws. Irish politics had been reduced to a period of pushing and shoving. O'Duffy himself swung some support behind the Franco-led nationalists in the Spanish civil war, which did not win him any support from the many Irishmen who favoured the Spanish republicans. Irish politics began to collapse from the centre, leading to the weakening of the IRA, the Fianna Fail and the Blues; eventually the Blues ceased to have much influence on pre-war Irish politics, but they still were able to throw a scare into the balkanised political system. Dr. Douglas Hyde, a protestant and champion of the Irish language, had become president of the new Republic. Others, like Sean McBride, threw in their support for the Republic. "But then the war came," said MacNamara, "and that had the effect of draining Dublin of young Protestants."

In those early years of a newly independent country still governed by the laws and statutes of its colonial enemy and a multitude of other regulations and standards, the capital was caught in the quicksand of privation. It was a city with little electricity, not much food but plenty of pubs. That at least was how MacNamara saw it. His view ran alongside that of J. P. Donleavy, who was to arrive as a former U. S. Navy enlistee in Dublin for a look around. He found it foul, polluted and unkempt but with a gritty charm and mystique. Nevertheless, he reflected that he had never seen such grinding poverty. MacNamara said that Dublin experienced chronic electricity

Growing Up

shortages – there was no economy, no money and no work. People in Ireland were living off their own fat as it were. In 1939, MacNamara applied to go to the College of Art. His mother's small savings had disappeared, and his father, who had died in the early 1930s, had lost his money on the London stock market."The cattle trade had gone and was not replaced till the 1950s."

Living in straitened circumstances was not that difficult for the Behans. Apart from the late Grannie's skills at rent collecting from marginal properties, the family was neither materialistic nor acquisitive. Two factors which spoke as much for the economic state of Ireland as they did for the economic state of the Behans were that few people had radios, television sets did not exist, nor any other such household comforts in Russell Street, near the Liffey, or in the northern suburb of Crumlin. Families gathered around a single drop-leaf table, and any heating that was available came off the kitchen cooker, usually of the trash burning variety. Behan's abode was no different from the others and was sufficiently uncomfortable to force its not-yet-famous tenant out onto the street for the long walk into town for a bit of action. On a typical day, a visit to MacNamara was followed by a drop-in to McDaids, then, if it wasn't too early, perhaps to The Catacombs, a lurid basement dive whose name has passed into legend and where eccentric, if not outrageous, behaviour was as guaranteed as a drink in a speakeasy. It is worth remembering that Behan's famed resourcefulness made him a valuable and streetwise companion capable of rounding up foodstuffs for supper. Anthony Cronin, the writer whose digs he would find 'taken over' by the sometimes intoxicated Behan, has recalled the undying image of the young Behan angling his way home in North Dublin with a sheep's head slung over his shoulder, then later becoming reacquainted himself with the same head, now exuding dubious odours from the steaming confines of the Behan elders' bathroom. Fergal Keane, a television journalist, recalled a family anecdote about Behan's extemporaneous eating habits: "Brendan's idea was to buy a pound of brawn and put in his pocket, and when hungry, take out a slice and eat it, washed down, of course, with Guinness."

But in the 1930s, Behan was still very much a youngster and was helpful and loyal to his mother, not least because he was the eldest of the five Behan children. Brendan, because of his seniority, no doubt learned how to play the angles for maternal affection. Kathleen, in an interview late in her life long after most of her children had died, denied that she had favoured her eldest son. It was a commonly mistaken observation made by many students of Behania over the years seeking to identify the various social tributaries that, taken together, formed the single character of such an unusual personality. On the contrary, Brendan's favourite adult in the family was The Grannie. unofficially the Queen Bee of Russell Street.

When she died she left many incidentals but also the then-huge sum of £3,000. She ensured that there never would be any food shortages nor would any friend or family member be denied shelter. It was to emerge too that she had persuaded Brendan to join her fairly regularly in discreet tipples, normally not a problem in the circumstances except that young Brendan was scarcely six years of age. Of course, in those days people did not drink socially at home as became the custom later in the century – that was why pubs were invented, as everyone knew. The reckless drinking with which Brendan was to become identified later in life was virtually non-existent. Who had money for such indulgences, Behan was to ask in the 1960s in his *Brendan Behan's New York:*

"To be an alcoholic is not such a good deal, I can tell you, but if you haven't got the money to buy decent liquor it must be crucifixion altogether. . . . I first learnt the use of whiskey at the age of six from my grandmother who said: 'Give him the sup of it now and he will never know the taste of it when he grows up,' which I suppose is the biggest understatement of all time; in my case anyway."

In Behan's early literary collection, titled *After the Wake*, assembled years later for publication by Peter Fallon, the reader encounters a lady in a pub whose character must have been based on the famous grandmother. She is accompanied by a youngster celebrating his fifth birthday

"In the pub, she sat n the corner and ordered a bottle of stout for herself and a dandy glass of porter for me. 'An orange or something would be better for the child,' said Jimmy the Sports.

'The drop of gargle will do him good,' said Mrs Murphy. 'It's only a little birthday celebration'."

Behan, in his youth, suffered from an embarrassing stammer and he certainly found drink something of an antidote, but it brought only temporary relief as the stammer never quite disappeared. It was to plague Brendan all his life. As he entered his teens, drinking became more accessible if only because it was so poorly policed. He would remain throughout the years a 'binge' drinker, prone to epic struggles for months on end. What happened was that his alcohol addiction was to collide with other physical disabilities and set up a snowball of troubles over which, in the long term, he was unable to prevail. Among these were diabetes and cirrhosis of the liver, not to mention the stupefying effects of strong drink itself.

But youth, brimming like a geyser, is a powerful counterweight to alcohol's ill-effects. Kathleen swore by Brendan Behan, the pre-school infant, for his being a model son and student, remarked upon for his equanimity and reading capacity. The reading was acquired from both Stephen and Kathleen. In those days, houses, even tenements, had musical instruments, ranging from pianos to spoons, with which to create music. If young Brendan was not reading himself, he was urging cousins and uncles to read to him from *A Tale of Two Cities* and other Dickens' works.

MacNamara, who left Ireland in the early 1950s and lived in London till his death on January 8 2008, described his friend as a 'sometimes boor, sometimes bad penny, who would turn up unannounced and promptly overstay his welcome. This was particularly so in the early days when Behan first got out of Irish prison having spent his mid-teenage years adapting to civilian life after some scary scrapes with Irish and British authorities.

"He could be a bloody nuisance in those days. I had moved from Grafton Street to a mews in Lower Baggott Street. He would have called on three or four people as he walked along through the Crumlin, taking a cup or two of tea or something else here and there before he got to me. I sometimes had to tell him to shut up, especially when he was drunk. Yet despite everything, you could not help but like him. It often feels that he is right here, now, in this room.

"I tend to measure my friends by thinking of something I want to tell them. I say to myself, 'I must tell so-and-so that, and this was frequently the case with Brendan, and then I suddenly realise that I cannot for they are no longer here. There are a very small number of such people, and Brendan was one of them."

That alcohol might have been wreaking a permanently damaging effect on young Brendan was now beginning to be feared, but if alcohol was having any ill-effects, it was being obscured by his affection for the Grannie. He displayed reckless possession of his grandmother and was apt to 'see off' any other youngster seeking to intervene in his drive for affection. Wrote Colbert Kearney, the Grannie was a benevolent and convivial despot "who always provided a jug of porter and a selection of dainty morsels during her levees . . . . "She plied him with alcohol and expensive food in order to ensure his good looks and his immunity from worms."

Stephan Behan continued to have a brusque relationship with his son, Brendan complaining that the father had never provide enough financial support for the family. Stephan Behan felt that despite his pub spending he had done enough. If money was tight then it was tight and that was the way it was in Ireland. Still Brendan claimed that he, the father, earned more than he let on. His income was that of a housepainter, He was head of the National Painters' and Decorators' Union, one of the organisations that provided a modicum of glue to hold Ireland's impoverished country together. If there ever was a trade that was a growth industry, it was house painting. In Dublin, lack of investment amplified the city's run-down look, much of it attributable to the lack of a 'drop of paint.'

Two decades later, at a reception in London when his fame was at its peak, Behan met the English novelist Kingsley Amis, another upstart writer who had indulged in a bit of literary iconoclasm of his own in the 1950s, notably with his novel *Lucky Jim*. Amis remembered later how the Irishman had lured him into a trap, Behan saying:

"I remember doing a bit of painting in Paris . . . ."

"Oh," said Amis, "I didn't know you went in for art, Brendan?"

"I don't mean painting fucking pictures," Behan bellowed, "I mean serious painting; painting fucking houses."

There are still traces of 'Behan the Painter' around Dublin. For decades, in a driveway outside Donohue's pub alongside St. Stephen's Green, there was a painted stencil that read, in black-on-white: **NO PARKING.**

"Brendan was very proud of that sign," said his old friend Garech Browne, a member of the Guinness brewing family. Browne with whom, it can be argued, Behan had a symbiotic relationship, Behan being a notable consumer of Guinness products and Browne a supplier of same. Browne, showing a visitor the playwright's handywork, pointed to a slight lack of alignment between **NO** and **PARKING**. Regrettably, the keen-eyed tourist of today will find that the sign has been painted over but, if the sun is shining at the correct angle on the narrow laneway, the barest outline of this example of Behan's native work is still visible.

Apart from his friendship with Browne, mere mention of the Guinness name was bound to prompt a riposte. It became assumed in Dublin that nearly all anti-Guinness humour was his doing. In his book of reminiscences, *Brendan Behan's Island,* he corrected a statement that was – and still is – misattributed to him.. "The Guinness family have always been very good to the people of Dublin, but as some wag has remarked, 'the people of Dublin are very kind to the Guinness's." So it was a wag and not him, but very much a classic Brendan-type remark that provided him with another chance to stick it to the 'haves'.

But times were changing. Behan had finished his basic schooling and acquitted himself well under the tutelage of The Christian Brothers and the Sisters of Charity. Practically all of Europe was politicised owing to various internal turmoils and the jockeying for position by national socialistic governments (a.k.a. fascists) and communists as the older, pre-democratic orders fell to the sidelines. Britain's empire may have been

Growing Up

at the flood tide in terms of size but the First World War had left it exhausted and there were pressures to devolve it, the French Republic was in turmoil, Germany and Italy were on the march and Ireland was locked in an internal struggle between a handful of power blocs. But for many Irishman the big action was in Spain where, in 1936, a civil war had broken out between the rebelling forces led by Generalissimo Francisco Franco, with the support of the church and big business interests, and the highly factionalised forces of the unstable but nevertheless democratically elected Republican government. Irish volunteers were queuing to join the many international brigades being sent to Spain to battle for the Republic and, by the same token, against the church. After all, was not Ireland's great leader, Eamon de Valera, of Spanish descent? Yes, but he wanted no part of any bloody conflict on Spain's Celtic fringe.

A popular view was that the conflict was about black against white. Franco, the military commander, represented fascism, enforced order and expected the support of the privileged classes as symbolised by the church, business and the military. Contributing to the conflict were Benito Mussolini's Italian forces and those of Adolph Hitler, the German leader, the latter having used his air force to bomb the north coast lumber town of Guernica, in one of the first atrocities of its kind in Europe.

For those rebellious Irish siding with the Spanish Republic, the cause was clear. History has instructed otherwise by pointing out that the differences between the Franco junta and the flagging government of the Republic were not so great, given Russia's eagerness to join the fray – on the side of the Republic. Nevertheless, the hunger for a just war whetted the appetites of many communities in Europe and North America, and many volunteers periodically filled Dublin's streets in response to the call to arms. It was at one such demonstration that

Behan, bobbing and weaving like rugby tackle, and otherwise distinguished only by a large mop head but with tiny hands and feet, collided with Desmond MacNamara. Behan, spoiling to put things right in Spain, was around 14 years of age. MacNamara did not know at the time just how close his first meeting with Behan nearly turned out to be his last.

Around that time, Kathleen Behan espied an ominous-looking envelope in the morning post. It was redolent of mystery, and Mrs. Behan quickly opened it. Its contents instructed the young Behan on how to travel to Spain for the purpose of joining the battle to defeat Franco and restore the elected Republican government. The letter contained a list of contacts to meet en route. For Kathleen, the mother, there was a sudden flood of tears and then the letter was destroyed and a veil dropped over the subject. Brendan didn't find out till much later, after the die was cast in Spain. In what could only be a mother's anguish, she said in her memoirs: "He never forgave me. Some of the family say I did the wrong thing to this day. He was already a man, they say. It should have been his decision and he might have come back a different Brendan. Yes, I say, but he might have come back no Brendan at all."

It was not surprising that Brendan was drawn into revolutionary politics and membership of the IRA The surprise, according to his brother Brian, was that he stayed. He never rose high in the ranks, though, and was never higher than that of courier. As a youngster, he fell in with a firebrand, the young Cathal Goulding, born in 1922. Goulding rose through the ranks to become the organisation's chief of staff in Dublin, succeeding Ruari O Bradaigh. As a teenager, Goulding joined the Fianna Eireann, sometimes described as the Boy Scout wing of the IRA (and described by others as the Hitler youth of the organisation). Behan was aboard also and together the two adolescents went on 'fund-raising' expeditions around Dublin. On one occasion, he was rounded up for a somewhat impromptu munitions and weapons training exercise at the south Dublin suburb of Killiney, where a small stately home was still in private hands – it is now part of a modern hotel complex. The two remained the closest of friends and 'minded' each other into and out of difficulties In 1963, Behan remembered his old friend fondly telling one interviewer about their joint membership in the Fianna Boy Scouts and how, as youngsters, they had been thrown out of the IRA, only to be allowed back in., Goulding would emerge as a serious IRA activist and political theorist who took a long view on the role the IRA would, or could, play in Irish national politics, whereas Behan would withdraw from overt activity in the organisation but not before making his own mark.

By the spring of 1939, the Spanish civil war was nearing its end. The siege of Madrid was over and the republican brigades were in flight out of Valencia and Barcelona for the French border. Franco had the Republican forces in a stranglehold and was on the verge of a 36-year reign as El Caudillo. The Franco victory was not welcomed in Ireland's Republican quarters because it would solidify the church's authority in Ireland. But there were still battles to be fought.

Behan received a call to deliver a message to an IRA Representative in London, specifically at the Goodge Street underground transportation stop in a fancy neighbourhood called Fitzrovia, now a centre of restaurants and computer equipment supplies.

He botched the job but did not lose his eagerness to support the cause. The cause, by this time, consisted of a stepping up of terrorist attacks in Ireland and on the British mainland as part of a drive to wrest the six counties of Ulster from British allegiance. In autumn that year, with another war in Europe boiling up, Behan somewhat bull-headedly dispatched himself from Dublin to Liverpool – marking his second visit to England

(and, hence, abroad) -- on a bombing mission. But his travel plans had been indiscreet and were noted by the authorities in England; they formed a surreptitious welcoming committee to meet him. He was promptly rounded up in a boarding house in possession of explosive devices. Thus, in ways that absolutely no-one could have predicted, this experience was to propel him into a career as a writer and in less than two decades one of the most talked about writers in the English language. He was little more than 16 years of age.

CHAPTER THREE

BORSTAL'S BOY

"Brendan...described borstal as the poor man's public school and such it definitely was for him since it was there he first began to write – and read – in earnest. Prison was also a place that forced him to put pen to paper under the influence. Neither would it take a genius to notice that most of his more serious fiction and drama concerned itself with character in captivity, be they thinly disguised versions of himself or people he had heard about..." – Brian Behan, in The Brothers Behan

MANY A YOUNG man may have gone through the British borstal system but there can be no doubt that there was only one who would be forever known as *'Borstal Boy'*. The term suggests menace and implies the sound of an iron gate being slammed back to allow a fighting bull, hooves pawing the ground and his horns lowered, to enter a bullring. It is a misleading analogy, for the term describes the reform school system for adolescents as it existed in the United Kingdom from 1902 till 1982. It eventually was succeeded by a new and better Act, or to put it in London Whitehall official-speak, "by provisions embodied under the Criminal Justice Act."

Its foundation lay with the Gladstone Committee in 1895 which was charged with putting together recommendations aimed at reforming young offenders. The committee was so named for William Ewart Gladstone, the British Parliament's longest-serving prime minister and one of the country's great reformers, at a time when various reforms – prisons, state pensions, taxation among others – were an agenda item in any party seeking to form a government. The operative term used to describe the benefits of Borstal detention was rehabilitation – notably through education, vocational training and group counselling. It was a new concept at the end of the 19th century. The first institution was established in 1902 at Borstal Prison, Kent, in southern England. Many others were subsequently established, some without walls or gates.

In 1939, Brendan Behan had just passed his 16th birthday. He had dabbled in writing but it looked unlikely he would make a career out of it; he was an angry young man a decade before the term had come into common usage. He was hell bent on causing mayhem on the British mainland, and for his efforts was rounded up in Liverpool following the channel steamship ride from Dun Laoghaire port in Dublin, across the Irish Sea into what many rebellious young Irish felt was enemy territory – England. The country that had London as its capital may have been known at large as Great Britain, but to the begrudged of Ireland, it was not the Welsh or the Scottish that were the source of ire, just the English.

It turned out that young Behan had been the victim of a tip off; the result was that he was rounded up not long after disembarking at Liverpool. He feared the likelihood of having to face execution for his ill-planned attempt. Instead, because he was under age, he was initially jailed for two months, and later, on February 8 1940 he faced trial and was sentenced to two years at the Hollesley Bay borstal Institution. The British authorities were especially on guard at that time about IRA activity given that Britain was again in a European war and facing trouble from Irish dissidents in its rear flank. The IRA had launched some attacks on the mainland and bombs had been set off in Manchester and in London's Tottenham Court Road area by those who would not accept the partition of Ulster from the rest of Ireland's 32 counties.

In the case of Behan's incarceration, there was a separate, highly emotional, strand that added poignancy to his time as 'His Majesty's Guest (HMG)'. Behan, for all his adolescent hell-raising, was deeply preoccupied with maintaining his Catholicism. To non-Catholics, this appeared to be an odd manifestation given the propensity for murder that dominated the two countries' relations during the long period of The Troubles. For all his braggadocio, Behan would be quick to admit that he could not manage in life without the anchor of his faith, regardless of how good or bad a Catholic he might otherwise be. He frequently referred to himself as a 'daytime atheist'. In his view, Irish nationalism and Catholicism were compatible, a view, if not a policy, which is held in many third-world countries to this day. In the Ireland of the 1920s and 1930s, this was contrary to official church policy, never mind how many individual priests privately felt about it. If anything, the church maintained a hard line and had overtly and repeatedly condemned the Irish rebels and republicanism. It was a classic standoff – in one line of thought, Catholicism was the church representing the poor and the oppressed, the self-same church having been persecuted by England under Cromwell. But in the narrow confines of the new nation of Ireland itself, the church played a central, if cautious, role so far as political support for the socially oppressed was concerned. In opposition to the more radical political movements of the day, the official church was playing the long game – the prize was Ireland itself.

Thus under the watchful eye of the Holy See and its many informers, the church condemned supporters of the IRA with the threat of excommunication. The idea of the church as a kind of 'trades union congress' whose priests would 'mix it' with the disenfranchised in order to improve their material, as well as spiritual, well-being (later to be known as liberation theology) had no momentum apart from its considerable charity work. This was not least because of the Communist-Fascist division arising from widespread civil unrest in Europe. To serious Catholics – even the likes of Behan – the threat of being kicked out of the faith was equivalent to a committal to hell-on-earth or to being cast adrift in a turbulent, endless, sea.

In a one-on-one battle between 'the Bolshie' young Brendan and a powerful institution, there was bound to be only one winner. Not a man for compromise, Behan at least would go down swinging. Some liberal Catholics held that the two views were not incompatible to the maintenance of one's faith, but conservative church members held that having it both ways would not pass muster in the church's inner sanctum. Behan v The Holy See was a small side show, even though it was a struggle that was not to be satisfactorily resolved. Asked not long after his arrest, why he didn't give up the faith, he would reply sharply: "In exchange for what?"

He spells this out in the final published edition of his autobiographical *Borstal Boy*, which at this juncture, 1940, was nonexistent and would not see the light of day for another 18 years when *Hutchinson's*, the UK publishing firm, agreed to go ahead with the book. By that time, Behan would be world famous and, like the boxer, Muhammad Ali, his own best promoter. But in the interim, his battle against the system was very much a private one and was little known about except for a coterie of his friends in Irish and British officialdom.

In his recounting of his first meeting in Walton jail with the prison chaplain, a Father Lane, in early 1940, he wrote: "I had been extra religious when a kid, and the day I made my First Communion, I had prayed to God to take me -- as Napoleon prayed --, when I would go straight to heaven. I was a weekly communicant for years after, and in spasms, especially during Lent, a daily one."

Then he reports having had difficulties when aged thirteen or so "with myself and sex (on this point he does not elaborate) and with the church because they always seemed to be against the Republicans."My father had been excommunicated in 1922 with thousands of others, and so had de Valera and the bishops were always backing the shooting and imprisoning of IRA men. It seemed the Church was always for the rich against the poor. But I had never given up the faith, and now I was glad that even in this well-washed smelly English hell-hole of old Victorian cruelty, I would be at one with hundreds of millions of Catholics at the sacrifice of the Mass."

But it was not to be so.

The following morning he wrote of being called to a meeting with Father Lane, who had said mass the previous morning and bluntly stated:

"When are you going to give up this business?"

"I don't know what business you are talking about, Father"

"You know all right – your membership of this murder gang – the IRA"

"The IRA is not a murder gang, father."

"Don't answer Father Lane back,' said a guard

"Cardinal Hensley said the Hierarchy of England have issued pastorals denouncing the IRA, and where you are going I cannot let you come to the altar, unless you tell me once and for all that you are growing up having anything to do with this gang."

"Why should the bishops of England be proposed to have the right to dictate about politics to an Irishman, Father?"asked the teenager

"I asked as steadily as I could," recalled Behan years later.

"The bishops of Ireland have denounced the IRA, Behan, time and time again, even early this year," said Father Lane. "The Church has always been Ireland's best friend in Ireland, here and England, and all over the world. I must inform you that your own clergy and hierarchy have excommunicated the IRA You are automatically excommunicated till you repent of your sin in being a member of it and promise God in confession to sever all connection with it. Surely you cannot set yourself up against the bishops, an ignorant lad against educated men who have spent their lifetime studying these matters."

According to his memoir, Behan, the rebellious teenager, let rip with a searing indictment of church and state, rattling off a long list of charges against the institution he had been thrown out of only minutes before.

"I didn't spend a lifetime studying theology, but I know that the Church was always against Ireland and for the British Empire . . . Wasn't my own father excommunicated and put in Kilmainham prison in 1922?"

Behan (according to Behan) in this exchange contained in *Borstal Boy* carried the day, but the act of excommunication which carries the steepest penalty in Catholic Christendom, the stripping of one's access to the sacraments, opened a wound in him that would not be healed for another 24 years. But just as his rift with ecclesiastical authorities created a terrifying seismic disturbance in his own life, the two-year term in Borstal, helped rid him of childhood prejudices about the English and laid the foundation for his later success as a writer. One reason was because of the availability of reading material, some of it in the Irish language to interested prisoners. Behan, although already well-read and competent in Irish, read aggressively and comprehensively, and the prison libraries themselves were even able to produce a digest of Irish language reading material. Behan, despite his natural tendency to defy authority, got on well while in English jails, his finding being that English lads were much the same as Irish lads. His was not a Damascene conversion, but being behind bars had the effect of knocking some chips off his shoulders and inducing in him a sense of realism about his situation.

An impression has developed over the years that Behan was an unruly prisoner, a James Cagney-type from the Dead-End Kids films popular at the time. Like Cagney, he was short but ready to deliver a punch, regardless of whether or not he was behind bars. While his pugnacity on the streets of Dublin would become known, misbehaviour inside jail was rare, particularly during such serious imprisonments as those in the UK and in Ireland, notably following an incident at Glasnevin cemetery outside Dublin. On the contrary, if anything he was as courteous before his masters and commanded their attention on interesting matters. A prison photo taken in 1940 shows the large-headed, curly-haired youth with protruding Adam's apple and tomahawk-shaped nose. He stands (at that time) at five feet, five and a quarter inches in height. His complexion is described as fresh. The photograph does not show his tiny feet and hands, key aspects of his so-called 'tulip shape', nor does it in any way indicate his aggravating stammer.

The Crazy Life of Brendan Behan

His inextinguishable humour seems to have been a source of amusement, if not mystification, to his English 'gaolers', as shown by his letter of December 23, 1940, a year after his capture in Liverpool. The letter is from a C. D. Robinson of Hollesley Bay Borstal to a M. H. Whitelegge of the prison Commission, Oxford.

"There is at Hollesley Bay Colony a youth named Brendan Behan, one of those convicted in connection with IRA activities, and the time has come for considering his discharge, for which, in the opinion of his housemaster and of the governor he is ripe . . . Bradley, the assistant commissioner who looks after Borstal institutions, saw Behan at a recent visit to Hollesley Bay and, in expressing the opinion that he is ready for discharge, Bradley says:

"He is a profound republican, but he assured me he had abandoned all ideas of violence . . . . I consider he was sincere in this assurance. He wants to be expelled to Ireland, for all his relations are there. He feels that the expulsion order will clarify the position and help him. He would go to sea if this was insisted upon, but he says he is always seasick and, being a good Irishman, he has a good deal of respect for Wellington but none at all for Nelson."

Particularly striking correspondence came from C. A. Joyce, the Hollesley Bay borstal. A week after Behan's death 24 years after the two men first met, Joyce wrote a letter to the *Sunday Telegraph* newspaper in London, very much a conservative establishment journal, referring to Behan's Borstal days. By this time, his own days as a prison governor were behind him. He was with the public relations office in an institution called the Ranier Foundation. The letter centred on Behan's continued torment over being excommunicated; it made particular reference to Joyce's efforts to alleviate the young Irishman's pain. It said:

"Would you be surprised to know that he was an intensely religious boy? He came to me as a member of the IRA and, as such, was excommunicated. It worried him a great deal. He said to me one say: "You must understand, sir, that the freedom of Ireland is me second religion. I was bred to believe in and work for it.' But very often he would come and say, 'Governor, couldn't you persuade the father to let me go to mass, for I feel all lost without its consolation?"

"I did ask the priest and he explained, so I told Brendan and he was very sad. Then I said, 'Listen, son, I'm not a Roman catholic, but I would like to go to Mass with you. We'll sit together and I cannot receive it for one reason and you for another, but I shall say my prayers to the same God as you will'."

The formula was ingenious and the two individuals put it to work. Sometimes the governor played the organ, the two joining in hymn singing. But there was also an impasse: "Brendan, I cannot recommend your discharge unless you promise you won't go back trying to kill my countrymen when you know that we are already fighting one enemy. Do you see?"

"The humour and wit of his character came up forthwith," said the governor.

"'Sure, I'll promise not to do anything until we've done with this bastard Hitler and after that I can always consider it again, can't I?"

Said Joyce: "He never lost touch with me over the years – often by telephone at 1 a.m, but never mind. You may think of him as the genius and the drunkard but I remember him as a boy of 19 *(sic)* who wanted to serve God and who loved his mother and his country."

His *Confessions of an Irish Rebel,* one of his funnier reminiscences, described the burlesque that accompanied the delivery of the release order that finally allowed him to return to Ireland. This was signed in November, 1941, two years after his initial arrest in Liverpool. It was read out by the prison sergeant:

"Take notice that His Majesty's Secretary of State for Home Affairs has made an order requiring you to leave Great Britain forthwith until further notice of this order has been made by reason of your instigation or preparation of acts of violence in Great Britain designed to influence government policy or public opinion with respect in Irish affairs."

Once that had been read over, Behan chipped in with a hearty 'hear-hear.'

"Shut up you little bastard," bellowed the sergeant. Further paragraphs were written, in effect reading Behan his rights."If you do not make representations within forty-eight hours of the service of this notice upon you, you will as soon as maybe thereafter be placed on board a ship about to leave Great Britain . . . . So take notice that you will be placed aboard a ship about to leave Great Britain . . ."

"Twice," said Behan with a grin.

"Shut up, you little git. Now (he asked the sergeant), do you accept service of this order?"

"I most certainly do."

The official, having finished his explication, put his arm around Behan and smiled gently, pledging to get him outfitted in suitable clothes and dispatched to Ireland. Thus, in December 1941, ended Behan's first stay in a British jail.

Behan's accounts of his triumphal rebelliousness must be taken with a grain of salt. Cursing in prison was forbidden, but for the privacy of one's own cell. Profanity of any sort, particularly in encounters with prison officials, was taboo and liable to be met with the brandishing of a prison guard's truncheon. That he said all he claimed to have said is doubtful, but the fact is that he at least wrote down what he claimed to have said that day, and that is a matter of record.

Behan would be in and out of jail, both Irish and English, many times over the next thirteen years. The most serious incident was the Glasnevin cemetery shooting in Dublin in 1942 which put him and a colleague on the run under orders to be shot on sight. No one was hurt in the incident, which happened on the anniversary of the 1916 April Rising. But Behan was sentenced, nevertheless, to 14 years penal servitude. He was sent to Mountjoy prison and released in November 1946 as part of a police amnesty. His many other bouts in jail were generally attributable to drink-related incidents consistent with those of a high-spirited Irishman 'out on the gargle.'

Although he was turning his hand to writing for a living – in both Irish and English – he continued to be at loggerheads with the British authorities, mainly because of his persistent violations of deportation orders. Under the order releasing him back to Ireland in 1941 he was forbidden to re-enter the U.K. This meant not using U.K. seaports as transit points to other ports. "Unfortunately, the immigration authorities did not take into consideration that the importance of England to an Irish person at that time was that it was only a stepping stone to France." That was Des MacNamara's view and it soon began to infect the young Behan once he'd had a taste of it. MacNamara would remember many times in the 1950s when the doorbell on his North London flat would ring and there would be Brendan skulking illegally in the shadows outside the door while en route to or from France. "Like an acorn, the idea began to grow in his mind that he didn't have to live forever in Dublin, a city he later said he loved deeply – but from a distance of say 3,000 miles."

The problem went on for years. A letter from the UK Special Branch police in mid-1949 reported that Behan had passed through the south coast port of Newhaven en route to France on August 19 and that Newhaven police knew nothing about Behan's police record, particularly his links with the IRA "He is due to return about September 2, and if he lands in England he will be arrested." The letter said:"It is useless to recommend that the life of the Prevention of Violence Act should be extended . . . . If steps are not taken to enforce it, Behan should certainly be arrested if he again lands in this country."

It was getting irksome for both sides. In January 1954 Behan himself wrote to the British Home Secretary. In a balanced letter devoid of invective, he explained that he was not permitted to enter the UK by reason of an expulsion order made against him under the *Prevention of Violence (Temporary provisions) Act 1939*. "I can only state that this order was made against me on account of my being caught in possession of a quantity of potassium chlorate and sugar at Liverpool in 1939. I was, at the time, 16 years of age. I do not deny that I was a member of the IRA nor do I deny that the material found in my lodgings was the property of that organisation. I further state that I was a member of the IRA when I was released from Borstal, and that I was sentenced to a term of imprisonment in Ireland in 1942."

At this time, Britain's problems with the IRA were becalmed as Ireland (minus the six counties of Ulster) had achieved full status as a republic, its brief period as a British 'dominion' having been consigned to the history books. Also his fame and infamy, for certainly he was the bearer of both, had not yet reached their peak, otherwise there would have been a more explosive reaction to his statement that he was "not now, nor for many years . . . a member of the IRA and I am not now a member of any political body or party or organisation of any description whatsoever. That my purpose in making this application to you to revoke this order is principally to facilitate my travelling between here and Paris."

A day later, on January 13, L. J. Burt of Special Branch wrote a memo: "Behan claims that he is not a member of any political party organisation and undertakes not to abuse the privilege of being allowed to visit this country . .. . I suggest that the expulsion order be revoked. . . .Thus, the end of the last traces of official bad blood between Behan and the British government,, underpinned with the statement that Behan no longer had any official connections with the IRA.

The story of *Borstal Boy,* the book, continued to gather shape and in the years between his first arrest and its publication in 1958.Behan's own development as a writer, thinker and human being. This is not to say that his famous short fuse had become longer, for it had not, but his barbs became more broadly directed. Nevertheless the English were always a good target. His brother Dominic remembered Brendan letting loose in defence of national heroes of the past. "The English claim Yeats but not Parnell, Wilde but not Pearse, and they wouldn't give you ten pence for Casement or Childers, but offer them Synge, Swift and Goldsmith and they would dance the walls of Limerick. The Yeats and Shaws live in Ireland as Irishmen and face the problems Irishmen have to face. They think of us as John Bull's other island, as Shaw said."

Borstal Boy is the story of two years in a young man's life although its composition would take nearly 18 years .before it made its explosive debut. Significantly, it blows away the author's entrenched phobias about the English – a people to be dreaded only two years before his IRA-sponsored trip to Liverpool and now found to be very much like his own countrymen. On steaming into Dublin, he says: "There they were (the hills) as if I had never left them; in their sweet and stately order round the Bay – Bray Head, the Sugarloaf, the Two Rock, the Three Rock, Kippur, the king of them all rising his threatening head behind and over their shoulders till they sloped down to the city"

It was as if he and his home town of Dublin were inseparable. Events were to prove otherwise.

CHAPTER FOUR

BRENDAN UNDERGROUND

"Fe fi fo fum
"I smell the blood of an Englishman.
"Be he alive or be he dead,
I'll crush his bones to make my bread..."
--19th century jingle from Jack and the Beanstalk

DESPITE HIS CHARM with women, Brendan Behan was probably more homosexual than heterosexual though he was scarcely discreet on either front. Rae Jeffs, when first interviewed for this book in 1979, dismissed suggestions that he was bisexual. She expressed it as a firm statement of fact and, as it turned out, it was an opinion held by many friends and observers and consistent with those times. She had been emotionally and professionally close to the playwright as well and her reticence was understandable. Unless one was overtly effeminate, as in the cases of the great Michael MacLiammoir and Hilton Edwards, partners and managers of The Gate theatre in Dublin, the subject was little discussed. Anyway Brendan wasn't the type.

But when the issue blew up over the kitchen table, the reactions were often far-reaching. The Behan family was still smarting years later from the cautiously worded published disclosures of writer Ulick O'Connor in his 1970 account of the playwright's life. O'Connor dated Behan's taste for the low life from his time in the British Borstal system, the boys' reform school institution where fraternising with young women was not possible and where sexual activities among young male prisoners were common. O'Connor implied that it was in Borstal that Behan developed a desire for fair-complexioned teenagers that never left hm. In Behan's case, argues O'Connor, it left a mark and led him to realise he could enjoy sex with young men as well as with women. The revelation certainly put him, O'Connor, on the outs with the Behan family, especially Beatrice, at least for a few years. Journalist John Walsh, writing for *The Independent* newspaper in London in July 2001, quoted brother Dominic as saying at the time of O'Connor's book that he would take Mr. O'Connor by the "scruff of the neck and sock him halfway round London."

That said, an aura of defensiveness persisted for years but the issue was finally blown away with the publication in 1981 of what can easily be described as a base experiment in biography titled *With Brendan Behan*, written by a boxer-sailor Peter Arthurs whom Behan and Beatrice met in Los Angeles at the time of *The Hostage* rampage. At Behan's bidding the two men formed a noisy and indiscreet relationship. Arthur's account, 17 years after Behan's death in 1964 prompted Clifford Irving, an American adventurer/writer who became famous by exploiting the secret life of billionaire Howard Hughes, to remark:

"This is a unique and unforgettable portrait of a sado-masochistic monster – a vicious tiny tank of a man rolling relentlessly through the mine fields of America crushing everything in sight until he blew up. I knew Brendan and couldn't stand him, but the bastard lived, he made his mark.

Peter Arthurs' book bursts with a dogged reverence, and at the same time is a stunning story of a worshiper's rites of passage toward freedom from the brutal writer who all but enslaved him. For that alone it should live too."

Desmond MacNamara came to the rescue with an artfully worded letter, eventually published as postscript material in O'Connor's study of Behan. It said:

"Surely, surely, the brouhaha caused by the reaction to a certain phase of Brendan Behan's sensual development is itself distorting and exaggerating the very complex truth of the matter. If a face is enlarged from a photograph of a football team or a school group, the result is a lie which interferes with the common process of perception. It can turn a sentient biped into something from a *Hammer* film production (*Hammer Films* being one of the big horror filmmakers of the time).

Behan, certainly because of his swaggering and aggressive personality, was not above 'trying it on' with acquaintances who had taken his fancy. He had well-practiced 'wandering' hands of the type bound to get one into fisticuffs. But among his circle of friends and buddies he openly joked about homosexuality while taking care to behave himself. As few of his friends were that way inclined and as they enjoyed his company, there was not the inclination to be distracted by his sexual pranks.

"It was quite a different thing to label somebody as gay (or queer) in those days when it was considered to be slanderous in comparison with today when it would almost add to the mystique of somebody like Brendan," said younger brother Brian in the 1990s. "A piece of graffiti I saw recently says it all – 30 years ago, homosexuality was condemned; 20 years ago it was frowned upon; ten years ago it was disapproved of today it is encouraged. I'm getting out before it becomes bloody compulsory."

Brian said of his brother that Brendan had never lost his sense of sin. But he didn't think there was anything worse about Adam and Steve committing that sin rather than Adam and Eve. . . . Brian remembered Brendan once being asked if he was homosexual. He gave a slashing reply worthy of tennis ace Jimmy Connors, low and just over the net: "Well, if I had to choose between Michelangelo's David and Whistler's Mother, who was ugly as the back of a bus, there'd be no fuckin' contest."

The fact was that he did not run with a 'queer' crowd and in any case, Behan was too busy raining insults, jokes, anti-religious barbs and assorted one-liners on any or all who might form up a pub audience somewhere around Dublin to share in the ribaldry with the possibility of punch-up as a bonus. There is no doubt that he learned a lot while in prison. In his Borstal memoirs, he wrote amusingly of an incident that occurred when he was installed at Walton Jail where he was told of his next destination, Borstal, by Tubby, a fellow prisoner. Tubby is a former Borstal Boy himself who is keen to impart advice. In an aside to a third person Charlie, Tubby says of Behan, "He'll probably go to Borstal and all. Want to watch his ring, though. Hey Jack'. He then shouted to Charlie, "Ever 'ad a length of the bo'sun's whistle? Any old three-batch stoker ever shown you the golden rivet'?"

He told also of an encounter with a Belfast man named Lavery, who in giving him a prayer book, warned him of some of the more seedy aspects of prison life. "The prisoners. . . though they are all right in their own way, they have as much respect for themselves, or for one another, as a bloody animal. They talk about things, aye, and do things that the lowest ruffian in Ireland, Catholic or Protestant, wouldn't put his tongue to mention of, things that you could be born, grow up and die an old man in our country without ever even hearing the mention of.

"You know what they talk about in the dormitories and you can't go and take a shower but there's some fellows making filthy jokes that you have to listen to you know. . . .Remember, you are not a cat burglar or a – a – a ponce, but a Republican soldier, and carry yourself as such."

Rae Jeffs, the very essence of Englishness, was charmed by Behan from the start of their friendship; to her he was kindness itself. Anybody inclined to be ill-mannered in her presence would be looking for a fist fight. Behan, though not big, was solidly built and possessor of an aggressive temperament, some of which could be put down to pent up frustration at his chronic stammer. In intervening years, up to 2009, when last interviewed, Jeffs was prepared to admit that he was as much one or the other. She said that if he went into a room filled with men and women he would be paying as much attention to the males as the females. The likelihood was that he had experimented while in Borstal. "He'd have screwed a sheep, he had to find out," she said. There were stories of group sex late at night back in the Behan house in Ballsbridge, south Dublin, and other assorted shenanigans. "I never turned a hair on all these things going on," she said, elaborating that in his later years, with the onset of alcoholism, he was quite incapable of having a sexual relations with anybody.

It is a moot point. There was the case of Shelagh Delaney, scarcely out of her teens who wrote the immensely popular *A Taste of Honey,* its production and staging making her one of the youngest playwrights in London's west end.. The play became popular in cadence with Behan's *The Hostage*. It was not long before Behan, the Dubliner, and Delaney, the Lancashire lass (but a Celt nonetheless), became an item in the gossip columns. Delaney's interest in Behan was not lost on Beatrice, an artist and fellow Dubliner who met and married the playwright in 1955. A quiet lady, she was not about to let her marriage founder over the affections of a girl scarcely out of her teens. Beatrice showed her fibre, promptly intervened and moved to break up the affair. With Beatrice, being married to such a man it was soon necessary for her to strike a balance between the entertainment value of her relationship and how much abuse of the institution of marriage she was prepared to live with. Rather more of the latter than the former as matters would turn out.

To those who knew him and had the presence of mind to stand back, Brendan Behan's life was becoming increasingly episodic, marked by a spirit of misadventure and knowing no boundaries. He was a teen-aged revolutionary, a jail bird in the UK and Ireland, then a house painter and raconteur in his early 20s, then a skilled, socially aware, playwright, a reckless vagabond, inside and outside marriage and a roaring artistic and commercial success at the age of thirty. With Behan, what you saw was what you got. It is intriguing to speculate how Professor Marshall McLuhan, the University of Toronto's modern communications guru, would have treated the phenomenon of Behan; it was McLuhan who coined the phrase *'The Medium is the Message.'* He must have had Behan in mind.

CHAPTER FIVE

HALCYON DAYS

'I remember being in the Blue Lion on Parnell Street and the owner said to me: 'You owe me ten shillings; you broke a glass the last time you were here.' 'God bless us and save us', I said. 'It must have been a very dear glass if it cost ten shillings. Tell us, was it a Waterford glass or something'. I discovered in double quick time that it wasn't a glass you would drink out of he meant – it was a pane of glass and I'd stuck somebody's head through it. . . ."-- Brendan Behan's island.

WHAT WOULD HAVE become of Brendan Behan had he not had his trade as a housepainter to return to? To be sure, his arrest and imprisonment by the British government in 1939 had been a close-run thing for him. Had he been older, he might have been jailed for much longer or might have even faced the death penalty. As it was, he was dropped into a liberally policed environment far from home among a people he had been taught to detest – the English. He had been out of Ireland for more than two years, he had been on a terrorist mission about which everybody knew and, what is worse, had failed to carry it out. He had also returned to an Ireland which was recovering from the 'emergency' and where some sense of political direction was starting to evolve now that the Second World War had ended. The de Valera government was also far less disposed now as opposed to just a few years ago to be seen offering tacit support for the more nefarious activities of the IRA. Within four years, Ireland would forgo its face-saving (for Britain) status, as a Dominion of Britain. It would, instead, be a fully fledged independent country that just happened to be on the American side of the British isles. Indeed, political and trade relations between the 26 counties of Ireland and the six counties of Ulster were going relatively smoothly and terrorist activity was at an all-time low.

Behan was freed in November 1941 and he returned home a somewhat different young man than the trouble maker of late 1939. For one thing, he seemed to have survived the terrors of jail relatively untroubled, having spent a calm, creative couple of years at Hollesley Bay Borstal institution the highlight of which was the discovery that incarcerated English lads were not much different from incarcerated Irish lads. Still, his Republican blood continued to run thick and fast, at least for a little while longer. Young Behan, only in his 20th year, became involved in a shooting incident at Glasnevin Cemetery, on the northern fringe of Dublin, at a ceremony to mark the anniversary of the 1916 Easter Rising. Behan, despite his bravado, was no Billy-the-Kid and cleanly missed what he was aiming at, went on the run, briefly, was captured, tried and jailed for 14 years, sent to Arbour Hill in Ireland and then the Currragh and after five years was released in a general amnesty. His next term behind bars lasted four months following his arrest by the British authorities in Manchester following his capture for helping an IRA prisoner escape jail.

By this time, the writer inside him had been scratching at its shell long enough and wanted to get out. Behan began to take a personal inventory of his assets – well read in English literature, capable in the Irish language, a budding love affair with France where, unlike England, he felt welcomed. His interests were widespread , and his political sensitivities were deepened by his time in jail. He claimed acquaintanceships with a number of literary folk, like Sean O'Faolain, editor of *The Bell,* and Samuel Beckett, the latter scoring a major international success with his classic play, *Waiting for Godot.* Furthermore Behan could type well and his experiences as a jailbird were enough to provide grist for the writing mill. He was not yet an alcoholic.

While Behan was getting settled back in Ireland, J. P.Donleavy, was arriving from the U.S. on what was known as the G. I. Bill to underwrite his studies while he was in Ireland. The term G.I., incidentally, meant Government Issue, a roundabout way of saying 'American Soldier'. To Donleavy, Ireland was a mesmerizing place. He was prepared to absorb its ambience while studying at Trinity in Dublin. It is a fact that one would not have to spend much time in Ireland in those days before encountering the likes of Behan, a noisy street personality but one passing into young manhood.

"I didn't know what to make of him," said Donleavy . "He followed no social convention, and he only once bought a suit, and when complimented on his purchase at once dirtied it up in the gutter. I remember him once pouring a pint of Guinness over his head, and then declaring 'now I'm having a shower.'

It was not easy to describe Behan and Donleavy as friends but they were 'confreres', though at times the American would take a wide berth if he saw the Irishman approaching. Once, when living in the countryside outside Dublin, he spotted Behan approaching, sockless, wearing unlaced shoes and covered in dust and sweat. It was Donleavy's view that Behan had advanced beyond his younger status as an IRA troublemaker;

instead, he had come to regard his stays at Borstal and other Irish lockups as akin to having been at Eton or Harrow.

In the early days of their acquaintanceship, when both were anxious to make their marks as writers, Behan, perhaps fearing the whiff of competition, challenged Donleavy to a fight outside the Davy Byrnes pub in Dublin. It is likely he did not know that Donleavy was an expert boxer capable of unleashing off a combination of seven punches in one second. Anyway, the two men, squaring off a-la-Queensberry rules, decided to call a halt at Behan's behest. 'What's the point of fighting," Behan said, "when we haven't been able to draw a crowd?'

Writing talent or not, one had to earn a crust and this meant house painting. One story, told by Garech Browne, reported the time when Behan was painting an outside wall of The Gaiety Theatre in central Dublin. The assignment was taking a long time as Behan had got into the habit of taking increasingly extended beer breaks at a nearby pub.

"There were footprints of white paint running from The Gaiety to the pub and back across the street – and they were not very straight. He was back up the ladder as the matinee was about to begin and people were queuing up," recalled Browne. "Brendan was painting and singing happily when the manager came out. Some people in the queue thought Behan a fine fellow and one woman said:

"Ah, begod, that's a grand lad you have singing up there," to which the manager, now fuming and drawn up in imperious pose, replied 'Maybe so, madam, but there will be no encore'. That was the end of that job for a while."

His painting assignments also brought him indoors. Once, while working in the loft of an old house in North Dublin, he was removing rolled up newspapers which had been put

Halcyon Days

between the joists years before as a form of insulation. An instinctive and voracious reader, he looked at the paper and saw that it was dated 1921 and that it had news of the death of, say, a Michael 'Ballymagool' in a shooting. Later, when he could get to a telephone, he located the next of kin, now 35 years older, and asked the operator to connect him. Within seconds, he was speaking to a surviving member of the family. Behan, posturing innocently, began: 'We've just read of poor Michael's death in The Troubles while crossing the bridge and a shame it was too and in a good cause but we'd like to send you our condolences. It was just in the paper there.'

Browne remarked that the conversation went on as if it had happened yesterday. Behan and the voice at the end of the line parted company the best of friends.

Actor Niall Toibin, a friend and an acclaimed Behan interpreter on stage, said that Behan could be inspiring in ways that he did not fully realise. Toibin, Behan and a friend, Seamus Ford, were drinking in a north Dublin pub in the 1950s when Ford noted Behan's distinctive rolling walk (which Donleavy referred to as a shambling duck walk).

"That's almost the same walk described in the production notes of *Juno and the Paycock,* by O'Casey, for Captain Boyle – a slow consequential strut." Toibin recollected that Ford drew this to his attention "should I ever play Captain Boyle. The coincidence was that I should use the walk to portray not the Captain but Brendan himself."

In the late 1940s and early 1950s, Behan went through a sociable phase which enhanced his reputation for being generous and made him more liked than disliked. Donleavy was cautious of some of the company Behan kept. The American recalled a Sean Daly, a Behan buddy sometimes known as Lead Pipe Daly or sometimes Daly the Danger.

The Crazy Life of Brendan Behan

He hadn't much of a head for alcohol at this time but his drinking in these years was more balanced all round, certainly a far cry from the state he was to find himself in just four or five years

One of Desmond MacNamara's favourite tales was of the time when he, Behan and a third person, a painter, were relaxing on an island in Dublin Bay on a warm summer day. "We had taken with us to this island a half dozen bottles of South African wine which we lowered on strings into the cold salt water, very, very deep, in order to keep it cool. Brendan was asked to pull in the strings with the consequence that all the wine went down to about ten fathoms. Naturally abuse was heaped on him. 'Never mind, never mind,' he said, and plunged into the water and swam out to sea. It was then that we noted two smallish boats about 300 yards out from the island; he had disappeared for a long time, and we wondered if he would ever get back."

"He swam back in about three quarters of an hour with a net back with one bottle of calvados and a Coca Cola bottle in the net. The boats were Breton fishermen, and he had noticed that. He had swum out and swum back and, in so doing, had repaid his debt."

Behan's agonising over the issue of excommunication from the Catholic church for failing to persuade him to renounce the IRA underlined his notion of faith but it did not stop him from unleashing anti-clerical fusillades on his colleagues. MacNamara was asked if Behan had ever shown any sign of softening his stance vis-a-vis the church. That is, did he ever yield to solemnity, prayerfulness or outright devotion? MacNamara said bluntly, 'no', he could not do so. Yet, while he could be outrageously condemnatory on matters religious, he sometimes would find himself deeply in need of some aspect of the faith for comfort and solace. In this, he would probably have needed to be armed with some religious weaponry to lever himself through a tough spot. When swinging the brickbats, Behan was likely to stand firm in defending his own arguments as well as rubbishing the same arguments to make a point. Behan was anything but lukewarm.

He claimed on several occasions to never swearing at home – the reader needs to be reminded that the Crumlin dwelling had but two major rooms, so the consequences of outbursts would be far-reaching. He admitted that if there was any cursing it was by Brendan '*pere*'. He had to concede a talent for blasphemy but again it was the old man's doing.

One of the more celebrated disagreements to take place in Ireland was between the poet Paddy Kavanagh and Behan. Kavanagh was vaguely anglophile and was known to have prompted a fight in a pub by demanding from the bartender an update on the latest cricket score from across the water. Overt affection for cricket in Ireland, particularly in those politically tense days, was seen as a dangerous way to behave mainly because it was indicative of an unhealthy affection for the British Crown. In the early 1950s, either by mishap or design, Stephen Behan, had heard of a paint job going at the Kavanagh household, so he subcontracted it to Brendan. Brendan did not get along overly well with his father, bearing a resentment against the elder's frequent absences from home as a result of extensive pub crawling. At some point the paint job was finished and the dwelling deemed to be safe for reoccupation. Kavanagh returned, opened the door and recoiled when he found that the interior had been painted black Despite their antipathy for each other, the two men have been filmed singing Irish folk songs while in a stotious state suggesting that there were occasional outbreaks of peace between the two.

CHAPTER SIX

A QUARE ONE

"He was often, ah, merry, to put it mildly, so we did not encourage him to come round to the theatre too often, but from time to time he used to come to rehearsals and he used to sit beside me and nudge me and say, 'I wrote that'. He took great delight in hearing his words spoken. He became very affectionate towards the actors and, until his death, he loved the actors who were performing his plays . . . . he realized that he needed actors to put over his lines. . . ." – Alan Simpson

THEY SAY THAT good luck, by its very essence, is accidental. So it was a lucky day after the end of the Second World War that brought Alan Simpson into contact with Brendan Behan. Simpson then was a part-time stage manager and an engineering student, and Behan, with his father's help, had resumed his trade as a house painter. In his spare time, he was trying his hand at writing at which, said many who knew him, he was a natural. Both men were just finishing up service to the Irish state, Simpson being demobilized from the official

Irish army – it was 1946 – and Behan, doing his last stint in jail as an IRA troublemaker.

Simpson, one of the underpraised pioneers of modern English-language theatre, was born in 1920. A few years older than Behan, he was an opposite in almost every way. He was tall, lanky and quietly erudite and not, to any extent, a big drinker. He was not an abstainer either. Born in Dublin, he was the son of Canon and Mrs. Walter Simpson, and was educated at Campbell College, Belfast, and Trinity College, Dublin, two of Ireland's leading protestant educational bastions. It was at both institutions that he first learned the rudiments of acting and theatrical presentation. Simpson, who had been studying engineering, eventually became an army engineer. He was to find the skills involved in engineering compatible with theatre for the stage, where he put on his first army shows for Ireland's modest soldiery. In the immediate post-war years, he divided his time between England and Ireland, busying himself with theatrical work and production.

"Brendan, who had a reputation as being a rather ferocious man, was scared out of his wits at my antipathy, but we became very friendly . . . . At that time, I really didn't know much about what he was writing, so we were really just drinking friends, as it were. Then a few years later I had started The Pike.

The Pike theatre was founded on a shoestring budget and, now long gone, was on Herbert Lane. It was a fringe theatre, a term then not widely used, and also sometimes known in France as a 'theatre de poche'. It was similar, as Simpson recalled, to the *Theatre Babylon* in Paris, where Samuel Beckett first saw the staging of his pioneering *Waiting for Godot*. The play had been written in French, as were all Beckett's plays, and because of its own brevity was very much theatre-de-poche material. The Pike, seating fewer than a hundred patrons, was in the same league; and was apt to run at a loss even when operating a full house, which it often did. Along with his wife and co-founder Carolyn Swift, Simpson brought the Pike into being out of the need for the couple to find a permanent home for a good company of actors they had been able to put together for a play written by Jonathan Swift.

"The Pike was very small, tiny in fact, and I started it because I wanted to direct my own selection of works. I found it would give me some sort of continuity to have my own very small place rather than get involved in bigger theatres. We had a couple of flops to begin with and then we had great success with a review starring Milo O'Shea. The next thing that happened was that I discovered that Brendan had written a play (some seven years had passed since they first met at MacNamara's flat). Brendan didn't submit it to me, but I had met a niece of the actor-manager Michael Macliammoir (the hyper-theatrical actor famous for his one-man shows and an early patron of the young Orson Welles), who told me that he (Behan) had submitted the play to The Gate and that they weren't going to do it, and I also heard from somebody else that the same thing had happened at The Abbey. Anyway, I asked him if I could have a look at it, and I immediately liked it. This was his first *play*, *The Quare Fellow*, and the minute I looked at it, I realised I must do it. That was in 1954, after I had started the theatre in 1953."

The play was a courtyard, not a courtroom, drama, and the story revolved around jailhouse anxieties among prisoners at the impending hanging of a convicted murderer, the so-called quare fellow. The story was set in a Dublin worthy of Welles' *Macbeth,* so dank and chilly was the atmosphere, and of course is took a big stab at the uselessness of capital punishment, very much the social issue of the time, and one that was delivering itself of a particular poignancy with the long drawn-out series of stays of execution in a celebrated California court case. The cast exceeded two dozen and all were male, adding to the play's unusual bite. The lines were delivered in rolling Irish argot.

Two years later, Simpson brought *Godot* to an English-language audience for the first time, followed a year later by Tennessee Williams' *The Rose Tattoo,* the latter accompanied by police intervention over the suspected deployment as a prop of a condom in violation of obscenity laws. The charges were eventually dropped, but not before a scare was thrown the freedom of expression movement in what was still a very censorious country. It was Simpson's firm view that *The Quare Fellow* was one of the pioneering plays in the revolution that was soon to sweep through the English-language stage pushing aside the Terrence Rattigans of the day and opening the door to the likes of John Osborne and a group of playwrights and novelists known as The Angry Young Men.

"There were two of them, himself and Samuel Beckett, at that particular moment. *Waiting for Godot* had opened in 1952 in Paris and of course *The Quare Fellow* opened with me in Dublin in 1954. It was not till 1955 or 1956 that *Look Back in Anger* appeared which was the beginning of the English revolution, if you like . . . In fact *The Quare Fellow* was the first play of a different type to hit the English market and, as such, had this incredible effect.

"It was really the 1950s when everything started to change for people who had experienced the war. . . and it welled up all over Europe and spread to the rest of the world," said Simpson. "Behan was not such a revolutionary at that point. In format. (The play) was very documentary, and his experience of theatre was not limited to but very greatly influenced by what he had seen in The Abbey by Sean O'Casey and J. M. Synge and so forth. It didn't occur to many Irish writers, until Beckett, to break away from the traditional format. Now this breaking away was more from the traditional content and using language which, in its way, though poetic was more realistic of its time in Dublin than (Sean) O'Casey's in his early days. . . . In *The Quare Fellow,* it was the content and the vividness of the dialogue that was the revolutionary aspect."

The Quare Fellow had the advantage, too, of showing that life imitates art; there were three real-life dramas dominating the news print and air waves of the US and Europe at the time which contributed to the rising tide of irreverence by Europe's and America's young.

First was the long debate on capital punishment. Behan had been an active if somewhat erratic campaigner for libertarian values at the time following the holocaust and other examples of blood spillage There was the Ruth Ellis murder trial in the UK -- she became, in 1955, the last woman to be executed in the UK, which added to the publicity for *The Quare Fellow.* Finally there was the prolonged detention on Death Row in the US of one Caryl Chessman (1948-60), a convicted rapist and kidnapper whose prosecution had been marred by numerous delays in applying the death penalty. Arrested in 1948 and finally executed in 1960, Chessman's incarceration was rarely out of the news and achieved an international following, *especially* with the surreptitious publication of his best-selling book about life 'inside'. It was titled *Cell 2455 Death Row.*

One feature of life that ignited the development of revolutionary theatre was the collective acknowledgement that the beginning of the end of the British Empire was nigh and with it colonialism and exploitation by powerful nations of subject peoples abroad -- themes all Irish people were acutely aware of. Some pundits argued that this could be pinned down to what has become known as the Suez Crisis and, at the same time the unopposed invasion of Hungary by Soviet forces. What was significant about these two far-distant and seemingly unconnected events was their disillusioning effect on western politics. The

A quare one

incidents underlined the recognition of the hollowness of the 'great' victory over totalitarianism in the recent world war. Neither British troops nor anyone else's for that matter came to the rescue in Hungary and the beleaguered government of Imre Nagy. As for Suez, the seizure of canal by Anglo-French and Israeli forces took place without any long-term game plan and, above all without US backing. This further underscored the fact that the British Lion, like Sampson, was fast losing its hair. The net effect was the deepening of the cold war and the growing disrespect for those in power by an increasingly emboldened public, notably the British prime minister, Anthony Eden, who resigned after just two years in office.

Closer to home, the primary inspiration on the budding author of *The Quare Fellow* came from Behan's own stays in prison. His time inside took up most of the first half of the 1940s and a quarter of his young life. But while inside, he became a voracious reader, "and you could say that his time in Borstal and subsequently in internment in Mountjoy prison in Dublin was his third level education. .

Just how personalised were Behan's researches into the character of *The Quare Fellow* was singled out shortly after his death by writer Benedict Kiley. It was during his spell in Mountjoy after the war, he found himself sharing space with the last man to be hanged in the Irish Republic. According to the story, Behan, two warders and the condemned man made a quartet to play handball. Behan drinking the *Quare Fellow's* allotment of stout, the condemned man no longer being sure that Guinness, the dark porter beer, was so good for you. Behan was in jail for politics; the condemned man in his play was a pork butcher who had murdered his brother and had dismembered and scattered his remains so thoroughly no evidence could be found. Indicative of Behan's quick and irreverent wit, the condemned man asked Behan if hanging hurt. Behan's quick reply was that he didn't think so but had never been through it himself nor had talked with anybody who had.

The decision to give the play its controversial name came down, in one instance, from Dr. Douglas Hyde, often called the father of the Irish language and the new country's first president. He had written a work called *The Twisting of a Rope*. Behan favoured a gentle plagiarism and opted for *The Twisting of Another Rope*, a play in which the protagonist, a man about to die, never appears on stage and, rather like Falstaff in *Henry V*, dies offstage. But despite his failure to appear, his presence still casts a giant shadow. The nigh the play opened, viewers were made aware of a last minute change of title from *The Twisting of Another Rope* to *The Quare Fellow*. The reason was simple -- the longer title would have taken up an extra line of space in the newspaper advertisement.

"Because the theatre was so small we could not afford proper publicity," said Simpson: "The interesting thing about the play is that it doesn't, in so many words, condemn anybody or anything, and the condemned man in the play is never seen. The play . . . shows a frightful psychological effect that in a sense it is the condemned man who is the lucky one it is everybody else who gets the psychological bruises and wounds . . . There is nothing preachy about it at all, and this makes for a remarkable play. But of course now (in 1979, when Simpson was interviewed shortly before his death) it has lost its impact, and in most countries, the idea of capital punishment, if not officially dropped, is not carried out very much."

Simpson described Behan as a careless writer, but said this was not necessarily a bad thing. He remembered: "He didn't have any feelings about (pruning his work down). One has had dealings with new playwrights who believe that every word they have written is pure gold; they create a terrific fuss if you suggest reorganising or removing any words. Brendan wasn't like that. He fully appreciated what one was trying to do that was good for the show, and we had no problems with him in that area at all. He was very happy to make changes or to let us make changes. But let it be understood that in making these changes of an editorial nature, there was never anything that I did or anybody that I know of that where other ideas were put in that were other than Brendan's, which makes dealing with his work after his death a very precise operation because one has to bring out exactly his ideas

"Brendan knew what he wanted to say and he just slapped it down on the page without cluttering it up with minute instructions of how it should be done, which is exactly what a creative director requires to make a production which is going to fit in with a freer approach to entertainment."

The world of the theatre got its first look at *The Quare Fellow* – and at its colourful author -- on November 9 1954. The tiny Pike was jammed. The curtain fell after less than two hours, and the play was deemed a success. Behan, only modestly into his cups, ascended the stage and delivered a coherent and much applauded speech. Said Simpson:"We did not afford to stage it for longer than one month. We did not actually make any money on it at all, but the impact was enormous . . . , We could have run it for months if we could have afforded to.

"As for Brendan, he was so enthralled. I mean he had written a play set in prison before The *Quare Fellow* but he wasn't happy with it and had destroyed it or lost it. If you are a novelist, it is wonderful to be published; but if you are a playwright, not to hear your words spoken by an actor must be extraordinarily depressing.

"He was often, ah, merry, to put it mildly, so we did not encourage him to come around to the theatre so often. But from time to time he used to come to rehearsals and he used to sit beside me and nudge me and say: 'I wrote that.' He took great delight in hearing his words spoken. He loved the actors who were performing his plays. He realised he needed actors to put over his lines."

Brendan's reaction was like that of a little boy who has just landed beneath the Christmas tree at the same time as Father Christmas: "I was at Joe McGill's house in London when the telephone rang (McGill, like MacNamara, was an old friend). It was Carolyn Swift and she and Alan had read my play and offered me a production of four weeks at The Pike. ''For god's sake, Carolyn, how much, and she replied, 'thirty pounds but we want to change the title to *The Quare Fellow*.

"For thirty pounds, you can change the title to any bloody thing you like," said Behan many years after, thus deepening the mystery over the provenance of the title. "I put down the receiver and far into the night the three of us lifted pints in the name of the Celtic god Led. In the morning, I left for France."

The triumph at The Pike that November night attracted attention in England, but it would be another 18 months before London's bright lights of would shine on the text. The rescuing angels would be Joan Littlewood and Gerry Raffles, who had been shaking up theatre in the UK, not least because of the emergence of political figures on the scene bearing names like Imre Nagy and Colonel Gamel Abdel Nasser.

CHAPTER SEVEN

A Shock at the BBC

"He had come to the studio, already quite drunk, and they had, as far as I could make out, poured more drink into him, and then realized that he was incapably drunk and exhibited him as a spectacle. I regard that as a horrible thing to do, particularly for a man who goes about being a Christian as Muggeridge does.. . . " – Conor Cruise O'Brien

BRENDAN BEHAN IN his prime was to the world of letters what Muhammad Ali a few years later would be to boxing, a quick, hilarious self-promoter, able to bob and weave his way into and out of trouble, a master of what Ali would call the 'rope-a-dope.' If he could not fly like a butterfly, he certainly could sting like a bee. His alter ego might also have been found closer to home in the person of George Best, the dazzling Irish football (soccer) star for Manchester United in the late 1960s whose on-field skills were matched by his off-field dramatics to the point where he was burnt out by the time he was 30 years old. Had the two men, with their remarkable capacities for off-the-field capers, been a few years closer in age, then a special Hall of Fame would have had to be opened for each of them.

A natural crowd pleaser, Behan was quite capable in a matter of seconds of seizing control of pubs or of gatherings of people and regaling those present with samples of his often scatological wisdom. This did not always work in his favour and led many to call him 'stage Irish', a shallow conveyor of blarney playing to the galleries. He also lost a few teeth in the process but so did his adversaries.

In the years of his greatest fame, these galleries were in theatres in New York, Boston, Toronto, Montreal, San Francisco and Los Angeles, cities with strong Irish Catholic populations where laughter could be expected even before Behan opened his mouth. He was, to many, an irresistibly humorous man , on the one hand spoiling for a fight and on the other genuinely fearful of being alone and in the grip of a stammer for which alcohol was the only cure. Behan thrived in the shared camaraderie of others, lighting up the dank atmosphere of Dublin pub life to the extent that it began to do serious damage to his health. So quick and precocious was his wit that he was quite capable of trampling over someone and causing real hurt, but if he was made aware of what he had done he would become as contrite as a child. As Anthony Cronin described it: "Brendan had a voracious appetite for attention and whenever he sought it he usually got it."

It was the diplomat and writer, Conor Cruise O'Brien, not necessarily a friend of Behan's but a contemporary and a supporter of his work, who once observed how the alcoholic had to be right to maximize the value of his company. "He was very good company, indeed, when he had had a few drinks, but he was not good company when he had had nothing to drink. Of course, it follows that he could be appalling company if he had had a hell of a lot to drink. So if you saw Brendan around, you took careful note of what the state of matters was before you made contact with him."

To underline the point, O'Brien recalled an early encounter in a pub with the playwright, sometime in the early 1950s at a time when Behan was trying to hawk *The Quare Fellow* around. Behan and O'Brien were dimly acquainted, but Obrien had not, at that time, thought of Behan as a writer. Valentine Iremonger, a friend of O'Brien's, from the Department of Foreign Affairs, had been given a typescript of the play to read and had passed it on to O'Brien for a second opinion. He was drinking at a very staid Grafton Street pub called Mooney's. "It was ultra-square, lower middle class, very un-Behanish, unlike the pub across the street he frequented, McDaids, sort of a Bohemian, rather raffish, literary pub which I used to avoid like the plague."

O'Brien was eating a frugal lunch while sitting as inconspicuously as possible between a man in a bowler hat who looked like a debt collector and a respectable lady who probably ran a boarding house. O'Brien himself was perusing with much admiration the typescript of *The Quare Fellow* when he spotted Behan swaggering through the front entrance. O'Brien's shoulders hunched up for he knew that Behan knew Iremonger had passed the script to him and that he was about to become the butt of a Behan joke.

"He came down the row of barstools towards me; he was fairly tight, which in fact was his best talking condition, that is, when he had had just a few drinks. 'Conor', he said 'would you lend me a quid?' I said no, I would not lend him a quid, but I would lend him a half crown. He said, 'That's not enough' so I said I was sorry. No was not enough for Brendan and he began to elaborate why. 'The thing, you see, is that I have a mott' (Dublinese for a woman companion of dubious virtue) across the street, you know what I mean. I think if only I had

had a few more drinks it would be alright this afternoon, you know what I mean?'

"My neighbours were getting a little restless at this intervention, so I said I knew what he meant, but I wasn't going to lend him a pound. You see, money was tight in those days. He argued a bit and then took his half crown, or whatever it was, and then he departed. This pub had a long rail and a long bar, very old fashioned. He walked down to the door and from the door he shouted at me: 'Conor, you don't mind what I said about the mott, do ya?' I said no but he shouted back, 'I mean, I'm a hamasexshul meself, but these days you have to take what you can get. Goodbye now, Conor."

O'Brien, with his head down in embarrassment, soon left the pub, but by the other exit. 'It is a scene I still remember vividly,' he said

Des MacNamara remembered that Behan, even before international fame engulfed him, had become popular on the streets of Dublin."People came to recognize him in the street and he loved that. On one occasion, he swept the entire top deck off a bus and into a pub. By everyone, I mean ladies, housewives, kids, pensioners. What happened was that when he got on the bus some old lady who had seen him on TV the night before recognized him again. They all spent several hours with him just chatting, talking and listening to him orate till some friend came to the rescue."

Behan, who at this stage of his public exposure became fond of the Irish counterparts of London's more famous open markets, Billingsgate, Covent Garden and Smithfields, "The pubs serving those markets were open very early hours and he would chat with anybody from market gardeners to Poles, Estonians to God only knows."

With the theatre and modern fiction breaking out of their traditional stranglehold, thanks to Osborne, John Braine, Keith Waterhouse, Alan Sillitoe and many others, and with an interest being shown in *The Quare Fellow* by Joan Littlewood's group in London, Behan's life had become as effervescent as a bottle of champagne. He may have broken through in Ireland in 1954 but that was not the same as a triumph in London. *The Quare Fellow,* in Littlewood's hands, loomed in importance after the London Arts Theatre presentation of Beckett's *Godot* on August 3 1955. Littlewood had established a big, if dusty and drafty base at Stratford-le-Bow in London's east end followed by a rival launching of John Osborne's *Look Back in Anger* by another theatre group, headed by George Devine, based at the Theatre Royal in London's Chelsea in the west end of London.

Behan's magic carpet ride out of Ireland and onto the London scene could not have been timelier and Littlewood's handling of her unpredictable charge ensured that Behan one day was going to make an international name for himself. It was only a question of waiting for lightening to strike. The bolt from the blue came when Behan agreed to accept an invitation to appear on BBC-TV's *Panorama* show, then an arts show and not the investigative news programme it has since become. *Panorama* went out live, and the host was Malcolm Muggeridge, then a journalist of much renown and satirical bent – not the somewhat priggish man he was to become in the 1970s when he converted to Catholicism. Muggeridge's journalism over the years dating back to the 1930s was closely followed by political analysts for it was he, more than almost any other English-speaking journalist at the time, who spotted the myth, the fatal flaw, of Joseph Stalin's vision of Communism which he sought to expose to a disbelieving western world anticipating the collapse of capitalism. In those days, too, the BBC was about the only show in town, independent television being in its infancy. To appear on the Beeb, as it was called, was a rare honour.

What was to become a TV show to remember – it is still talked about in the bowels of Broadcasting House, the BBC's London headquarters, by senior journalists – began ordinarily enough early in the evening with drinks at the famous Garrick Club, a gentlemen's club mainly peopled by writers and located close by Covent Garden. Muggeridge recalled in his memoirs that Behan, accompanied by his new wife Beatrice had already had a head start, by which he meant that some alcohol was coursing through his guest's veins. No matter to Muggeridge who years later were to sum up his professional philosophy with a single line: "if journalism stops being fun then it is time to get out of it."

Then it was off to the BBC studios at Lime Grove. Muggeridge, not being disposed to turning off the tap, ensured that more drinks were poured in the entertainment bar before show time. Behan was to be the third of three guests on the live TV show. The first were officials from the War Office, then a finishing school headmistress and several of her charges. He recalled the girls filing into the entertainment room, only to encounter this rough-hewn Irishman bellowing; they abruptly filed out again. Behan, suddenly turning and asking: "Didn't I see a lot of pretty girls in here just now?" Muggeridge's reply: "I explained that he had been dreaming; we were in a place of dreams."

Just before lights, action, camera, Leonard Miall, BBC official in charge of *Panorama,* feared the worst. "If he uses the word 'c---', don't laugh," he instructed Muggeridge. What the TV audiences saw was the saturnine smile of the interviewer trying to prompt answers to his questions from a by-now-incoherent Behan. Such behaviour on the state-owned broadcasting network was something of a first and led to a flood tide of ribald headlines in both the popular and serious newspapers the following day, not only in London but back in Dublin. Said Muggeridge: "When the cameras came on us I put my first question and, allowing Behan to mumble a little, answered it myself. All television interviews are really like this – Behan's was simply an extreme case."

Behan, he said, "was extremely considerate and friendly in his references to me. I liked him except, of course, that like all drunks he was a frightful bore."

There were many who did not share Muggeridge's delight, feeling that it was another tiresome example of an erudite Englishman exploiting a drunken Irishman, an extreme case of victimization. Rae Jeffs, who did not yet know Behan but knew much about him (and who would come to know more), said five decades after the event that the show was disgusting. Even Conor O'Brien, who would go onto a life of international controversy in the world of United Nations African diplomacy (the Congo crisis) and then as editor of *The Observer*, one of London's Sunday newspapers, remained steamed up for years.

"My reaction was one of anger, possibly an unjust anger, but we are talking about what one felt at the time, at the people who had exploited his drink problem on television . . . . I think it was a most dreadful thing to do. He'd come to the studio already quite drunk, and they had, as far as I could make out, poured more drink into him, realized that he was incapably drunk and proceeded to exhibit him as a spectacle. I regard that as a horrible thing to do, particularly for a man who goes about being a Christian as Muggeridge does (Muggeridge died in 1990, aged 87).

Nevertheless, the incident, in a paradoxical way, served to internationalise Behan's fame, a fact underlined in the following day's popular press. There was not a taxi driver in London who did not know who Brendan Behan was. It is probable that his TV appearance marked the first time anyone ever appeared on the BBC in such a state, and the fact that it was an Irishman won him over to the English working man as a kindred spirit. The affinity was natural, brother Brian observed, saying that until then there was been no West End interest in *The Quare Fellow*. Soon Behan's telephone was ringing with offers from managers seeking an option on it.

"Suddenly, all London was at my feet and everywhere I went I was hailed like a fucking taxi." Indeed, he had made it big in London, in fact, far bigger than he ever could have imagined.

CHAPTER EIGHT

'BEATSIE'

"'You are not suited to a regular life, Beatrice, you are an artist. you'd be better off with me than with that civil servant....' 'Until then, I do not realize where our friendship is leading, but at this point I decide to marry him, and once my mind is made up I have no further apprehension.... "*– Beatrice Behan*

BEATRICE FFRENCH-SALKELD ,WAS 27 years old when she first met Brendan Behan, aged 31, in 1954 at the house in South Dublin where she lived with her father, Cecil ffrench-Salkeld. He was a skilled avant-garde painter. He liked to drink and was an equally vigorous political debater. Beatrice, or Beatsie as she became known, was to inherit most of her father's attributes. She had a head for drink and was a capable artist though she did not quite achieve her father's apex of painting a mural for Davey Byrnes pub in central Dublin.

But just as Beatsie had drawn from her father's odd but considerable talents, so did he from his mother, Blainad Salkeld, born in 1880 and died 1959,a published poet and friend in her later years of Dublin's literati, Flann O'Brien and, Patrick Kavanagh. The Salkelds came from a long line of empirical stock, in the main from what used to be called British India – she was born in Chittagong, in East Pakistan (which in 1970 became known as Bangladesh). She was sent back to Ireland for her early education, while her father stayed on as a doctor. She married and returned to India in 1902 where her husband took up work in the British medical service. Her son, Cecil, was born in Assam, the tea-growing area in northeast India. By 1909 the family was back in Ireland, although Cecil, as a youngster, advanced his education at art academies in Germany, returning finally to Dublin in 1925. He had entirely missed the turbulent years of the Easter Rising and the struggle for independence from Britain. Her mother, Florrie, of German blood lines, had none of the artistic dispositions of Cecil.

The family house was on Morehampton Road in south Dublin and its style suggested a degree of middle-class comfort not known to the Behans and, at a stroke, put a little abrasiveness into Behan, the outsider, and Beatrice, the becalmed daughter who lived there with sister Celia. Nevertheless, Brendan and Cecil had become acquainted when Cecil heard Brendan holding forth in an ale-house on behalf of the working man. The man who would become Behan's father-in-law was impressed, invitations were extended. Several house visits to Morehampton followed, and Behan catching the eye of the shy Beatrice, a long-limbed, sandy-complexioned junior botanist who listed painting as her main hobby. Behan and Beatrice then crossed paths in January 1955 at one of the last performances of *The Quare Fellow,* then being run on a shoestring by Alan Simpson and Carolyn Swift.

Behan, whose inclinations were well-known among his closer male colleagues, nevertheless made his move when Beatrice's then-escort briefly left her unguarded to fetch cups of coffee. Behan filled the hiatus by inviting Beatrice on a date the following week. The possibility of marriage in what, up to this point, was a scarcely active relationship, loomed with remarkable speed. As Behan specialist Ulick O'Connor wrote, the two were at another theatrical performance at the Pike a few weeks later when Behan, in an attempt to sandpaper away some of his rough edges, told her: "You know, I'm really respectable." Her answer was: "I don't care whether you are or not."

The words sounded like those of a woman enchanted or, at least, in deep and blind infatuation. Whatever inhibitions Brendan had about cranking up the relationship another notch while he got to know this young lady a little better were quickly swept away by Beatrice's dreamy naivete and the naturalness with which she was prepared to take on the responsibilities of marriage.

She didn't care about Brendan's faults. She would take him warts and all. Dublin's sages regarded the relationship as odd but were taken aback at the swiftness of the union. Thus was set in motion one of the literary world's most unusual and, ultimately, tumultuous relationships. Comparisons are as inevitable as they are elusive, marriages and their terms and conditions being unique to the individuals concerned. But in the world of books and writing one considers the union of F. Scott Fitzgerald and his wife; Zelda, Welsh poet Dylan Thomas (for whom Brendan would develop an irrational contempt) and his wife Caitlin and even the fictional characters of Johnny and Kathleen, played by James Mason and Kathleen Ryan, the doomed couple in F. L. Green's IRA novel *Odd Man Out*.

It was an odd pairing and, as one of the partners was Brendan Behan, the raucous singer, joker and writer who had pulled himself back from the abyss, it was bound to be marked by controversy and incident. In this, Behan-watchers were not disappointed. Certainly, his rebelliousness stemmed in large part from his social background and compared with that of Beatrice, whose family was seen as more genteel and middle class – more south of the Liffey. As Ulick O'Connor has pointed out, Behan, for all his accomplishments "still indulged in drunken outbursts and public horseplay" while her father, "a man of Bohemian habits . . . was associated in the public mind with an upper class background."

It was probably because of these different backgrounds and the couple's utterly different personalities that the suggestion of marriage was met with amazement, dismay, disapproval and downright shock. This was particularly so within his circle of drinking companions, who knew too well this ribald and decidedly unconventional lifestyle and his taste, when well into the gargle, for 'a bit of rough.' Behan, to his friends, was decidedly not the marrying type. This view was held by denizens of such establishments as Davey Byrnes, Grogans, the Harbour Lights and McDaids.

But unacknowledged or unseen by his more sceptical colleagues was the presence within his chest of a big heart, unforgettable sense of humour and magnanimous personality, topped up with chunks of blarney, which made him much fancied by the opposite sex in spite of his many shortcomings. Nevertheless there was genuine stupefication at the news in a town famous for its capacity to accept as fact any scrap of information that tickled its collective fancy. In the case of the marriage, Dublin found itself scooped. Decades after the event, publican Paddy O'Brien, a long-time fixture at McDaids before decamping in the 1980s to nearby Grogans, still talked with alacrity about the marriage; it was as if he had just heard about it.

"She was really a quiet person, the reverse of Brendan . . . I suppose that is why they hit it off. She could sit all day long in any company and never utter a word. Apparently, she was a good listener and a lovely person. As a matter of fact, when they married, it was the biggest mystery of all because no one ever thought of Brendan as the marrying type at all. It was just men and drink and pubs and jokes and yarns. That was his life.

"The evening before they got married one of his pals came and said to me, 'guess who's getting married tomorrow?' I says, 'I don't know', and he says, 'Brendan Behan!' and I says, 'If you t'ink you are going to spin t'at yarn around the shops, you had better t'ink again!' Then he says, 'I'm not kidding ya, Paddy, you know who told me? It was the clerk of the church (Westland Road Church) and I told him the same as you just told me. I met him in a pub and he says, 'It'll be on Baggot Street and then he says, 'It is a fact, it's at seven o'clock in the morning.' 'Then I says, "Who's he marryin?" and he says, 'you know, that young woman, Beatrice', and I says 'You mean that quiet girl? Jaesus!' So it turns out we're not tellin' anybody because I don't believe it, even now.

"Anyway, the following morning, Dominic (Brendan's younger brother) who was out of work at the time and had been agitating for workers' rights, lying down in the road and obstructing traffic, arrived at the pub and I said to him:, "What's this about your brother's wedding? ' and he says 'What fookin' brother's wedding?' and I says, 'Brendan. Anyway, Brendan went home in a taxi to tell his mother and collected her and brought her out for the day and that was his wedding."

In an interview years later, Beatrice Behan said that it was a secret and was something Brendan had wanted. "I was working at the National Museum and he used to drop in occasionally, we had only been going around a few months. The first time I met him was with my father. He had gone out drinking with my father.'

As for the wedding day, hardly anybody knew. The ceremony took place at seven thirty in the morning. Beatrice's family knew because she had told them, but not Brendan's. It was not till later in the morning, when they had taxied past Mrs Behan and had stopped to pick her up for a trip to the pub that Beatrice had met her."We called at the house on Kildare Road to collect Kathleen, but she had gone shopping. We met her later on the road with her shopping bag. Brendan asked my father to stop the car and he called to her. 'Come on mother, we're going for a few drinks.' We went to Kennedy's bar and it wasn't long before Kathleen was singing. She had a beautiful voice and a repertoire of songs the like of which I had never heard before. It came to two thirty in the afternoon, closing time for pubs in Ireland at that time, and I bade farewell to Kathleen. What I never knew about that day was that she had no idea that we had just been married. We often laughed about it years later. It had been a day to remember."

In that interview, Beatrice stressed the importance of a church wedding, complete with the sacraments, to Brendan. It took him a few days to get ready for confession. He did so and to the surprise of many received holy communion at the wedding mass. "I know nowadays people think all pomp and ceremony and the dresses. . . . I wasn't really interested with that; I was concerned more with the spiritual side of things. I suppose I felt it would be a lot more lasting thing for me if I could be married in a church with the sacraments. I don't think Brendan was that worried . . . No, he would never have settled for a registry office. No way!'

(This raises an interesting point. Brendan must have believed himself to be in an excommunicated state because of his refusal to toe the line while in Borstal in 1940. But the fact of the church wedding, however unorthodox, suggests that he had been able, through confession, to put the earlier supposition about sacrilege – which arose because of his refusal to denounce the IRA -- behind him.)

The newlyweds went to France for their honeymoon. Brendan was still constrained from transiting the U.K. owing to the 1939 offence. On their return, they set up home in a flat in Waterloo Road in Dublin. Behan, chuffed by the success of the *Quare Fellow* and a few coins earned here and there from the publication of other, shorter works, believed he could make a living at writing and filing for the *Saturday Press*. A quick and natural writer, he settled into a creative work pattern that would lead to the publication of Borstal Boy, his much agonized-over autobiography, and what would become his biggest play, *The Hostage*.

Although he was a heavy drinker he was capable of working with discipline, rising early and working till midday. He would work from about eight in the morning till midday and then he would go out, sometimes for lunch, sometimes for a drink, said his widow. He never worked at night unless, maybe, he had a deadline for *The Evening Press* or *The Saturday Press*.

But misfortune struck. It was not long after the wedding that the couple learned that Behan was suffering from diabetes, one of those potentially gravely debilitating illnesses that require abstinence from alcohol. There were those who recall him from his early days, before the success of *Quare Fellow* and *Hostage*. At that time he had started to bulk out and was losing some of his rugged good looks. Within a few years, the diabetes had developed company in the form of cirrhosis of the liver. But Behan was remarkable for his stamina and, in any case, it was not conceivable for a man with a personality like his would yield to such a medically-induced regime.

Beatrice was not going to crack the whip. Said Rae Jeffs: "Her father had drinking problems and she did know what she was in for, but I suppose if you marry a public figure you have to share him with the public, and part of Brendan's public image was to drink. But it was really very sad for she would follow him as much as she could."

Younger brother Brian, as recently as the 1990s, said of Behan: "Brendan's philosophy of marriage was that a woman was there to administer to a man's wishes and then bid a hasty adieu when she wasn't needed any more . . . . She took up her cross and followed him; if he was happy, she was happy; if he was sober; she was happier still; and when he was working hard and the money rolling in, well that was very heaven."

Beatrice, in the years after her husband's death, said she had no regrets about taking a back seat in the relationship. Brendan simply enthralled her for the full term of their life together – despite the opinions of many who knew the couple "I was a housewife, but I was new at it. My mother never let me inside the kitchen, so I never did a lot of work. I didn't know much about cooking but I learned as I went along. But I was painting at the time and exhibiting, I always took second place and I only painted when I had the time for it."

"I enjoyed some of it; there were moments now which were tremendous. There was the time they presented *The Hostage* in Great Britain and at the Theatre des Nations in Paris. Afterwards the audience stood and applauded. We were introduced to this Dominican priest afterwards, and the priest asked Brendan: 'Why aren't you representing Ireland,' to which Brendan replied sharply: 'The same reason you're not married – I wasn't asked'."

CHAPTER NINE

SUSSEX LADY

". . . . Borstal had made a man of him. It had certainly taught him a great deal about himself and about life in general; it had sharpened his perception, taught him to use his comic gifts as a means of survival, granted him leisure to read widely and given him his first literary award. . . ." – Colbert Kearney

ON A DAMP spring day in 1957 in London, Brendan and Beatrice Behan turned up at the head offices of *Hutchinson and Company,* the publishing concern. For years it had been located on Paternoster Row, under the giant shadow of St. Pauls, but those premises had been destroyed in the Blitz; in recent years it was shifted close to the head office of the BBC, a few streets north of Oxford Circus in the heart of London's shopping district.

The Behans had come to discuss the publication of Brendan's autobiographical memoir, *Borstal Boy,* then well into its second decade as a talked-about work but which few people had actually seen. There to meet them was the firm's publicist

Rae Jeffs who was promptly assigned to 'mind' the erratic Irishman till a deal had been struck to publish what promised to be a successful book. Behan now was 35, and had achieved widespread and colourful fame, and it could be said that wherever he went, especially pubs, he found that his reputation had preceded him. With a little imaginative packaging, whatever he affixed his name to was guaranteed to sell, ranging from compilations of newspaper clippings to the deepest and most heartfelt memoirs. In an interview nearly five decades after the event, Jeffs recalled the meeting with Behan as if it had just happened.

Firstly, he was sober – she knew of his reputation in London pubs and in front of any kind of company for that matter. Secondly, he did not have the manuscript of *Borstal Boy* with him, an irritating but not insoluble problem given that he was famed for his untidiness. As to the matter of drink, she recalled: "He was a cunning man, it was then after 3 p.m. when he and Beatsie turned up and he asked for a drink while we sat in the office. By that he meant Irish whiskey, though he knew the pubs were closed (usually for two to three hours) in the afternoon in those days and that we would not be able to buy a bottle. I went to the local pub, knocked on the door and asked the man if he would sell me a bottle; he said no, that it was against the law. But he thought a minute and said that he could actually give me one, which was what he did, and when I produced the bottle back in the office, Brendan thought I was a secret drinker. This was completely untrue, but we got on well after that,"

Jeffs was a Sussex lady which usually meant a high standard of breeding, comfortable country living, and the inevitable la-di-da accent. All these served as social barriers to keep the coming and going of tradesmen, riff-raff and other examples of rough trade that might disturb the equanimity of England's bucolic southern counties, a million miles distant from the over flowing sewage mains of Dublin. But the Sussex connection meant a great deal to Behan who, like any rebellious Irishman, had an instinctive sense of mistrust when around English people. No-one could have been more English than Rae Jeffs, sophisticated, poised, nicely spoken, in possession of those social qualities that opened doors in the upper seams of English society. A knighthood in the family did no harm either. The fact that she was from Sussex served to sweep all these interpersonal impediments away, for it was in Lewes prison in West Sussex that Behan was jailed in the early 1940s after being arrested in Liverpool in possession of bomb-making equipment. This was his dramatic baptism of fire in England; the story about it he would vividly recall in the opening pages of *Borstal Boy*. If Jeffs played her cards right it would soon be filling the bookstands across the country. It opens:

"Friday, in the evening, the landlady shouted up the stairs:

'Oh God, oh Jesus, Oh Sacred Heart. Boy, there are two

gentlemen to see you.' "I know by the screeches of her that these

gentlemen were not calling to inquire after my health or to know

if I'd had a good trip."

Nevertheless, once jailed, Behan enjoyed good treatment, especially when transferred to southern England, and the impression it made on him, linked forever with the county of Sussex, turned out to be lasting and favourable as far as his relationship with Jeffs was concerned. The fact that she was a Sussex lady was good enough for him. It was rough ground in which to grow the seeds of an enduring relationship but it worked.

As for the book, Rae Jeffs was shocked to learn there was no completed manuscript, at least not that day, though one was to be produced shortly afterwards. Behan was possessive about the book and it seemed that he did not want to let go of it. "I think (it) pulled more out of Brendan ... the emotional strain of writing *Borstal Boy* was something he never quite recovered from," said Jeffs. "He was a most possessive man with the manuscript. He never really wanted to give it up. In a funny way, he was glad to get it out of his system, but he didn't want the world to see the vulnerability."

Thus it fell to Jeffs, with a reputation in the publishing trade as a disciplined, get-it-right, promoter and publicist, to coax the manuscript into daylight. (She hastened to add that she was not at that time working as his editor - that would come later.) The manuscript had a life of its own and behaved like a prop in an Ealing comedy, its hefty 300-plus pages proving tough to pin down. The lubricant that freed it was the whiskey. Brendan was 'on the gargle', and after a bottom pinching rampage around the office, he disclosed that the text had been left back at the BBC which the Behans had visited earlier in the day to discuss broadcast of a radio play, *The Big House*. A taxi chase ensued, bearing the protagonists across town to the BBC and to nearby pubs where the rumpled text, of which there was no copy, was eventually found.

So began the laughable-tragic saga of the rise and fall of Brendan Behan. The text of *Borstal Boy* was in surprisingly orderly condition, for those who did not know him, when finally completed the following September. The word was out, another fine Irish play was in the works and with luck *Borstal Boy* and *The Hostage* (or *An Giall* in its Irish language version) might be hitting the bookshops at the same time. There was further good news from New York where Jose Quintero, the *enfant terrible* of New York theatre direction, gave Behan a U.S. off-Broadway debut that year with *The Quare Fellow*.

When finally published in 1958, *Borstal Boy* boomed well up the best-seller lists in the U.K. (though not in Ireland where it was banned), assisted by Behan's highly public antics and the coincident success of *The Hostage*, his second play. The play had already broken through to critical acclaim in Joan Littlewood's Theatre Royal at Stratford East, in London, and was being readied for a shift to Wyndham's theatre in the heart of London's west end. Armed with these 'advances', it was not difficult to find a peg with which to introduce the author to a reading public especially since practically everybody, by this time, knew who he was. The publicans at The George on Mortimer Street, near the BBC's Broadcasting House, knew him so well; they grew to fear his visits, eventually banning him and Jeffs from the premises but not before milking Behan for his out of pocket expenses. The ban stayed on well after Behan's death ('in case he should return!')

The two plays and the book confirmed his reputation as a writer of quality on both sides of the Atlantic. The original *Borstal* text was not published in the form in which it was submitted, the original 'vulgate' being replete with F-words, and censorship was such in the UK that freewheeling use of obscenity was unlikely to get past the men with red pencils. "It could be published now, of course, and it is my view that an author's works should be published in the way they were written, but we couldn't do it at that time," said Jeffs.

For Jeffs, the association with Behan marked the start of a six-year – at times life-threatening – commute between London and Dublin, and later New York as she took on editorial responsibility for virtually the rest of his output till the time of his death. It is without doubt that her involvement with Behan changed her life. Becoming absorbed into Behan's entourage and lifestyle meant taking health risks, she was to laughingly recall – she was not so prim that she didn't like a drink now and then, but in Behan's company there was no such thing as now and then; it was *'hold your hour and have another'* (the title of one of his books of collected writings which meant basically, 'forget the train schedule, for we're having another').

She soon found herself swept up in her client's lifestyle, Dublin and London pub-crawling, media appearances and transatlantic voyages to New York where rambunctious behaviour in bars, on talk shows, and above all, on stage served to broaden Behan's reputation. The relationship between them made for an odd pairing, but people who knew them both got used to it given that his relationship with Beatrice was sacrosanct. But from time to time questions about its propriety were raised. Jeffs has acknowledged developing a close affection for him to the point where she had to scotch rumours of an affair, underlining the point that she was his editor and, where possible, his minder.

"That was nonsense, I don't think Brendan was capable of having an affair with anyone in the time I knew him," she said. "I was with him more or less from *(Borstal Boy)* till his death in 1964. I worked with him constantly from 1960-61 till the time of his death. I gave up my job at *Hutchinson* to work directly with him in the hope of keeping him alive because he had a great deal more to say."

The rumours of an affair had their comical aspect. Kathleen Behan, the writer's ebullient mother, learned in 1960 that her son was going off to America 'with a woman'. There was only one response. 'Jesus, Mary and Joseph – he's left Beatrice." She soon learned that the woman was Rae Jeffs, whom she did not know and that the trip had to do with a book-writing project. "Only afterwards did I learn that Beatrice was going as well."

Things between them might never have developed as they did if *Borstal Boy* had been just another book requiring a little promotion. Jeffs felt at the time and maintained the view a half century later that the memoir was a work of exceptional quality and of deep humanity.

"As for Brendan, he was the most understanding and human of persons I should ever meet. I very often did not have to say anything at all, he would know I was sad or that something had upset me or that I was putting a brave face on things. He would say 'what's the matter, daughter, what's happened?" I learnt such a lot from him as a human being. I learned a lot about tolerance and I learned that nobody actually fits into one pigeonhole, you cannot put rubber stamps on people."

After *Borstal Boy,* Jeffs set herself up as Behan's agent. She did not know how grave Brendan's health problems were. What she did learn was that Hutchinson's back in London, after the first flush of success with *Borstal Boy,* was getting no work out of him now and that he had yielded to the publicity bandwagon. Everyone was after him to write other things, short stories, reviews, "this and that and the other, and he just could not work," said Jeffs. He had once again become the *Borstal Boy* to all and sundry. Under her ad hoc management, some sense of purpose returned when he was commissioned to write *Brendan Behan's Island,* a light and witty commentary about Ireland which he described as an Irish sketchbook, complete with illustrations by Paul Hogarth. Although he was beginning to accept that his best writing was behind him, he agreed to meet Jeffs and Beatrice at the Behan household in Dublin to establish some workable modus operandi. After some coaxing from Jeffs, he agreed begin to dictate his sage reminiscences and tales of the Irish people and of personal misadventure. The arduous process worked, but it took months of taping, followed by even more time transcribing the tapes before a working text was available. What resulted was a lively book that served to reassure the reading public – particularly outside Ireland – that he was alive and well and still had lots more work in him.

About four years later, under Behan's name, *Hutchinson* produced *Brendan Behan's New York,* a sequel to the 'island' book and, to many, even a funnier book about his adventures in the new world, a far cry from tales of life aboard the immigrant 'death ships' at the time of the famine. By this time he had become something of a caricature of himself. It was getting to be plain to all that his addiction to alcohol, plus the diabetes and other problems was cutting short his life and his work output. *Confessions of an Irish Rebel,* eventually to become a big sales success in the U. S., would only be published after his death. To his North American readers, the steady appearance of books with the Behan name was proof that all was well with their Celtic hero and that he was in for the long haul. To those nearer to him, in England and Ireland and in the eccentric atmosphere of New York's Algonquin, Bristol and Chelsea hotels, the prognosis in the face of his dependency indicated otherwise.

Surprisingly, Behan managed to stay sober for much of this period. Never once, recalled Jeffs, did he fall off the wagon nor slio out of the house for a beer break. "I would sit with a tape recorder in my lap and say, 'now Brendan, please tell me about such and such.' Once I got him going he was absolutely marvellous," she said. But she was prepared to admit that his tape recorded works were not the same as his plays. "Once I got the transcriptions done, I was expecting he would edit them, but I think he was ashamed that this had to be pulled out of him. The result was that it was not the same as a proper book . . . . It was a manufactured book and not a book from the heart'."

She explained that all the works were done almost entirely from his home and not, as was often reported, done on the run from London or Paris or New York, the latter conjuring up misleading images of a towheaded Irishman lurching through western capitals with Jeffs chasing behind with a tape recorder.

While it is true that some work was done while they were on promotional tours, the manner in which it was organised was both correct and professional. "He was very professional on this. We only recorded in the privacy of his room –- wherever he was living -- there was never anybody allowed in, and even Beatrice and he would drink only tea or soda water."

However, neither she nor Beatrice could keep him off the drink forever, so that a certain amount of life on the razzle at Behan's side was inevitable. "Because I was around so much I got rather involved in the booze-ups," she said in a voice of crackling, elderly gentility without evident regret.

Behan had a musical voice in those days, which survived despite his gargantuan cigarette consumption. His musical ear was shown regularly at pubs when he would easily break into song, two particular favourites being The Old Triangle (which was used to accompany *The Hostage*) and The Laughing Boy, associated with *The Quare Fellow*. The musical ear came from his mother who had an endless repertoire, much of which was eagerly absorbed by her eldest son. "He might, all of a sudden, say: "C'mon, then, we're off now and we're going to Timbuktu.' Next thing you knew, we were on our way to the airport – nothing ever stopped Brendan from getting on a plane. You never knew what he was going to do next."

His unpredictability led to some hilarious encounters of which, perhaps, her favourite was the time in March 1960 when she set out with him to get him outfitted in a new suit of clothes at a tailor's shop on London's Euston Road, near King's Cross train station. The occasion was the arrival of Behan's parents, en route to London to see the London debut of brother Dominic's play, *Posterity be Damned*. Dominic too was a writer and a playwright who had not had an easy time of it making his way under Brendan's large shadow. For his part, Brendan was apt to be annoyed at having some of his thunder stolen by his least favourite brother, hence his recourse to the protection provided by another prolonged binge. As Jeffs told it:

"Brendan had gone on a blinder the night before and he was staying with Joe McGill. I had to call round very early in the morning to collect him, and when I got inside the flat it was obvious Brendan wasn't going anywhere. He hadn't been shaved. Joe said he'd shave him and wash him. His clothes were not fit to be put on. I said to Joe, 'Well, leave him to me.' I had an old car. I decided to stop somewhere not too well known and get him a suit and a shirt and a tie and another coat. He needed them anyway; his clothes were all like rags by this time. We stopped back at Euston Station where there was a gentlemens' outfitters. I said to Brendan: "We are going to stop here and buy you a suit,' so he gets out of the car fairly quickly and he was already in the shop by the time I had found a parking place and had got out of the car. When I arrived, I was met by a whole lot of people running out. I thought Brendan had done something terrible. I didn't realise he was inside stripping in the middle of the shop. Absolutely true. Stripping!" There were three shop assistants. One did vaguely make the gesture, 'Would you like to come in here sir,' but Brendan told him in no uncertain words what he could do and went on as before till he was standing without a stitch on. By this time there was no one in the shop at all. Those three assistants didn't raise an eyebrow. It was as if it was a perfectly normal occurrence to have a naked man in your shop every day. They redressed him in the middle of the shop. As it turned out, we arrived at Euston Station to meet his parents looking like a million dollars. We just left those dreadful old clothes in the shop. I shall never forget their faces, there was no shock, and they were beautifully behaved."

Such scenes were becoming commonplace as Behan's life and behaviour became more exaggerated and bizarre, but the passage of time did not diminish Rae Jeff's fondness for the

Irishman. "He was a most generous man, and Beatrice has told the story about how they were invited to the Guinness' family home one Christmas. Beatrice didn't think she had a good enough coat; it was shabby. She told how Brendan stayed up night after night writing articles to raise the money to buy her a new coat."

CHAPTER TEN

THE LITTLEWOOD FACTOR

"Joan was the first theatrical director to put the working class voice on stage with dignity. Until then, such accents represented figures of fun – your 'funny' little maid, your 'comic' policeman, the 'comic' waiter. Joan took it up, put it on the stage and that is why it was so populist, it was because people recognised their lives. . . ." – Murray Melvin, first Littlewood 'Hostage'

JOAN LITTLEWOOD AND Brendan Behan, like Adam and Eve, could well have been created for each other, so similar were the politics, disposition and temperament of each person. The one big difference was that Littlewood did not have Behan's predisposition for alcohol which probably contributed to her longer career in the theatre.

Littlewood was a feisty, leftist theatre director given to profanity, both backstage and onstage. She was firmly reliant on her instincts as to what made good theatre. She was absolutely sure just whom she was fashioning her productions for. She was at the forefront of the new roughhouse theatre that was coarsely and unceremoniously elbowing aside the more measured and mannered, if not outright, snobbish works of the likes of the dilettantish theatre as best represented by Terence Rattigan or even Noel Coward despite his adroit skill at challenging the establishment while sounding and acting every bit a central part of it. Although Rattigan had it in him to be able to shake up audiences and win back some of his critics to his carefully crafted manner of writing and storytelling, particularly with such works as *The Winslow Boy* and *Separate Tables,* his manner and style, and those of many of his contemporaries, served as a stark and unappealing reminder to many Britons of the nose-in-the-air personalities, deemed responsible for committing the country to war. Thus, he had not the style or type of personality desired by a new genre of theatregoers after the war. The public wanted carnivorous theatre, after all, there were scores to settle on stage after two world wars.

Littlewood, with the face of a boxer dog and a bark as loud, certainly did not have time for deferential theatre nor was she afraid of taking on her own playwrights themselves. She was not wedded to the convention that a playwright's words, once written, should not be changed, and it was commonplace for her to bellow aloud when the quality of a particular text offended. Littlewood, a leftist of the old school to whom the notion of the ownership of property was theft, was accustomed throughout her long theatrical life to working on a shoestring. But deadlines had to be met, and this meant everybody connected with a particular work had to pitch in. The work at hand was not just her property and that of the playwright but belonged to the actors and backstage crew as well. It was participatory theatre at its most exciting and busy. The play, as Shakespeare wrote, not the playwright, was the thing!

Littlewood was a northerner and effectively began her career in theatre in Manchester in the mid-1930s after teaming up with Ewan MacColl, better known later under the pseudonym as a folk singer but at that time simply by the name of Jimmie Miller. Together they formed the Theatre Union, dedicated to anti-establishment revolutionary theatre, a much-needed escape valve for the working classes who were very much immobilised by the exploitative contribution of Britain's industrial classes to the Great Depression. In the post-war years, Gerry Raffles brought his organisational and administrative skills into Littlewood's troupe, MacColl and Littlewood eventually parted company as Raffles took over, becoming Littlewood's companion, partner, organisational rudder and collaborator for the next 22 years till his death in 1975.

The Theatre Union's U.S. counterpart was called the Group Theatre, founded in 1931 in New York by Austrian immigrant Lee Strasberg, the theatrical director later to be identified with the 'method' form of acting and later still as Jewish gangster Meyer Lansky in Godfather II.

In the UK, a competing organisation was George Devine's Royal Court theatre, set up in southwest London far enough distant from London's West End to escape the bourgeois label that applied to mainstream theatre. Devine, who died in 1966 at age 56, went on to spearhead the creation of the Young Vic Theatre Company, and the English Stage Company, and benefitted from his association with Tony Richardson, the film and stage director, and William Gaskill, who eventually succeeded him at the Royal Court.

The Littlewood – Devine rivalry was aggressive – Devine on one occasion manoeuvred to appropriate Behan's *The Hostage* from her east London bunker at Stratford East, for his Royal Court. The first person to play the role of the British hostage in the play was Murray Melvin, boy and man a product of the Littlewood theatre and a keen observer of workers' theatre at the time. In an interview in 2006 – he was still on stage and also in charge of archives at the refurbished Littlewood theatre

The Littlewood factor

-- he observed: "The Royal Court was a progressive socialist theatre, but it had a very middle class clientele whereas Joan's Theatre Royal (at Stratford East) was the opposite . . . anything but!"

Both benefited from the new theatre trend sweeping through the British isles and the new writing that grew out of the cynicism that infected British society at that time. Just as Devine had won plaudits for Osborne's profane *Look Back in Anger*, so did Littlewood for her adventurous renderings in the 1950s of *Volpone*, of teenager Delaney's *A Taste of Honey* (including a memorable supporting role by Melvin), *Fings Ain't Wot They Used to Be,* and the outrageously iconoclastic *Oh What a Lovely War.*

Said Melvin: "There was a freedom after the last war and those class barriers started breaking down. Works by Terence Rattigan were no longer pertinent. What would this (east end) part of London have to learn from Rattigan? She set a precedent for she knew her European theatre, she knew about Stanislavsky, these were the fields in which we worked."

By this time, the lid was off. While censorship had not entirely been lifted it was in retreat under the onslaught of new works that all looked back in anger. Devine and Richardson were producing the full portfolio of Osborne's plays, Samuel Beckett, an Irishman, was standing the play-going world on its head with *Godot, Krapp's Last Tape* and a handful of reductionist works. The kitchen sink was 'in' in British fiction and film-making thanks to works by John Braine, Sillitoe, Waterhouse and Kingsley Amis. And across the Irish Sea, a wild Irishman was making a modest mark for himself at Dublin's Pike theatre with his first play, an anti-capital punishment drama that was so unusual in its concept and execution that the outside world was bound to take notice.

The precise details of what prompted the initial meeting between Behan and Littlewood on a late winter's day in 1956 are enshrouded in the mists of time, but it is clear that, according to Littlewood, a 'tattered bundle' from Ireland arrived at the Theatre Royal, Stratford East. It had originally been addressed to former partner Ewan MacColl and was forwarded to Littlewood who found favour with the text after ploughing through the untidily-typed manuscript that she said bore numerous beer stains – one assumes they were stains made with the stout porter for which Dublin was and is well-known. The Irishman was in fact a skilled typist but of the first-draft-is-all-you'll-get variety. He was not one to start sub-editing what he had written or subjecting himself to any arduous tidying up process. Behan, unknown to Littlewood at that time, was duly checked out and it was found that he was from a thoroughly Irish Republican family and was a roustabout. But his work bore the mark of an original talent and after a couple of 'injections' of air fares – the first of which was liquefied and therefore required a second – he traversed the Irish Sea for London's main airport and the meetings that would mark him as an important playwright. In Littlewood's view, *Quare Fellow* did need pruning and editorial adjustment. Hence, the need to meet the author and establish a modus operandi, an immediate obstacle being that Behan, the ex-Borstal boy, had no legal right to be in England, Her Majesty's Government still not having forgiven him for incidents against HMG dating from 1939.

This was a mere trifle for Littlewood who proceeded to get on with the show. The first challenge was to trim out the surfeit of sub-plots and get the story down to manageable form; this meant converting what was an essentially Irish prison play, revelling in all the argot of Dublin tenement life, into an English depiction. One reason for this was that she did not have any members of her crew who were Irish, apart from those Britons with Irish names like Yootha Joyce and

Brian Murphy. Many of the rest were Welsh, from the West Country of England and in one case, a Jew. Help that would restore some of the ethnic balance came in the form of a Limerick-born Irishman named Richard Harris who, in a few short years, would be playing rugged roles in major motion pictures, and would reach the apex of his fame as King Arthur in the durable and often-revived Arthurian musical *Camelot*. Living in a bedsit near the theatre, Harris needed almost no rehearsal before being selected to play the role of Mickser, one of the prisoners, a role he was to alternate with Eric Ogle once the play was launched. Finally, Behan agreed Littlewood's proposed cuts, a decision which, later on, would add to the controversy surrounding Littlewood's apparent free hand with playwrights' copy. But she found no opposition from Behan who, with Beatrice, would sit in the second balcony lazily watching rehearsals. He said simply that the revised version "was better without all that old rubbish" which Littlewood explained later as references to his Catholic childhood.

"He was very good (about the changes), and Joan got on with him," Melvin said in an interview. "She felt every author had to be part of the company. There were no prima donnas. I have been there when authors would say: 'no no, I cannot change it, and Joan would say, 'well, get up there and do it yourself, then', and they would do so and make fools of themselves."

As for Behan, there was something of the time bomb about him. He was very much his own man, striking fear into critic Ken Tynan with funny, if gross, obscenities. Beatrice, as ever, would stand behind him despite the fact that the popular media would never let him alone, knowing that if they bought a round of drinks they would get a story. He would also hold forth before the cast conducting ribald tutorials.

"He would not just sit there and let you NOT drink. You could not say 'I've had enough', not with Brendan, in the early days.

He was just a loveable character. Everybody in the building was around him. He was tiny, short. He is thought of as a big bruiser but he was not. Joan would get him talking and he would bring in a case of stout and would talk two, maybe three hours. . . . Then you had to go away and do your homework and put down all the pertinent remembrances you had just heard and incorporate them into his work."

While Behan and Littlewood got off to a good start, in the years to come familiarity would breed fatigue as the two strong personalities began to wear each other down, invariably over the issue of missed deadlines. While the rewritten version of *The Hostage* – starring Melvin in the title role – would be presented at the Theatre Royal in 1958 and would go on to be his most successful play, Behan grew more erratic and ultimately would fail to deliver a follow-up work such as *Richard's Cork Leg*. There is one story of the stark naked Raffles chasing Behan across a field near their southeast London house in an attempt to wrest a copy of the overdue script from him. *Cork Leg* eventually was produced but only after Brendan's death. But all of that was in the future. Right now, with *The Hostage* being hammered into shape, there was all to play for in the life of Brendan Behan, west end playwright.

CHAPTER ELEVEN

HOSTAGE TO FORTUNE

"Hawkins had begun to say something else when Donovan fired, and as I opened my eyes at the bang, I saw Hawkins stagger at the knees and lie out flat at Noble's feet slowly and as quiet as a kid falling asleep, with the lantern light on his lean legs and bright farmer's boots. We all stood very still, watching him settle out in the last agony. Then Belcher took out a handkerchief and began to tie it about his own eyes – in our excitement we'd forgotten to do the same for Hawkins – and seeing it wasn't big enough turned and asked for the loan of mine . . . ." – Frank O'Connor, Guests of the Nation

THE HOSTAGE, EASILY Behan's most popular and successful play, began commercial life at a Dublin opening in June 1958 as *An Giall* and was staged at a small Dublin theatre owned by Gael Linn, one of several organisations set up to help promote the Irish language. Because Ireland was officially bilingual, with Irish gaelic promoted *de jure* to equal status with English, any cultural enterprise likely to involve the promotion of Irish, was likely to win some government backing and promotional support. State-owned or state-operated institutions, such as Aer Lingus, the airline, Bord Failte, the tourism board or the Post Office, among others, were expected to make services in the Irish language available where possible. It was to be a long haul, reality dictated that English would be the first official language, and the teaching of Irish only got under well beyond the half-century.

An Giall/The Hostage was controversial from the start, poking fun at the mores of the times and ushering on stage prostitutes and homosexuals while lampooning the English, the Irish, the IRA, and the solemnity of 'the cause'. *An Giall* was seen by some as a bold statement by Behan against the IRA. But how could this be given that Behan was Republican stock? One could not be sure just where Behan truthfully stood despite his statement to the British immigration authorities that he was no longer involved in any way with the IRA, not strictly true given his close friendship with Cathal Goulding, the head of the IRA in Dublin. While he had put himself into the position of an ex-communicant from the Catholic church in 1940, shortly after being jailed in the UK for failing to renounce the IRA, he had occasionally turned to the church and had even married , complete with having made his own Confession. But he was also an iconoclast and any sacred cow spotted ambling across his bow was asking to be bumped into.

An uninhibited wordsmith, Behan was what is known in the British Isles as a 'quick read', not only in English but in Irish and other key European languages such as French. So it was that his proficiency in Irish, a language he had partly learned while in an English reform school. Exhilarated by Behan's potential and the success of *The Quare Fellow,* Joan Littlewood liked the story line of *An Giall* and pressed the author for a translation. In Littlewood's case, it would be more than a translation but a fully fledged adaptation.

Hostage to Fortune

In its Irish language form, it should be thought of as a *succes d'estime* and nothing more as the Irish language version would be impossible to present to a commercial audience in England. With Littlewood and Gerry Raffles pounding on the door for access to this new work from this wild Irishman who had two years earlier drawn *The Quare Fellow* out of a hat, Behan eventually got round to reworking the new play in English. By coincidence, both Behan and the Littlewood theatre workshop needed money. Such triumphs as *Fings Ain't Wot They Used to Be* and *Oh What a Lovely War* lay ahead. Money was needed now to keep the group going. Littlewood knew that with the success of *The Quare Fellow* – and the boundless capacity for publicity-generation by its author – a follow up piece, this one with a little heft, was in order.

It has long been a matter of debate among purists whether *An Giall* was a better play in Irish than in English when it became, once and for all, *The Hostage*. In its Irish incarnation, it was a contemporary play and, despite its focus on The Troubles – well before the civil unrest that exploded in northern Ireland in 1968 – it retained a lot of broad and topical content. Satire it was, but not without a blaze of humour: two characters, Pat and Meg, speaking about one of their colleagues, a certain character named Monsewer, get into an argument over whether he is Irish or English or something else, Pat finally declaring that he is Anglo-Irish. And what is that? He is asked, riposting that an Anglo-Irishman is a protestant with a horse. The Anglo-Irish, Pat explains, only work at riding horses, drinking whiskey and reading double-entendre books in Irish at Dublin's Trinity (then a very protestant university). Ever ahead of his times in humour, Behan has Pat approving Monsewer "even though he has a slate loose."

The story line emerges in Belfast with the retaliation kidnapping of an English soldier by the IRA, seeking revenge for young members who have been arrested and are facing the death penalty for shooting two policemen. The scene shifts to Dublin where the soldier is held and as such he becomes the 'hostage'. The dialogue is rich and bantering, and arguments, some sound and some specious, about the cause and the morality of such struggles all receive an airing. The reasons for the guerrilla war are discussed logically, but the conclusions are found wanting. Love flourishes in this infested hothouse between the prisoner and one of the female captors, but death, too, pays a visit, underlining the folly of war and the needless waste of a life, at a stroke turning the play from a tragic-comedy to a comic tragedy.

In the *An Giall* version, stripped of its supporting music and the jollity of the English-language version, these themes are dealt with simply, or as Niall Toibin, the actor, put it: "It struck me as a simple story of love, naive and underdeveloped but cleverly set in an era and location unfamiliar to the Gaelic theatre, such as it was." He commented that the story line was lean, but that the play worked thanks to the acting. "The quality of the play sustained the show," he said.

According to Colbert Kearney, a cousin and a Behan specialist, *An Giall* is not propagandist, nor is it a tract, just a play. "It would be wrong to describe it as pro- or anti-IRA -- nobody takes Monsewer and the Officer to be accurate representations of the IRA any more than anybody believes Leslie's (the English hostage's) attitude to Ireland to be that of the British government. The characters are, at once, individuals in a specific time and place, and symbols of an action which is not defined by time or place in one sense they show the insignificance of this squabble in the universal history of conflict. The play . . . presents two sets of people, those who have been scarred and those who are crushed by ideology . . . Behan has dramatised the poignancy of two young people caught in a conflict which they neither desire nor comprehend. . . ."

But in getting the play ready for presentation to the east London stage and later the West End, some changes had to be made and a certain amount of editorial bullying was required. Littlewood used cockney jokes, introduced an upright piano and gave it the atmosphere of musical hall, her trademark styling that would mark most of her adaptations in the 1950s and 1960s. (She would benefit from the recently army demobilized Murray Melvin, a lean and feline tyro actor just breaking into theatre. He would be destined to play the role of the British Tommy held hostage (Melvin would follow through with Littlewood's adaptation of Shelagh Delaney's *A Taste of Honey* in the role of Geoffrey. After an intermittent film and stage career Melvin would return to the Theatre Royal as historian and archivist.)

Brendan Behan's *The Hostage* made its debut on October 14 1958. It was adapted in preparation for presentation at the Paris Theatre des Nations festival on April 3 1959. The French success once again reaffirmed the Irishman's love affair with Paris which in his dreams would have been his home away from home had life dealt him a different hand of cards. On June 11 that year, *The Hostage* was transferred to Wyndhams Theatre in London's west end. Its success was paralleled by *Taste of Honey* which made its debut on May 27 1958 and which moved on to Wyndham's on February 19, 1959.The coincident appearance of their works and of themselves in London sparked an outburst of gossip by Fleet Street's columnists more interested in whether or not Behan and *Taste of Honey* creator Shelagh Delaney were a 'an item.' In the short term, there was some truth to the gossip. Delaney's interest in Behan was not lost on Beatrice, an artist and fellow Dubliner who took marriage seriously. She was not about to let her marriage founder over the affections of a girl scarcely out of her teens In a brief exchange, Beatrice told Delaney to cease and desist – if she wanted Brendan she would have to take him warts and all. The rumour soon faded and, in any case, Behan was to find himself with bigger distractions.

As for *The Hostage,* Toibin observed:

"In the Behan way, *The Hostage* worked, the culmination being an affecting and side-splitting version of *The Captains and the Kings. The Hostage* attracted much in the way of theatrical showings in the late 1950s and throughout the 1960s becoming a big hit in London and an exceptional success in New York and in various American tours." It was not until the late 1960s, with the explosion of renewed violence in Ulster province in Northern Ireland, that its retail value as a commercial enterprise temporarily waned. Even at that, a successful revival of *The Hostage* was shown at London's Barbican theatre, staged by the Royal Shakespeare Society, in 1994.

As with *The Quare Fellow*, Behan's works brought out the best in Ken Tynan. He wrote of the new play:"It seems to be Ireland's function every twenty years or so to provide a playwright who will kick English drama from the past into the present. Mr. Behan may well fill the place vacated by Sean O'Casey (then an octogenarian and very much alive and living in England. "Perhaps more important, Miss Littlewood's production is a boisterous premonition of something we all want – a biting popular drama that does not depend on hit songs star names, 'spa' sophistication, or the more melodramatic aspects of homosexuality. . . ."

Harold Hobson of the *Sunday Times*, the dean of London theatre critics, weighed in with the following: "I do not know whether *The Hostage* is a masterpiece or not. It made on me the impression of a masterpiece . . . It crowds in tragedy and comedy, bitterness and love, caricature and portrayal, ribaldry and eloquence, patriotism and cynicism, symbolism and musical hall songs, all on top of one another, apparently higgledy-piggledy and yet wonderfully combining into a spiritual unity."

The cognoscenti, while admiring the play's brio, sometimes found fault with its borrowed origins, one example being Frank O'Connor's powerful story of the Anglo- Irish civil war, *Guests of the Nation*, to which *The Hostage* bears a striking resemblance. Set at the time of the first troubles, the short story tells of the capture of English soldiers, their brief incarceration, their budding friendship with their captors, and then their abrupt execution, the uncomprehending cold-bloodedness which underlines the status of the short story as a great example of anti-war writing. Some have likened it to Erich Maria Remarque's *All Quiet on the Western Front* and others to such works as Dalton Trumbo's *Johnny Got His Gun*. There too is plenty of O'Casey and his *Shadow of the Gunman* and *The Plough and the Stars*. While *The Hostage* lacks the originality of *The Quare Fellow*, it benefits from being able to be played out before an audience at that time becoming aware of the civil rights movement in America and the changing face of discrimination. As a play, it packs its own punch, as Behan himself found out. According to Littlewood, Behan was sitting at John Ryan's Dublin bar, The Bailey, in Littlewood's and Beatrice's company. Littlewood heard a man whisper into her ear: "Yer man stole Frank O'Connor's work for his *Hostage*. Did you know that?" Behan, never out of earshot, exploded:

"That's a lie, you pox bottle." Blows were struck and injuries sustained, Behan finally being bundled off to the pokey for yet another night behind bars.

At first, Behan and Littlewood worked quickly and, according to Kearney, the London version was ready for the Stratford East stage just four months after the gaelic version was put on at the Damer Hall. However, the brief honeymoon was about to come to an end. Littlewood and Raffles began to encounter in their erratic charge the effects of drink, the lack of attention to detail and the indifferent interest in getting the work prepared for presentation. Littlewood took the script into her own hands while Behan succumbed to the lure of the pub. Behan, rather than fight his corner to ensure the integrity of his writing, yielded to Littlewood's demands to get the work out and on time. At one point, Littlewood and Raffles had all but written off *The Hostage*. Littlewood recorded that she feared the disappearance of the script when Gerry intervened and, armed with a pistol, bellowed outside Behan's door only in language the Irishman would understand.

"See that? If you don't finish that 'effing' play, I'll kill you." The sound of fingertips hitting typewriter keys resumed and the play's third act was completed only days before opening night. As Kearney also observed: "Her theatre was a genuine workshop, a community in which nobody was allowed to dominate. The dramatist was simply a member of the team and his script was by no means sacrosanct."

It eventually was all right on the night and it can be said that *The Hostage* gave more than one actor a needed boost to stardom. One of these was Victor Spinetti, a Welsh-Italian actor and a great admirer of Littlewood who found himself in blunt head-to-head conversation with Behan, whom he scarcely knew. At issue was the impending (1960) U.S. run of *The Hostage*. Behan, short and rugged, and Spinetti, cat-like and pointy-nosed, squared off after Spinetti had been asked to take a role in the US version. He answered: "Brendan, what can a Welsh-Italian (actor) play in an Irish play?" Behan snapped: "Why the fockin' IRA officer, of course."

Littlewood went on to global fame with her production, later filmed to remarkable reviews, of *Oh What Lovely War,* a punishing satire on the insanity of the First World War. Alan Simpson joined forces with Littlewood to see what could be done about *Cork Leg*. He wound up having to retrieve the production from her. At a meeting with Behan in Dublin in 1961 – by which time his international successes in London had catapulted him into the heady world of Broadway -- Littlewood reviewed his scattered text for *Cork Leg* and found it long on colour and short on story. Further discussions were held in a pub, but unruliness prevailed, a fist fight with the patrons ensued and Behan was taken to jail. In the end, the play was never completed.

For all their differences, Littlewood admired Behan's innate talent and revived *The Hostage* in 1973. It is a play that has been performed with remarkable regularity at smaller theatres in the US, and to a lesser degree, the UK during the 1970s and 1980s, mainly because of the fun it pokes at the IRA. But it is only lately that *The Hostage* has been able to attract interest at larger venues, the most sanguine reason being the controversy of the theme against the background of renewed troubles in northern Ireland and a death count of more than 3,400, mostly by shooting, in the 1968-2000 period.

BOOK TWO

CHAPTER TWELVE

A TASTE OF THE APPLE

"I knew an old Irishman who went (to New York) when he was seventy-five and ill, and like a Lourdes of light, New York cured him and he lived for years afterwards, a healthy and happy old man . . . " – *Brendan Behan's New York*

IT IS NOT clear when Brendan Behan first began to take seriously the innate desire shared by many Irish to live in New York, to actually pull up stakes in Dublin and ship off to the New World, and sod all the rest. He had certainly got the taste for the expatriate life with his noisy escapades in France beginning in the late 1940s. He had begun to write and the buzz that came from living in a writer's city – for Paris was a great hangout for many foreign writers after the war – was enough to sustain him. Also it was cheap to live, and in any case if he didn't feel up to it, he could fall back on his trade as a house and bridge painter. He would drop in whenever he could at the Irish embassy in an effort to keep up with the gossip. Some embassy staff found him to be a nuisance – his works up to that time were little known – but he hung in and did so with ever greater zeal once fellow Dublinman Samuel Beckett, a long-time expatriate who wrote in French and struck it big with the publication of *Waiting For Godot*. He immediately counted himself a friend of Beckett's. This friendship he invoked once he made his own breakthrough with *The Quare Fellow*. There were to be occasional pub crawls through Paris with Beckett or sometimes in search of Beckett who indulged Behan's company more out of duty than any illusion about friendship. Noted the English writer Anthony Burgess:

"Brendan Behan never learned to understand that Beckett was not his kind of Irishman. Irish was Irish, and if you are Irish come into the parlour but the flabby drunk with 'Erse' on him was not the cup of tea of this wiry, scholarly, reticent, tennis-playing intellectual aristocrat." Behan's liking for the City of Light did not stop him from burning a short fuse about the French. After all, he started writing *Borstal Boy* in Paris, and by 1958-60 was running *Quare Fellow* and *Hostage* in the French capital. On a flight back home from Paris, the aircraft was struck by lightning forcing the pilot to return to base. Behan, good at insults in foreign languages, snapped:

"Je suis prepare a mourir pour la France, si c'est necessaire, mais certainment pas pour l'Air France."

France, for all its charms, was not New York. Millions had undertaken the big move before him in search of a better life, and the haemorrhage would continue long after he was gone. But Behan's situation was different. Almost overnight he had become a man with cash flow.

That was the rub, for unlike most of his countrymen, his was not a mission to alleviate personal poverty or to flee the famine. It was to obliterate the past. Money was beginning to roll in from his writings, and he began to see himself atop a throne, his head filled with illusions about personal liberty, American style. He would be preceded by his own publicity machine that, by dint of his expansive personality, he had built up following his London success with *The Hostage*. He

A taste of the Apple

was unaware of what a deeply conservative land America was, despite all the chest-beating bravado and egalitarian energy of New York and its polyglot of nationalities.

It is certain that he had already rounded the clubhouse turn in life; whether or not he knew it was another matter. It mattered little to him that his quest for exhilaration and fame might have a price attached, such as the by-now noticeable deterioration in his health. He looked like a boxer who had taken one hit too many. The simple fact was that he was making little or no attempt to look after his health, particularly his diabetes. It is likely Behan knew that opting for New York, with his wife Beatrice as accompaniment, would lead to his ultimate destruction, but the impetus to escape the 'ould sod', not to mention the constraints of marriage and all its obligations, was unstoppable. Brendan loved to be on the jar with a crowd around him, and where better to be so deployed than in New York and the many other corners of Hibernian America that already knew about him.

Word of Behan's exploits had travelled fast; with a little patience, transatlantic telephone calls were now possible and international air travel by jet was on the rise. It was soon going to be possible to beam TV signals from Europe to North America and videotape was about to replace celluloid as the way in which TV programs were played and saved – roll on instant replay. A revolution was taking place in English theatre and Behan was a part of it. It was often difficult in Behan's case to tell the bombast from the substance.

A year earlier, Behan had had a taste of American television thanks to a brief but memorable appearance on Edward R. Murrow's public affairs programme, *A Small World* broadcast by Columbia Broadcasting System (CBS) on August 12, 1959. Murrow was a giant figure in the early history of television news and public affairs. He made his reputation through his memorable broadcasts from London during the Blitz, with the opening line, "This. . . is London." After the war he fashioned his news-gathering team into one of the leading news organisation in television (the Murrow years are still talked about – and their passing is lamented - a half century later), featuring such stalwarts as Fred Friendly, Charles Collingwood, Robert Trout, Douglas Edwards, Eric Sevaried and Walter Cronkite.

By the late 1950s Murrow had developed an unimpeachable reputation for journalistic integrity through the *CBS Evening News* and associated 'lighter' programmes such as *See It Now, Person to Person* and *A Small World*. Under Murrow's guidance, these soon became 'must' viewing for those who owned TV sets.

Small World was something of a pioneering effort for the network. The intent of the half-hour programme was to provide a forum for the exchange of ideas, and to be incisive, as it almost always was, given Murrow's exacting standards. But, as Alexander Kendrick, a Murrow biographer, noted at the time:

"The programme was not always intellectual – as Brendan Behan, Ireland's bibulous playwright, demonstrated when he became progressively more maudlin on camera and finally disappeared mid-channel – but it was always cerebral."

Kendrick's view of the programme was perhaps a little too brief, for there was more to it than that. For one, Murrow was using the programme to do a simulated feed from London to New York – this was the early days of over-water, broadcasting - with an input from Dublin. The guests on this particular night were American intellectual and critic John Mason Brown, an amusing if aloof individual of a type bound to get up Behan's nose; actor and comedian Jackie Gleason, representing Irish-

A taste of the Apple

America and inputting from the US, Murrow co-ordinating from London and Behan , adding to the expected debate from Dublin. The theme of what was intended to be a free-wheeling discussion was 'the art of conversation', with Murrow, trademark cigarette clenched between his right index and middle finger, leaning pensively on his fist.

Behan, possibly because of his nervous stammer, looked calculatingly rumpled and half asleep as he sank slowly into a spongy sofa. But he wasted no time in letting the audience know where he was coming from, his performance being uncannily reminiscent of the infamous *Panorama* programme of three years earlier. It was up to the guests to make something of the theme sufficient to fill thirty minutes of air time. Behan was fast off the mark, declaring that the art of conversation was dead, nuclear bombs (this was the era of nearly rampant nuclear testing by the superpowers) had intimidated everybody and "had scared people witless". This point was not taken either by Mason-Brown or Gleason who commented that conversation among the group seemed to be going well. Behan stuck to his guns, Gleason, as famous for his healthily rotund physique as Behan was for his debauched tulip-shaped form, beamed and chuckled throughout, referring to Behan as 'Brendan, bye', as if to show that he was au fait with the vernacular from the old country. The nearly comatose Behan opened an eye and said he was nobody's 'bye'. If his intent was to rile Gleason he failed for the comedian continued to chuckle as did Mason-Brown when Behan called him 'a liar'. Gleason, obviously enjoying the discussion and a man who genuinely liked Behan, said: "I could do 'a night with Behan' and extend an invitation to the Irishman to come to New York. Behan then broke into rebel song, prompting the remark from Mason-Brown that "as songs go, you are a fine author."

A commercial break severed links to Dublin, leaving the arena occupied only by Mason-Brown, Gleason and Murrow. Noting

Behan's disappearance, Mason-Brown asked whether this was down to an 'act of God or an act of Guinness', the black Irish beer being something of a novelty in the U.S. at that time. Gleason replied that Behan "had come through here at one hundred proof." Murrow thereupon wound up the programme with his traditional: "And now from London, good night and good luck." Thus ended an early appearance by Brendan Behan on American television.

About this time, a young reporter for London's popular *Daily Express*, Michael Parkinson, was sent to Dublin to interview the Irishman about the success of *The Hostage* and the impending New York run set for autumn, 1960. There was another thing, in a previous encounter with Behan, the newspaper had agreed to pay for a set of false teeth; it thought that the Parkinson interview might provide the *Express,* a high circulation newspaper owned by press magnate Max Aitkin, better known as Lord Beaverbrook, an opportunity to find out how its expense money had been spent. It didn't take the newspaper long to find out. On his arrival in Dublin Parkinson was greeted by a near-toothless man He broached the question and was immediately told that the teeth were ill-fitting and were loaned to a street merchant who sold linen handkerchiefs. Parkinson, who retired as a TV interviewer in 2008, went on: "The man was easily recognisable because Brendan's teeth were too large for his mouth, which was stretched into a permanent rictus grin. Moreover, he had to take them out to speak and tell us how generous Brendan had been."

Fortunately, Behan was going through a dry spell and was in good humour as they made themselves comfy at their newly bought row house on Anglesea Road, South Dublin. This was despite an exhausting pub crawl accompanied by Beatrice in which her husband took no alcohol, but danced on tables and broke into song. One prophetic number was the haunting 'Oh, my old Irish tomb, I'll be there soon', a little folkloric that he would soon inflict on New Yorkers queuing to find out more about this man called Brendan Behan.

CHAPTER THIRTEEN

THE BEHAN TRAVELLING ROAD SHOW

"In 1936, I began writing for the Irish Democrat about Spain, and they are the only articles I have written that I was not paid for and enjoyed writing. Any writing I have done since I have done purely for money..." – *Brendan Behan*

IT WAS ON a late summer day in 1960 that the Mr. and Mrs Behan settled in for a comfortable, if noisy, propeller-driven flight bound for New York to ready themselves for the U.S. debut of the Littlewood version of *The Hostage*. Not all the in-flight noise came from the engines; indeed passengers sitting in the back could hear the enthusiastic refrains of *I'll Give you a Golden Ball* and *The Old Triangle*. The Behans disembarked at New York's Idlewild Airport (later to become John F. Kennedy Airport) 12 hours later that day. It was September 2 1960. Deplaning with the couple was Beatrice's actress sister Celia Salkeld, who was to appear in the play. They had little more than two weeks to warm up the crew for the debut scheduled for September 20 at the Cort Theatre at 136 West 49th Street. There to greet them were the duet of Joan Littlewood and

Gerry Raffles who had set out for New York ten days earlier in a pre-emptive effort at damage control – after all, it was their play as much as Brendan's. Better to have feet on the ground in the host city rather than having Brendan cutting loose with the verbal grapeshot to an as-yet unfamiliar New York press corps.

Brendan was buoyed by Joan's earlier arrival, it amplified his attitude towards New York. Not so Beatrice, ever the small-town girl, who wasted little time in deciding that she wanted no part of New York, knowing well that the bright lights of the big city would pose as great a threat to their relationship as any street corner temptress, but to no avail. According to her, there had been a choice – to see the play staged in Moscow or New York. She favoured the Russian capital, but Behan's left-wing politics notwithstanding, the choice was hands down for New York despite the inevitable temptation of the gargle. His younger brother, Brian, saw the trip and Brendan's sight-unseen love of New York differently. Brian observed that most people's lives tended to slow down at 40, but not Brendan's.

"He wanted the Behan Travelling Road Show to go on, regardless of the consequences," Brian wrote. "He still wanted to be first into the boat and last out, regardless of how the barmen, or even the other patrons, might feel. There was always a story to be told or a song to be sung."

He was already having intimations of mortality and he confided as much earlier to an acquaintance, Desmond Mackie, who instinctively knew that the bright lights of Broadway would only be bad news for his friend. "I sat with him (Brendan) at a pub in Ballsbridge, Dublin, and he told me, "Desmond, I am going to America. They're going to put on the *The Hostage*", I said, "Brendan, you're fucked," and he asked me, "Why do you say that?" and all I could say was 'You know that, don't you', and he had to agree."

Mackie immediately thought of a boxer named Jack Doyle, a huge heavyweight, of six feet, seven inches tall, who was variously known as the Gorgeous Gael or the Prince of Cobh, formerly the port of Queenstown, near Cork, whose one other distinction was that it was the last port of call for the Titanic. The rudely-educated Doyle, born in 1913, was plucked from His Majesty's Irish guards in the early 1930s and went to find fame in the U.S., winning a number of preliminary fights until he was knocked out by heavyweight Buddy Baer, a giant of a man who was the brother of Max Baer, a heavyweight champion in the mid-1930's. Doyle married a now long-forgotten starlet with the stage name of Movita, lived extravagantly and, like Behan, favoured a tipple with outgoings far exceeding incomings, but no matter. He won most of his 23 fights but never the big one. He died 'short of a bob or two' in 1977.

Thus it threatened to be for Behan who by 1960 was just past his peak as a literary force, at least in the view of many literary and social friends on the other side of the Atlantic. Despite his ability to make headlines or obtain strategic mentions in the gossip columns, many began to ask when did he find time to write. But for the moment, the New York public was all adoration and was held in thrall by this most charming of individuals. In any case, Irish New Yorkers were always enthusiastic for a visit from the old country. In Behan, they had the perfect mark. Behan had little idea that the pulsating theatrical crowd on the Great White Way was replete with fair weather friends. The newspaper columnists, Earl Wilson or Leonard Lyons, both of the *New York Post,* loved a star, but like Norma Desmond in *Sunset Boulevard,* they were just as apt to forget them once they were out of the limelight. Desmond Mackie was worried for his friend, observing that Behan had already spent the best years of his youth in jail.

"He had been a long time in the nick, either up at the Curragh concentration camp for the IRA men, then in jail in England, then to Borstal and then he's famous. You're suddenly brought up and thrown late into the middle of Broadway. How do you live with that?"

Yet Behan himself said that he never felt so much at home anywhere as in New York forgetting, perhaps, that New York was not one and the same as the rest of the United States. It was the greatest city on God's earth, he told a fellow guest while staying at the Algonquin hotel. Dublin must have seemed puny, insular, claustrophobic and, above all, penurious. "You have only to look at it (New York) from the river, from Father Duffy's statue. New York easily is recognisable as the greatest city in the world, view it any way and every way – back, belly and sides," he said. "A city is a place where Man lives, walks about, talks and eats and drinks in the bright of the day, or electricity, for 24 hours a day. In New York, at three o'clock in the morning, you can walk about, see crowds, read the papers and have a drink . . . It is the greatest show on earth for everyone."

There is much to what he observed. In Dublin, the city was buttoned up tight by ten-thirty in the evening, maybe a little later. The shops closed early, provided there was anything to shop for, and the pubs took off two hours each afternoon as a matter of routine. The mid-afternoon closing was brought in by Westminster under the Defence of the Realm Act, ever since known as Dora, and the regulation stayed on the statute books long after Ireland's independence.

Thanks to the vibrancy that accompanied the rehearsals for his play, *The Hostage,* he became something of a boulevardier, albeit a ramshackle one, and developed his own haunts in town through whose swinging doors he would crazily propel himself in hope of finding the old magic – a gullible, good humoured audience game for an evening of Behan's brand of blarney. He met the literati soon after arriving, including novelist and essayist Norman Mailer, a feisty literary force whose domain was Manhattan. He was the founder of *The Village Voice* newspaper, the voice of New York's Bohemia. With about the same build as Behan, he was a natural playmate for the Irishman. Behan had been there only a matter of weeks when he and Beatrice were invited to a huge party hosted by Mailer who had just announced his candidacy for mayor. Mailer biographer Hilary Mills quoted litterateur George Plimpton as being inundated by calls from Mailer about who to invite to the party. "He wanted to impress his constituency, the fire commissioner, the police commissioner, then he wanted me to get Saluradin Aga Khan who had an important position at the United Nations, Tammy Grimes (the actress) who was to represent Broadway and, for some odd reason, Behan. God knows what he was supposed to represent."

A handsome and charming Irish-American, John F. Kennedy, complete with pretty wife with an exotic French name, Jacqueline Bouvier, was running for president and looked like emerging the victor over Richard Nixon, the Republican party candidate then seen as a throwback to the tired cold-war politics of the 1950s when he served as vice-president under President Dwight Eisenhower. There would be no prizes for guessing which side Behan would be on, though he had no voting right in the U.S. Despite the fun of it all, the outcome of the November poll showed an extremely close result, but the right man had won and the Behans happily were invited to the inauguration in Washington set for the following January 20. From his vantage point, it seemed the whole country was Irish-American.

New York, in those days, had nine daily newspapers, so there was no shortage of wordsmiths to keep the wheels of publicity turning. Behan soon became an old Broadway hand (for anyone who lived in New York this can happen with extraordinary speed). In addition to pumping himself up for the delectation of the gossip columnists, he made appearances on the *Jack Paar Show,* a precursor to the NBC-TV *Tonight Show* hosted for subsequent decades by Johnny Carson. In Behan's first appearance, Paar was absent and the charming Arlene Francis, well-known as being a regular on the American version of the *What's My Line* quiz show, was the hostess. She corralled Behan, Arthur Schlesinger Jr., the biographer of John F. Kennedy, actress Constance Cummings and humorous playwright James Kirkwood for the show, thus giving Behan a national platform. Unlike his still-talked-about appearance on Muggeridge's BBC show *Panorama* years before, he acquitted himself well, having kept off the drink. It appeared that his reputation as a drinker extraordinaire was behind him and that he was truly 'off the gargle.'

The Behans were put up in the heart of New York's theatre- and night club land with the best restaurants that Manhattan had to offer. These included Jim Downey's steak house, Sardis Restaurant, the Silver Rail and Costello's. Behan also was invited to appear on the *David Susskind Show,* where he was a welcome guest because of his quick wit and the perception that he was an intellectual. He returned to Paar, with the host actually there this time. He became something of a regular on Paar. As Ulick O'Connor, the writer, found out, these appearances were doing his reputation no harm and were helpful in turning him into a noticeable man-in-the-street, the kind of person one stops and asks for autographs.

Behan may have been in his element, but Littlewood and Raffles put their moistened fingers to the New York air and sensed turbulence. They were grateful at Behan's abstemiousness despite the fact that he was behaving as if he had lived there all his life. With him were members of the cast, including the camp Victor Spinetti, who was thrilled, like the others, with the bright lights. Everyone was on a roll, no-one more than the playwright. Where ever he went, incidents were bound to follow, for instance when he first noisily tried to clear customs on his entree to the big city. He was asked:

"Are you queer, Brendan? We've thought so since *Borstal Boy*"

"Well, if I had to choose between Michaelangelo's David and Whistler's Mother."

"What are you going to do in New York?"

"Visit the Empire State Building in honour of King Kong and swim at the Jewish boys' club"

"But I'll be the only one with a foreskin."

And so it went on, to be followed by days of rehearsals and antics with cast members like Spinetti and Dudley Sutton and the welcome arrival of Chicago columnist Studs Terkel. The visit, for Raffles and Littlewood, could not go on forever – they had the financial health of their east London group to preoccupy them. Littlewood recalled that it was just as well, for Behan was back on the gargle and many of the Irish pubs were beginning to take a cautious view about their noisy customer. "Nevertheless, he and Beatrice came to Idlewild to see us off, said Littlewood. "As our flight was called, Brendan gave each of us a hot greasy hand and , half drunk, sang his ominous and unsettling song:

> ". . . . me ould Irish tomb,
>
> I'll be in there soon…."

The Behan travelling road show

Not long after opening night, Behan, fuelled by a large amount of champagne the need for which had been sparked by a silly domestic spat with Beatrice, went on to put his personal and very public, stamp on the play. The evening began with an uproar at a restaurant and a bulldog like rampage at the Cort that night. The repercussions were serious "Whilst the audience enjoyed Brendan's impromptu appearance, Perry Bruskin, the stage manager, smashed a photographer's camera in order to keep the story out of the press and was arrested for assault."

CHAPTER FOURTEEN

THE HEMINGWAYS

"As I stood in the hotel's lobby that day, I could not help noticing that the short, stout, unquenchable bundle of effervescence that was Brendan had transplanted very well from Dublin to New York. Fame had not changed his countenance . . . " – Valerie Danby-Smith

IN THE RUNUP to the debut, Behan had been taken in tow by the *New Yorker* magazine's Brendan Gill, an urbane American of Irish ancestry assigned to tag along with Behan and write a lengthy profile on him while listening to him busily feeding one-liners to the rest of the New Yorker writers like James Thurber and visiting celebrities like the rotund Robert Morley, who were it not for his English accent could easily have been mistaken for Behan's doppelganger. .

Behan also allowed himself the distraction of renewing a friendship with an aspiring journalist, aged 20, from Dublin whom he had known for several years. Her name was Valerie Danby-Smith and her claim to budding fame was her *ad hoc* work the previous year in Spain for Ernest and Mary Hemingway. The Hemingways would probably never have brushed the sleeve of the Behan group had it not been for a big contract from *Life* magazine for the American to write up the 1959 Spanish bullfighting season. A galvanizing factor was the increasingly sour relationship between the U.S. government and Cuban revolutionary leader Fidel Castro. What is often forgotten now is that about that time the Castro revolution enjoyed considerable popularity among the young in the U.S., largely thanks to the romantic image conveyed by the young rebels as Fidel's tanks rolled into Havana, the rebels sporting thick dark beards and flourishing cigars. In Washington, the jury was still out on Castro, but ill winds were blowing across the Gulf Stream which were to prove unsettling for the island's most famous resident, Ernest Hemingway. He and his wife, told that Washington could not guarantee their safety if they decided to stay in Cuba, Hemingway felt he had no recourse but to return to the U.S.

The Hemingways, with great reluctance, were now packing up their belongings in Havana where they had lived for nearly two decades in preparation for a reluctant but urgent return. Hemingway cared little about the revolution – there had been others, he felt, and there would be more again. That was the way it was in Cuba, and in this case a complicating factor was his less-than-robust physical and mental health.

It was a weird coincidence that a year earlier, Irish-born Danby-Smith, still in her teens, told her friends in Dublin that she was going to give free-lance writing a 'try' and would base herself in Spain, perhaps picking up some supporting work in the meantime as an au pair child minder.' (It is to be noted that, in 1960 Danby-Smith was one-third Hemingway's age.). One of her confidants back in Dublin, it so happened, was Brendan Behan who, fascinated by the young lady's pluck, wished her well and asked to be kept informed on how she made out. Oh, he added, there was a possibility that his play, *The Hostage*, might be readied for staging in a year's time in New York and if she happened to be there at the time there might be some work for her.

Within months, the adventuresome lass, was in the foyer of a Madrid hotel flagging down a large grey-haired man whom she had never heard of for a story she had been asked to write for a Belgian news agency. Hemingway was in town to write about bullfighting, a subject of which he was an undisputed authority. Weeks later she was running with the bulls in Pamplona as a member of the large Hemingway entourage of VIPs, matadors and well-connected friends. She was also taking dictation and keeping up with the paperwork that began to pile up as the group hit the bullrings of Spain. Hemingway, American entrepreneur William Davis who was providing accommodation at his villa in Malaga, and Mary Hemingway all agreed to take her on as an assistant during the Spanish assignment.

Meanwhile, events in Cuba began to build up. Valerie was asked by Mary to stay on, at least for a short while, and this necessitated a reconnaissance trip to Cuba and New York with the writer to assess the future of the Cuba house. Valerie had continued to keep Behan, still in Dublin, up to date on her achievements during her first phenomenal year in journalism. He in turn kept her posted on the proposed New York staging of *The Hostage* and repeated his offer of a job for her, not unlike what she had been doing for the Hemingways. The Hemingway job had proved doubly useful: firstly it catapulted her into the high profile world of the bullfight in Spain, and secondly, as luck would have it, exposed her to the media capital of the world, complete with an opportunity to hob-nob with Hemingway's old writing and sports cronies, all of this happening under the effervescence of the Castro's political revolution and Brendan Behan's theatrical revolution. It was a breathtaking sequence of events, especially for one scarcely turned 20 years of age. But in a matter of months, it all looked like coming to an end when her work arrangement with the Hemingways began to look unfeasible after Valerie's and the Hemingways' reconnaissance trip to Cuba and New York began to look unfeasible. Told her services were no longer needed, she wondered what to do? Why, what else but to take up Brendan's offer to join the *Hostage* entourage as it was mobilizing its forces to sweep New York off its feet, so she took up Behan's offer, complete with a New York opening night ticket for Mary Hemingway, should she be in town. The invitation would have extended to Hemingway himself but he was not much of a theatre-goer and in any case was back in Spain wrapping up the bullfight research for the *Life* magazine article. Danby-Smith's coquettish appearance with a 'comp' (complimentary) ticket to come to New York to work as a 'circus barker' for Behan set off an alarm signal with the ever-alert Beatrice who was all too aware that her husband was in-demand by the opposite sex. She had already fought off expressions of interest in Brendan by Shelagh Delaney and did not fancy having to run up the defences again to reinforce her marriage. She knew, however, that trouble could be brewing.

That there was interest in other tactile relationships was also taken on board by Victor Spinetti, who was enjoying the bright lights of New York in advance of opening night. He was thrilled at the buzz around the theatre and the big characters seeking a share of the action. One of these was Tennessee Williams, an Olympian figure in American drama. He could be counted on to have a big city production of any one of his plays running somewhere in North America and the UK at any given point in the late 1950s. Being a risk-taker himself, he was attracted by the successes of the Littlewood team, especially with their staging of *The Hostage*. According to Spinetti, who was to portray an IRA officer in the forthcoming play, Tennessee Williams became not only smitten with the play but with its author, the two having only just met and Danby-Smith having just checked in at the Algonquin hotel.. Herewith Williams on Behan:

"Youah ah a good looking man, Brendan, you know, you really ought to get yourself some teeth," The reply was characteristic Behan. "Who needs fockin' teeth, I threw them in the Liffey."

Although both men were understood to have the same sexual tastes, Behan, a natural wolverine, was wary and asked Spinetti to chaperone the playwrights when Behan and the feline Williams were out together. He elaborated; "I cannot understand a fockin' word he's talking about".

But it was early days yet. Practically without precedent, a full page advertisement urging the public to see *The Hostage* appeared in the *New Yorker,* subtitled *A Letter from Brendan Behan*, complete with a drawing of the tow-headed playwright and a rambling display of utterances and aphorisms.

The letter acted as a salvo from the old country and in it Behan expressed concern that while America was a fine country, one noted for its hard working people, he would have none of that. "I hope it is clearly understood when I come to New York in September that I am allergic to shovels and do not want to go tunnelling under the East River in case it gives me the shakes – I know a more amiable way to get them."

He went on: "In *The Hostage*, older folk are torn between youthful loyalties and so-called adult wisdom, which comfortably concludes that the world doesn't really want to be improved. And when the struggle between their memories of the good old days and the science-ridden real world becomes too difficult, they usually settle for another beer."

From time to time Behan found himself asked what his 'message' was, and his invariable reply was "Message? Message? I'm not a fockin' postman." It was a one-liner that Behan's camp-followers would hear him blurt out countless times. In his open letter he allowed himself the luxury of elaboration and it is about as close as he came, in corporate-speak, to what might be called a 'mission statement'.

"You see, in *The Hostage* I have nothing to sell – not religion, not a political system, not a philosophy and certainly not a panacea for the ills of the world. I respect kindness to human beings first of all and kindness to animals. I don't respect the law. I have a total irreverence for anything concerned with society except that which makes the roads safer, the beer stronger and the food cheaper and old men and old woman warmer in the winter and happier in the summer."

The Hostage drew the crowds to the Cort Theatre, perfectly positioned in the center of theatre land, and these included noisy appearances by Behan himself. Its staging was at a particularly fertile time for the Broadway stage which enjoying a long run from Fiorello, the popular musical depicting the life of Fiorello La Guardia, the big city's most popular mayor, the revival of Arthur Laurents' rousing musical *West Side Story*, the political satire, *The Best Man*, by Gore Vidal, particularly apt given the machinations propelling John F Kennedy towards the White House, and some avant garde theatre represented by *The Connection, The Balcony,* Samuel Beckett's Krapp's *Last Tape* and Edward Albee's *The Zoo Story*.

Behan's ploy to self-promote the play through a explosive burst of public relations paid off. *The New Yorker* praised the work of Maxwell Shaw and Avis Bunnage, who headed the cast, and Joan Littlewood for her production. It said of Behan's play: *"The Hostage* (is) a rousing romp with Brendan Behan, who makes the disorderly conduct of his creatures a virtue, not a vice."

Brendan Gill, in a later memoir of a long career spent working for the magazine, respectfully noted some detective work undertaken by fellow writer, Susan Black, who was fascinated by the writing style of *New York Herald Tribune's* Walter Kerr, a senior man about town in the world of theatrical criticism (and after whom a theatre has subsequently been named). Kerr, also was impressed by *The Hostage*. It was Black's finding that Kerr metaphors were drawn from the world of food. He described Behan's masterpiece as a 'pot-au-feu' and 'a broth', and said of the author himself that he was 'an original piece of salt.'

Clearly the play had impressed as it would again the following winter after it returned from a lengthy and noisy road show. For its second New York go-round, the play started to develop a patina of respect. By then, Behan had almost become an establishment figure in the world of drama and was drawing mature reviews, such as this one from Edith Oliver, which the *New Yorker* ran. She wrote:

"The only news of any value about Brendan Behan's *The Hostage* ... is that it seems as wonderful now as a year ago, and that it has lost none of its spirit in transit from one cast and director ... It is as hilarious and bawdy and poignant as ever .... Comparisons with the Broadway (Cort Theatre) production are inescapable, though I wish they weren't. Perry Bruskin, the stage manager, has followed Joan Littlewood's ideas pretty faithfully, and the form the play takes seems about the same to me . . . On the whole, the performance is somewhat broader and more deliberate that the one on Broadway. It doesn't have the same snap and rightness, which means that Mr Behan's occasional fumbles are exposed since none of the actors throw away or camouflage a dud line. This is a small objection, though, when you consider the meats they do provide. . . "

"What a play! Its freewheeling rambunctiousness and its fast changes of mood (can anyone turn laughter on or off more quickly than Mr. Behan?) are never pointless or frivolous. From the beginning of this century, it seems to me, most of Ireland's writers have been trying, with ridicule or poetry or whatever, to snap the country out of her bondage to worn out standards and attitudes and to . . . injustice, which should be worn out. In *The Hostage* Brendan Behan shows himself to be one of the best of the rescue squad."

Behan was winning the praise of the critics, and business opportunities arising out of his pledges to write more plays and essays were beginning to pile up. His skill at self-promotion knew no bounds. Two weeks after arriving in New York, he was holding forth before students at Vassar College, up the Hudson River in Poughkeepsie. Before the girls, he was a tour de force, acting out skits and scenes from some of his plays. As if to confirm his new found friendship with Tennessee Williams, he mimicked the southerner. "Will you have a drink, Ebenezer?" "Wha bless you mah deah, ah prefer mah drewgs."

He liked the money and the endless line of credit that went with it. He also found that he liked the ether of fame. According to Rae Jeffs, for $3,000 he contracted to produce for *G. P. Putnam* a photographic book on himself. Each illustration was to be captioned by Behan witticisms, and he promised Bernard Geis that, in return for $12,000, he would write a sequel to his autobiographical *Borstal Boy*. Geis would turn out to be a patient contact for Behan who was prone to sign off publishing rights to anyone who handed him a pen and paper. Geis believed in Behan's artistic ability but wanted to do serious business with the Irishman. Geis had taken gambles before and was prepared to do so again. He was often described as a maverick publisher attracted by high-risk publishing ventures and his most renowned efforts were the publication of *Sex and the Single Girl* and the racy best-seller *Valley of the Dolls* by Jacqueline Susann.

It was on a cold December morning at the end of 1960, two months after the Behan's thunderous arrival that they departed for Ireland aboard the small Cunard liner, the Saxonia. The first trip to New York had most of the hallmarks of a great success, but to some, the seeds of self-destruction also had been sown -- and this time alcohol had little to do with it.

CHAPTER FIFTEEN

FROM COAST TO COAST

"I would have liked for Brendan to have seen his own books available in the shops in Ireland. He never had the pleasure of seeing his favourite, Borstal Boy, in the bookshops. It was only released in Ireland about a year after he died It was on the banned list, and that was rather sad . . . ." – Beatrice Behan 1979

FROM A STRATEGIC distance, the arrival of *The Hostage* in the U.S. looked to be an unqualified success, the critics liked it, the man in the street liked it and so did the Sons of Erin and the gossip columnists. Behan, readers should be reminded, was, or at least looked to be, all that the punters could have wished for – if you wanted to go to New York for the 'craic' then what better than the Behan extravaganza. In short, he was a super human personality who could write. No point in dwelling on the *New Testament* account of Christ's triumphant entry into Jerusalem, to be followed within a week by his crucifixion. Behan believed he was the native son come home when in fact the reverse was true. What Americans had heard about him from overseas in preceding years was now the real thing, the talented madcap was loose among the masses, a lion escaped from his cage. His adoption of New York was irreversible and he saw no problem in making the Big Apple his permanent abode. He was not taking into account the staying power of Mrs. Behan. The invitation to the Kennedy inaugural on January 20 1961 had been sorely tempting but as the inaugural date drew closer, Behan, in a rare moment of wisdom, declined the invitation, perhaps fearing that he could not guarantee being on the wagon and, therefore, might unintentionally find himself the author of an incident that might bring embarrassment to the new resident of the White House.

But New York offered other forms of bait. Behan had been making business commitment to promote his works. The structuring of some of these commitments was somewhat careless, but he did have real assets for sale such as U. S. rights for *The Quare Fellow, The Hostage* and *Borstal Boy*, not to mention compilations of newspaper articles and even a short novel written a decade before called *The Scarperer* (Irish slang for one who might otherwise be described as an 'escapist'), as well as a film version of *The Quare Fellow*. Behan was in talks with Geis for the promotion of his works in the U.S. There was travelling to be done, palms to be pressed and books to be signed, disciplines which all went against the grain for one who would rather be telling jokes in a nearby tap-room. He had his own distinctive style and anarchic ideas on promotion. Not for him sitting down in a main street book store nodding politely while jotting down dedications to his latest best-seller. Nevertheless, as Beatrice pointed out, promotional trips out of New York were part of the deal and the several that he did took him to Montreal and Toronto, each 450 miles to the north. No-one worried more than Beatrice, and she was to remain bitter for years about how Brendan had been manhandled by his promoters. "You know, this is a human being you have, this isn't a machine. You can't tell him to travel so many miles today and get up to give a witty speech and then travel another lot of miles tomorrow and to the same thing," she was heard to complain well into her own old age.

And so it was that Brendan and Beatrice set off from Dublin for New York again, Beatrice fearful of the turbulent waters that lay ahead and genuinely beginning to fear for her marriage, and Brendan, like a farm ox, ploughing forward, ignoring every danger sign he encountered. He was truly becoming 'quits with Dublin', the city of his birth, and his contempt for the place often showed itself in the form of various contusions and bruises received from some fellow drinker who had heard just one snide remark too many in the course of an evening. Dublin, he once said, was a good place from which to receive a post card. He may have thought he had got the measure of New York in his triumphant first visit, and, with his renowned gift of the gab, who could dispute it. But New York had got its measure of him as well, to the extent that he found himself banned from participating in a St. Patrick's day festivity in March 17 1961. But nothing is at it seems in the mysterious world of Behania for the heads of St. Patrick's day committees in Jersey City and Boston rallied to Behan's support. He was given the keys to Jersey City and thus found himself baptised into Irishism-American Style. He and Beatrice had only been in New York four months. One thing he was to find out was that St. Patrick's Day in many cities in the United States and Canada was celebrated in a far livelier way than in the home country where dreariness prevails.

Word of his arrival in the New World did not take long to reach Canada where, in the depths of winter, he found himself recipient of an invitation to speak to students at McGill University in Montreal. The invitation was a pleasant surprise and owed its provenance to a post-graduate student named Tony Aspler who had met Behan in a pub the year before when Aspler was studying in Dublin. At McGill he sat on a committee whose purpose it was to arrange guest speakers, and with Behan holding forth in New York, the school was able to invite him to speak. Aspler, now a wine writer and specialist living in Toronto, said that the prestige English-speaking university on the slopes of central Montreal got more than it had bargained for.

With temperatures plummeting to levels that not even the defiant Irishman had reckoned on encountering, Behan managed to disappear into a blizzard and was found unconscious and close to death from hypothermia. Aspler said he was sure Behan would not survive the night but with his unusual recuperative powers he was helped to the university where he gave a long, rambling incoherent discourse which the students loved – and which the elders hated. According to guests that night Behan rattled off a few stanzas of French-Canadian folk music, made the obligatory jibes at England and criticised France for what it was doing to the Algerians, then fighting for independence. But for all the laughs, Aspler's recollection of Behan is not a pleasant one. "Behan didn't care anything about the rules of social behaviour – he was bound by no rules." But Aspler still found the Irishman fascinating, if gross and coarsely behaved, and fictionalised him as a self-destructive Irish poet named Bart Shea in a novel titled *The Streets of Askelon,* published in 1973.

A few months later, in early spring, 1961, it was Toronto's turn to feel the lash of his tongue. Toronto then was a very conservative, industrial city, and a cultural backwater compared with Montreal (Ensuing decades have seen the roles reversed.). Behan was asked to appear at the new O'Keefe Centre, along with such other performers as Nina Simone and drummer Art Blakey, all participating in a new revue. Jazz would not seem to be a natural domain for the likes of Behan, who would be more comfortable staging an old-fashioned 'hooley' by jumping on a pub tabletop. But George Avakian, the jazz promoter, remembered him in those days turning up at jazz seminars held by Marshall Stearns, a jazz specialist. Behan, of course, was on a binge and naturally provided grist to Toronto's journalists. Behan was arrested and sent to hospital in the neighbourhood of Sunnyside, a policeman posted outside his door, following a ruckus at the stately Royal York hotel, a huge granite edifice. Local news reports said he had had to be subdued after going on a rampage in the hotel's corridors "stampeding like a great, naked bull." The inevitable altercation broke out with hotel officials and the police, with Behan at the centre demanding a bottle of drink, even though it was after hours.

His uproar had forced the backers to cancel the revue. Toronto still had a crushing WASP image at that time and when bars were shut nothing would prise them open – a far cry from Dublin and even nearby New York. Hundreds of cranes and derricks marked the flat city's skyline and Behan, despite his intoxication, still managed to take this in and, thus, had already formed strong views on the city as a kind of Canadian Belfast. After the arrest, he was recumbent in his hospital bed with his eyes closed when, according to company legend, a reporter from the broadcasting division of *The Canadian Press* news organisation, known simply to Canadians as 'the CP', turned up for an interview, tape recorder slung over his shoulder, and looking for a memorable quote or two. Behan, opening his eyes, obliged him:

"Who are you?"

"I'm from the CP," said the reporter.

"And what'll that be," Behan replied, "the Communist Party or the Canadian Pacific (the latter Canada's biggest and most capitalistic company)." A little while later, he said of Toronto, "It'll be a great place when its finished."

But his trip to Canada rankled and he wasted no opportunity to express his irritation. "The attitude here seems to be, 'if you don't like it here you can leave, and that is what I want to do. I want to be let out. I have no desire to bolster the sagging cultural economy of this country."

Chicago, the melting-pot prairie city with a long history of Irish-American machine politics, would have seemed a natural place to show off the wit of Brendan Behan, such were the anti-English sentiments rampant in the city. One mayor famously remarked in the 1930s that 'if George the Fifth were to visit Chicago, I should punch him in the nose.'

By 1960 Mayor Richard Daley, was able to deliver key support from Cook County to the Kennedy campaign. He may have liked Kennedy but in Chicago he was the boss, which meant there was no room for the likes of Behan. Chicago writer Studs Turkel said that Daley had nixed a requested visit by Behan, whose Hostage play was on tour. To Daley, known as The Big Dumpling, Behan was an affront and the answer was no.

A more agreeable environment would assuredly be found on the West Coast where *The Hostage* was being taken for the final phases of its American road show. The most promising stop began on April 30 1961 in San Francisco, that most Irish of west coast American cities. It was ready for Behan in the sense that the citizenry had foreknowledge of what he was like and was prepared to enjoy his excesses during the week-long run of his play, at the Geary Theatre near the centre of the city.

Behan was not without competition for space in the news pages – the stories that week were dominated by the Cuban revolution, the U.S. calling on all Americans in Cuba to pull out and Fidel Castro declaring no more elections and the creation of a socialist state. The trial of the Nazi, Adolph Eichmann, was nearing its inevitable close in Jerusalem. Local baseball hero Willie Mays had struck four home runs in a single game, a feat that happens in that sport about once a decade and is somewhat akin to Sir Gary Sobers' famous six-for-six in cricket. Film star Gary Cooper, a good friend of Ernest Hemingway, lay mortally ill in a Los Angeles hospital from cancer. Hemingway, whose own fragile mental state was unpublicised and unknown to the public at large, was slipping into serious decline and was under psychiatric treatment at the Mayo Clinic. Mary Hemingway had dispensed with the services of Valerie Danby-Smith following the Hemingways' return to the US after exiting Cuba. Similarly, Danby-Smith's short stint working for Behan for whom she admitted to having developed a deep affection, appeared to be over now that the playwright was on his western tour. In April 1961, after Behan's Toronto episode, Danby-Smith picked up a job as a researcher for *Newsweek* magazine on a $55 a week salary. But her Irish charm and willingness to put in long hours won her many friends at the magazine, and at the start of May 1961, after angling a couple of days off, she was en route to San Francisco to test the waters with Behan.

The jetliner bearing the author taxied up to the San Francisco airport terminal where a mobile staircase was wheeled out. Behan, unaccompanied by Beatrice who, afraid of air travel, was making her way across America by train to join her husband, emerged, clad in grey suit, blue tie and black sandals, his thick Roman hair tousled and his manner pugnacious. He was sober and much in need of a 'cup o' tay'. He reassured reporters that he was 'off the gargle'. "Any of you who can put up with the Barbary Coast (San Francisco's Gold Rush era nickname) can put up with me," he said.

The crowd greeting him knew of his escapades back east and he was prodded with some questions. "You know, I don't really think that place (Toronto) is finished. Those Canadian writers asked me if I didn't think that the Russians had shown you guys up (Russia had put an astronaut into space). I told them to stick to their focking ice hockey." He beamed toothlessly to the crowd then was taken by car to a capacious hotel on Union Square and was heard singing a bellowing rendition of something called 'Don't muck about with the moon.'

He took a little time to warm up, but within 48 hours he had exploded into print. A headline bursting out of the *Chronicle*, the so-called Voice of the West, declared that "Behan Upstages the City." What had happened was a reprise of his New York debut seven months earlier. Behan was described as "cutting a musical swathe" through the hard-drinking town. Tangle-haired and red-eyed, he entertained patrons by jumping up on stage in the first act and sprayed the contents of a glass of beer on the cast like so much holy water being converted to wine, then disappeared into the wings then across the street to the aptly-named Curtain Call Bar. Such noisy debuts were not necessary, given the interest in and quality of his plays, but audiences were going to get them, no matter what. He liked to brag that he was "the only playwright to get thrown out of his own out of his opening night."

The next day, May 3, Herb Caen, the dean of west coast gossip columnists, was back in town and on form after a trip to Chicago. He wrote of Behan's bar crawling and his enjoyment of the critical and popular acclaim for his play while he lapped up the contents of four bottles of champagne in the basement of the Geary Theatre. Intriguingly, Caen, in his column referred to an unidentified young lady, obviously a close acquaintance, seen clinging to Behan's arm entreating the playwright not to drink any more. Was this the young lady from *Newsweek* who had just spanned the continent so as to be with Brendan in San Francisco? Behan and the rest of the crowd then taxied across the Golden Gate Bridge to the bohemian North Bay town of Sausalito, famous for many things including its Bar With No Name, where the evening pulsed on. Behan was described as being accompanied by a young brunette, arm in arm, singing the Internationale.

Caen, who had not met Behan before, sagely noted the similarity in his behaviour and that of Welsh poet Dylan Thomas. Caen had a way with words for it was he who a few years earlier, with the launch of a Russian satellite, the so-called sputnik, coined the word 'beatnik'. Prescient praise also chattered off the typewriter of Paine Knickerbocker, the drama critic who concluded that if there was any 'hostage' at all it was Behan himself. To the actors, led by Beaulah Garrick, Eileen Kenelly, Aubrey Moris and Donald Moffatt, the play was an ever-changing thing given the antics of the author and the free hand the actors were given to vary their interpretation. That was one way of looking at it, but one actor said Behan's erratic behaviour and on-stage unpredictability was the stuff of heartbreak.

It was inevitable that his 'return to the gargle' would take its toll, and by May 5, he was in the coastal city's St Mary's hospital, an event that earned him a substantially under-researched front page story in the *Chronicle*. Fortunately Beatrice had caught up with her husband and, on arriving in town, found a scene of carnage – according to local reports - in her husband's hotel room. Details, however, were to remain obscured for some years till she wrote her own memoirs after her husband's death in 1964. She disclosed how life-threatening his escapade had been. According to Beatrice, she found Brendan in his hotel room, unconscious and lying among piles of papers and correspondence, much of it unopened. His ability to bounce back again proved remarkable for the next day he was sitting up and talking with the nurses, most of whom were Irish. For the moment, Beatrice's instinct was to cover up. As for the local wags, who were unaware of the gravity of Brendan's drinking and diabetes problems, the stint in the hospital was just another amusing adventure in this Irishman's life. It was, of course, much graver than that, underlining once again Behan's liver damage, diabetes and an unyielding need for alcohol.

On June 23, seven weeks after the San Francisco visit, an odd thing happened: Valerie Danby-Smith wrote a letter to Mr. and Mrs. Bill Davis, the wealthy expatriate American couple who had hosted the Hemingways at their villa in Malaga, southern Spain, 18 months before. It was on that occasion that Danby-Smith, based in Madrid, met Ernest Hemingway, and set in motion a cavalcade of events that would lead to her being in San Francisco with Brendan Behan.

In her letter to the Davises, she told them of her trip to the West Coast and the high spirits and general revelry that accompanied the Behans in their post-*Hostage* celebrations at the Mark Hopkins hotel and various other venues such as the popular 'hungry i', Fisherman's Wharf, Chinatown and the City Lights book shop. In all, it was a tale of a good time being had by all. But the letter was economical with the truth and in her own memoirs, published in 2004, the salient details of those days and nights in San Francisco – and their consequences – surfaced. She wrote:

"There was one incident I did not mention to the Davises. After the closing party for The Hostage, which took place at the Mark Hopkins Hotel where the Behans and I were staying (sic) I retired to bed exhilarated but completely exhausted. I was awakened a short while later when Brendan let himself into my room with a key he must have acquired when he made my hotel reservation. I learned then that the romantic fantasies he had hinted at during the preceding months were not just attempts at lightheaded flirtation, it was a night that would change my life forever."

TAKING FLIGHT –
Behan gets set for New York
© REX Features

HAPPY DAYS – Brendan, Beatrice with all to play for
© *REX Features*

ON THE GARGLE – Behan, Donleavy et all test the waters
© *REX Features*

TWO OF A KIND –
Behan meets Jackie Gleason in New York (circa 1961)
© REX Features

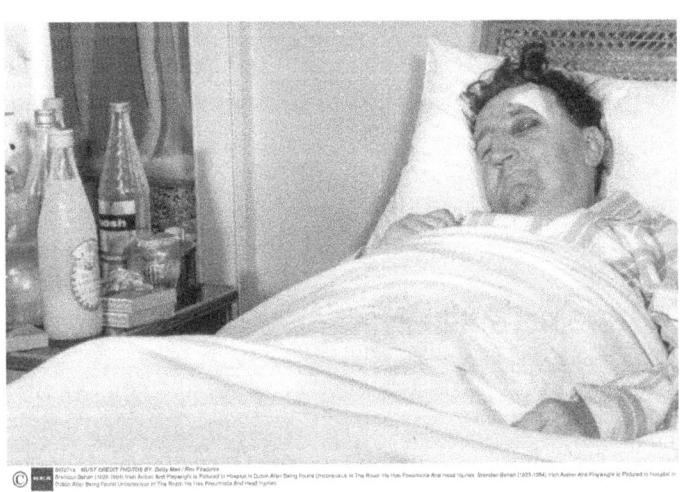

LIFE ON THE EBB – The Meath hospital, Dublin, 1964
© REX Features

CHAPTER SIXTEEN

AT THE PRECIPICE

"Brendan was a live one; at one time he had managed to get himself banned from most pubs in Dublin; now they are all clamouring for pictures of him to go on their walls...." – Dublin taxi driver

THE LIVES OF Brendan and Beatrice Behan were about to enter their most precarious phase. Not only was the playwright displaying a harrowingly indifferent attitude towards his diabetes which was now becoming a day-to-day worry his creative juices were drying up at a fast rate. Despite his promises about a sequel to *Borstal Boy,* none was reliably evident, at least not along the lines originally promised. This impasse was of continuing concern to his British and American publishers and to his arch-supporters running the Theatre Workshop at London's Stratford East theatre, Joan Littlewood and Gerry Raffles. Indeed the pair remembered well the difficulties in extracting *The Hostage* from their recalcitrant 'artiste'; that proved ultimately to be a triumph, leading to west-end presentations as well as to the Sarah Bernhardt theatre in Paris in 1960 and now to the Cort theatre in New York. The triumphs were one thing but the need for a follow up was another, and Littlewood and Raffles had speculated that Behan, given his behaviour patterns, would be in danger of seizing up entirely once he had established himself as New York's laughing boy.

It was true that he had offered *Confessions of an Irish Rebel* as a sequel to *Borstal Boy,* although it would lack some of the former's authenticity once it had been dictated (not till 1963) into a tape recorder, with Rae Jeffs at the controls. *Confessions* did fill in many blanks in the author's post-Borstal life after the end of the Second World War, but no text was yet available to sate the thirst of his publishers. His much-promised backup pieces, *Brendan Brendan Behan's New York, Behan's Island* (eventually destined for syndication in London's *Sunday Observer*) and which also would turn out to be tape recorder jobs, were not yet extant. In short, as Behan might have said, he was one cover short of a book and his hungry public would have to wait.

As for that elusive 'third' play, *Richard's Cork Leg,* originally conceived in Irish as *A Fine Day in the Graveyard,* it had not reached the stage where it could be called a contribution to the Littlewood-Raffles 'oeuvre'. What had been completed was inadequate, despite the many entreaties of his patient promoters and publishers. It was play rather than work which increasingly dominated his time as Behan wallowed in a life of debauchery and otherwise erratic behaviour. In a self-reproachful moment, Jeffs recalled hearing him cry out: "Everyone should try being famous for three months." It was the cry of a lost soul being leached to death. Behan's sad lament was to ring in her ears long after his death. She had contracted to work with him to extricate from him further memoirs but told friends of her shock at his physical deterioration. His perpetual puffiness and a further loss of teeth, someone remarked, was making him look like a grouper, the large fish which is said to have swallowed Jonah. Both Beatrice and Rae knew that they were working with an unexploded bomb and their duty was to manoeuvre the host – Behan – towards some sort of creative life as best they could in hope the bomb within him would never go off without extinguishing him in the process.

His own weapon, as always, was his sense of humour which he always seemed able to tap into when he needed it. On one occasion, the three of them were motoring from Dublin to London. Behan was in the back seat snoring as usual. The three had landed in north Wales off the Irish Sea ferry before resuming their journey south towards London. The embargo banning him from touching down anywhere in the British Isles had long since been lifted. At some point, on a quiet part of the motorway, their car sustained a flat tire and they were forced to pull over to the shoulder. After a time, a police car drew up. The policeman asked what the matter and then set off to find a garage or a tow truck. Leaning in the window he saw the puffy and inert form of Behan, apparently asleep, then asked Beatrice and Rae what car breakdown service club they were members of so as to facilitate the car repair. Was it the A A (Automobile Association), he asked, or was it the RAC (Royal Automobile Club)? A swollen eye opened and Behan chipped in: "As a matter of fact, it is the IRA," to which the policeman, nonplussed, replied, "They're all much the same, sir." With that he sped away, the repair van duly arrived and presently they proceeded on their journey.

Brendan Behan's women problems were not as easy to laugh away. They were gathering pace which some friends said was unusual given the perverse nature of Behan's appetites. There were the expected dalliances as one would expect with a person of such fame, but the serious relationship – that involving Behan and Danby-Smith – was another matter.

At the precipice

Many of Behan's friends regarded Beatrice as turning a blind eye to her husband's complicated relationships. She would say: "I had no illusions. There would always be women infatuated with Brendan." Danby-Smith acknowledged that her pregnancy by the Irishman dated from spring 1961, just after the San Francisco bacchanal. She would bear him a son, also named Brendan, and there would be personal wrangles and protracted disputes over how to parent the boy. There also would be painful correspondence between Valerie, now 22 years old, and Beatrice that would last for the duration. Beatrice was anxious to block any more adverse publicity and would not acknowledge any culpability by her husband on the question of pregnancy She wanted him out of the gossip columns whereas he wanted in. Behan, his marriage starting to come adrift, was able to maintain a relationship with Danby-Smith – a big reason for his wanting to stay in New York -- but it would be the source of many tears. After much bitterness, she did resolve to take over the rearing of the child by herself and, as long as she was based in New York, she was able to maintain a carefully balanced relationship with Behan. She resolved, also, that the baby would not be brought up in Ireland, very much a clericalist republic at the time and dominated by the church. She also underlined that Baby Brendan would not be raised by Brendan's mother Kathleen. In the end, the baby was born in the United States and it took the name Hemingway, after Gregory Hemingway, the author's third son, who would marry Danby-Smith, the two having met at Ernest Hemingway's funeral in July 1961.

The death of Ernest Hemingway - which was still in the future - was to have a profound effect on the world of literature but would scarcely rate as a footnote to anyone trying to conjure up a connection between the names of Hemingway and Behan. True, the two men had read each others' work with much admiration. Indeed, the fact that Valerie knew Behan was a factor in her being hired to join the Hemingway 'quadrilla' in Pamplona. The fact was that Hemingway was already on the downward slope, a well-kept secret by his closest allies, notably A. E. Hotchner, who was whip cracking the author's bullfight treatment into shape for use by *Life*. What was going on in the Behan camp after the San Francisco layover was real enough to the parties concerned. Behan had recovered from the degeneracies of San Francisco, thanks to Beatsie's help, but he would yield to the shapeless temptations of Los Angeles and Hollywood. that would test the marriage as never before – there would have been no inkling about pregnancies at this time.

Brendan and Beatrice had not long been in Los Angeles when Behan struck up, literally, a relationship with one Peter Arthurs, a sailor from Dundalk. The two met after colliding at a local swimming pool. After this 'incident' the two men became companions and were to form a triangular relationship with Beatrice turning a blind eye. On top of this state of affairs, Brendan employed Arthurs, an amateur boxer, as his minder and chauffeur, whose chief function appeared to be to convey Behan to and from the city's homosexual bars and private VIP residences of Hollywood's great and good where he sought to bask in everybody's mutual fame, It was as life-style light years from life in Ireland . Indeed, Behan was in his element. Beatrice managed to ignore the sordid goings on at their suite at the Montecito Hotel and instead made good use of Arthurs-the-driver to fetch her husband from encounters with the police or bartenders seeking to terminate his custom after the inevitable fracas.

It may well have been that she was not surprised at Brendan's other side. She was certainly forewarned. On their honeymoon in 1955, which took place in France, he broke down and told her that he was not a great lover. Put another way, he did not like the physical side of marriage, an embargo that did not apply to physical relationships outside marriage. She said that

At the precipice

she was never embarrassed by Brendan despite the drinking, bad manners, fights and unconventional hours. All she had wanted of him at that time was that he take confession, which he did when they got married (though only he and his confessor would or could ever know the details of what he said in the confessional booth).

Having compartmentalized her husband's relationship with Arthurs, she found it useful to be able to rely on the handsome pugilist's broad talents, especially his reliability and his skill at keeping her husband out of trouble. But there were things Brendan wanted to see in and around Los Angeles that never would have been possible to take in without the man from Dundalk. Los Angeles also had a modernistic dazzle which, at least in those days, would have been impossible to replicate in diminutive Dublin. Arthurs was reliable and she knew Brendan was in safe hands when the two or sometimes three of them set out for the Mexican border towns of Tijuana and Ensenada, communities otherwise tremendously seedy and vice-ridden. Arthurs, being an Irishman, was quick to understand Behan's interests. He had his own motives, one of which was the hope Behan might be able to propel him to a stage career of *his* own – after all, he had a modicum of acting experience behind him, and was not *The Quare Fellow* being filmed in a grainy black-and-white version starring Patrick McGoohan and Celia Salkeld, Beatrice's sister. He hoped that his relationship with Behan might lead to something better than just being a merchant seaman.. Ultimately, Behan's support for Arthurs came to nought and the shooting that had been done involving Arthurs did not make it past the cutting room floor as the film, under the direction of Arthur Dreifus, departed substantially from the text of Behan's original, all-male, prison masterpiece. Despite Behan's expletive-filled entreaties on behalf of his minder, the creation of a script that would provide an opportunity for Arthurs seemed fated not to happen. Finally, a brief scene in which Arthurs, as prison guard, kills Mickser, one of the prisoners, was recorded but did not survive the trip from Los Angeles to New York where the film was given a debut in 1962. The grounds for cutting the scene was that it was 'too violent.'

Arthurs remembered the playwright's rendering of what was meant to be his third major play, *Richard's Cork Leg,* a version of which eventually ran posthumously on the London stage, thanks to Alan Simpson, and with critical acclaim but little else. Said Behan in his best holding-forth style:

"On me way to America, I told a joke to a steward on the boat. He laughed his bollox off. There and then, says I to meself, I decided to make a play out of the cunting thing. I'm calling it *Richard's Cork Leg.* It was an old line of James Joyce's. Not that I'm a fan of that interior-minded degenerate cunt. He should have been hung in my estimation for desecrating valuable paper."

Behan, said Arthurs, exuded a rare charm, an ebullience and an enormous human sensibility. Apart from Beatrice and Rae Jeffs, few saw him at his self-abasing worst, sick and vomiting, drinking uncontrollably and hell bent on self-destruction. Arthurs was reaching a point when he could take little more of Brendan's excesses and decided to return to sea, hence his periodic get-togethers with Brendan. Behan and Beatrice returned to New York and then hopped to Dublin, thus putting an exclamation mark on the prolonged and ill-defined California visit. Dublin, however, was fast fading from his life as a rendezvous point or as a place in which to recharge the batteries. New York was, he insisted, his adopted home. Other events were evolving and were about to remind the writer of grave matters that required the attention of a mature adult male. The life of perpetual adolescence could not go on.

Or couldn't it?

At the precipice

Sitting with Beatrice at table back at Anglesea Road one night, Behan absented himself from the house for a 'short meeting' with a friend. A few hours later, he was moving at more than 500 knots per hour over the North Atlantic en route to New York, Beatrice still wondering what had become of her dinner companion. It was perhaps just as well, for there lay a certain predestined 'appointment in Samarra' which neither of the Behans could avoid. Firstly there was the dawning knowledge that Valerie Danby-Smith was bearing Brendan's child. She can scarcely have been aware as yet of this given her quick visit to San Francisco only in May 1961. Of course parenthood for her meant parenthood for him, except that he was married to Beatsie. But that was still a little way off. More immediately ominous were the warning sounds from two gunshot blasts heard around the ranch house at Ketcham, Idaho, early in the morning of July 2, 1961. Behan, in New York, found himself with a rare reason for a binge and he took advantage of it. According to Arthurs, also in New York, Behan telephoned him and blurted out:

"P-Peter, its HH-Hem. . . H-H-Hem. . . . s-shot h-himself. P-Peter, he's dead. P-Peter."

There was little to be said except that Behan took to the bars and had to be taken into custody. He was briefly hospitalised thanks to the attention of his restaurant buddy Jim Downey. That very day, Valerie Danby-Smith was playing tennis with friends on Long Island. She had not heard from Hemingway all winter, nor had she expected to. She was aware of his melancholic state but did not know the details of the shock treatments nor that he was all but incommunicado. In the dawn hours of July 2 the news broke and was followed by a telephone call from Mary to Valerie to confirm the news reports. Brendan contacted Valerie and suggested they meet. Valerie had been invited to the funeral but didn't want to go till Behan persuaded her in soothing terms that her attendance was necessary. Behan was at his best, urging, cajoling, soothing Valerie and finally persuading her to attend and funding the air ticket as well as asking that a wreath be laid in his and Beatrice's name. Behan inscribed some words on letterhead: they were in English and Irish.

'Around the Hearthstone every night/The storyteller lives forever/

Timcheall an teaglach gac oice/Maireann an scealuf go deo.'

The funeral took place and the occasion, though sad, brought together many different factions of the Hemingway family, extended by various marriages. It also brought Valerie into contact with Gregory Hemingway, who had fallen out with his father a decade earlier. Shortly afterwards, the Cuban government was in contact and were inquiring what Mary's plans were regarding the disposition of the writer's belongings, particularly now that he was dead. Mary, still distraught, saw a solution in the hiring – again - of Valerie to help with the paperwork, an offer Valerie promptly accepted in the face of the pressure on her from practically anyone in the U.S. to talk in probing detail about the suicide. It would be a relief to escape from the U. S., and as she was an Irish passport holder getting papers for Cuba was no problem. Valerie Danby-Smith and Mary Hemingway wasted little time, and within six weeks had tidied up the files and arranged for their delivery home.

For all of the trauma, the link with the Hemingway family proved to be a godsend, at least in the near term, for it gave Valerie a bolt hole in New York; although she was not yet sure about whether she was pregnant. But she became aware soon enough. She took an apartment in Manhattan's Upper West Side after deciding that continued residence in the Algonquin Hotel would not work. She recalled in her memoirs that she saw plenty of Behan at that time – he was once again on the transatlantic commute -- and even helped type some of the script for *Richard's Cork Leg* as she had typed basic text for Hemingway's *A Moveable Feast* a couple of years earlier.

By early 1962, Behan was in an ever deepening struggle with Beatrice over what was to be called home. Certainly it had to be New York. But what kind of home would it be? There had been much to-ing and fro-ing between New York and the British Isles, but as far as Brendan was concerned, it was New York that formed the axis, not Dublin. In little over a year he had become an old hand, though he had shifted his favourite bars and hangouts away from mid-town Manhattan down to more traditional Irish bars and pubs on the lower west side. He was behaving as if he had lived there for years or, indeed, been born there. He also had shifted hotels, from the Algonquin down to the environs of Greenwich Village. One tolerant hostelry was the Bristol hotel, a place accustomed to eccentrics and bohemian types. He made his mark there just as firmly as a burglar leaves an incriminating fingerprint. He was accustomed to treat the hotel as if it were all his own, and it was not unusual to encounter his scarcely clad squat form burrowing about the corridors.

But there were important matters at hand; in early 1962. Valerie gave birth to baby Brendan, a juicy item of gossip that managed to stay out of the news. Beatrice was continuing to dig in her heels to shore up the timbers of her constricting marriage. She simply did not accept the notion of divorce or separation, though the Behans had spent plenty of time apart and were to continue to do so. But separation is not divorce and in the case of Brendan and Beatrice , they were guided by Dublin Rules, whether they liked them or not – well entrenched Roman Catholicism, a church-dominated state and, for that matter, the non-availability of birth control pills or even the use of condoms, not that it made any difference since their use was sinful anyway. According to Valerie's account of this time, it almost became possible to work out some modus operandi by which Brendan could play a parenting role for the baby, but at some point Valerie concluded, there was no way forward but to raise young Brendan by herself. This she felt she would be able to do and stay based in New York, remaining at work for Mary Hemingway and *Scribners,* the author's publishers, in what was becoming the mountainous task of sorting out the Hemingway papers and keeping an open-door arrangement with the Cuban cultural affairs contacts in Havana. In death, Hemingway loomed nearly as large as in life, such was the global interest in his life and works. There were rumours of a cache of books by him and there was just as much interest in the literary community in books about him.

Valerie acknowledged that Brendan senior was devastated at not being able to play a substantial parenting role in the relationship. Friends of Beatrice have made it clear that the pregnancy had dealt a serious blow to the marriage. Brendan had got into the habit of referring to Beatrice as 'my first wife', implying a special arrangement among the three. Relations between Beatrice and Brendan were never to be quite the same again.

CHAPTER SEVENTEEN

HELP FROM ASTOR

"He made endless trips abroad. He never told me about them, he would just go back to his home, on a whim, take his passport and off he would go to the airport. Beatrice sometimes would hide his passport, but in the end he didn't need the passport. He would just get on the plane and off he would go to America. Every one in Dublin and America knew who he was...." – Rae Jeffs

THE DUBLIN-NEW YORK air run was turning into an air shuttle. Then there were fleeting side trips from Dublin to London just to remind people in England that he was still alive and well and living dangerously. Brendan Behan would often turn up, unannounced, at the London homes of Joe McGill and Des MacNamara, loyal and tolerant friends throughout his life. Sometimes he was on the gargle and was good fun, other times, his alcohol intake was at such a level as to fill him with remorse and self-recrimination, disagreements would ensue, followed by tears and then sleep. Beatrice, ever stalwart, was finding it difficult to keep up the pace. She was gravely hurt by Brendan's affair with Valerie and the letters intruding into Beatrice's and Brendan's married life. But Brendan was also hurt that he would not be able to test his paternal skills with the newborn infant who was his son. He took what opportunities he could when in New York to show off the boy and to equally show off his own pride, but this was not easily done – and in any case would have to be done in secret. Furthermore, the issue of divorce was not on the table; the affair with Valerie was far from over, but it was holed below the waterline and its prospects looked bleak.

An important supporter of Behan's was David Astor, editor of the *Observer*, Britain's oldest regularly operating newspaper and a 'must read' for the quality of its news, commentaries and arts criticism on the weekend. Astor, a member of a branch of the property-rich Astor family, was a close friend of the *Hutchinson* publishing family and was anxious to help Behan. He had a reputation for taking care to hire top quality, searching editors to contribute to the Sunday publication and would spare no costs to help get a story right – or to help extricate one of his writers from a tight spot. Surprisingly, the *Observer's* editorial content in the post-war to 1970s period, Astor's heyday, was frequently anti-establishment and avant garde, not that that was unusual in itself, but to outsiders it seemed so given the Astors' extraordinary pedigree.

The *Observer* had been preparing to run extracts from *Brendan Behan's Island,* but Astor could not provide personal help unless asked. The process by which this step was initiated came in a letter from Beatrice to Jeffs. In it, Beatrice acknowledged that there had been rows, drunken escapades and the draining away of a lot of goodwill by people in Dublin towards her husband. A consensus was emerging among his friends that some form of enforced cure or regime of recuperation might serve as a catalyst for change. Finally, Beatrice expressed the fear that unless he got on the right track soon, he likely would be pulling up sticks and heading for New York again – with or without his missus. The portents from Anglesea Road were not good.

The letter – perhaps better to call it a lifeline -- eventually sent by Astor in reply was a model of diplomacy and friendliness. If Muggeridge and Behan were opposites back at the time of the BBC TV interview, then Astor and Behan were even further apart, or at least apparently so. The fact that Behan, through his serialised *Brendan Behan's Island,* could be contributing a big spread to the *Observer* was seen by some as the backslapping Phineas T. Barnum, the circus king, getting pally with King George V (observed broadcaster Alastair Cook in another context). In reality, the aristocratic Astor was well inside the pale, owning the venerable newspaper, and employing several of the country's best reporters, such as drama critic Kenneth Tynan, who was so impressed by Behan's two stage plays that he regarded them as keystones in the Anglo-Irish theatrical revolution that had sprung to life in the 1950s.

At the start of his entreaty, Astor apologises for not having written sooner and cleverly says that "I gather from newspaper reports that you have travelled a lot, but one learns little from these reports." Then off-handedly he asks that if Brendan would wish to take up a 'reconditioning programme' in London then he would be pleased to provide assistance. No admonitory remarks, no reference to alcohol, no en-passants about noisy rampages, just a letter from one gentleman to another, concluding with "Do let me know if you are ever over here with a little time to spare."

Jeffs' recollection, to this day still a source of anger, was that Behan ignored the letter for days, then finally he opened it and felt himself seduced by the charm. He could not say no to such a gesture of kindness, and made plans to cross over to London and take the publisher up on his proposal. It was suggested that he be accommodated in an east London clinic specifically to dry him out and begin the reconstruction of his health. It was almost as if he were a section of dilapidated structure with roofing tiles missing, bricks askew and loose fitting sash windows prey to unhealthy draughts. Jeffs met Behan and Beatrice at Euston Station and, probably unwisely, agreed to stop off at a pub in Soho for a 'restorative' before pressing on to the York Minster public house for further rehydration. It did not take long for Behan to say what was on his mind, and he did so only after Beatrice had absented herself for a few minutes. As Jeffs said in her reminiscences:

"He wanted to return to America, he said. There, he was understood, but Beatrice did not like the idea. She would rather he remained in Ireland, an invalid. I interrupted to remind him that as long as he craved publicity, there was little hope of him recovering his health. Treatment in hospital now was exactly what he needed."

But it was not to be. Behan, forever stubborn when confronted by marching orders and perhaps sensing coercion by those closest to him, refused to be holed up in a London hospital unless Beatrice was there with him for the full length of the stay. This emphasised his reliance on Beatrice for as much as he beat his chest as an independent and free spirit, he really could scarcely do without her. He argued that such a type of treatment was inadequate and that it would be better if he sought to cure himself. A clinic was selected and offered to provide extra accommodation for Beatrice, thereby meeting one of Behan's terms and conditions, but Behan continued to object, bobbing away from each attempt to save him. Finally the couple erupted into a row and Behan said that a divorce and a 50/50 split in their joint assets might be in order. With tensions volcanic, Jeffs posed the question as to who would telephone Astor to break the news. Rae checked the Behans into a hotel near Holborn tube stop, on the fringe of central London itself. It was then agreed to make Brendan call Astor to

Help from Astor

explain the situation. This he did, pleading with Astor for just one more try to recover from his problems in his own way.

Clearly Behan had other things on his mind. Uncharacteristically, he returned to Dublin, then he booked a flight to New York where *The Hostage* was undergoing another revival– and where he would find Valerie and baby Brendan, at this moment the two most important people in his life. Jeffs, speechless with irritation, stayed on top of her editorial obligations for the Irishman on bringing *Behan's Island* into print for *The Observer*. As for Brendan, more than ever a loose cannon, all one needed do was read the popular press to pick up his trail. The news reports were of endless binges culminating in hospitalisation then temporary recovery.

By mid-1962 Hemingway had been dead a year. At least the business side of Behan's life had begun to proceed with some normality. *The Observer* obtained the serial rights to *Brendan Behan's Island*. Astor, while hurt at Behan's rejection of his offer of help, pressed ahead with plans for a serialisation in *The Observer;* Bernard Geis in the US had obtained the American rights. What with these positive blips on the commercial radar screen, it turned out to be a bumper period for Behan. Colin Macinnes, the writer, had termed Behan an outstanding writer and was chasing him on behalf of BBC's *Monitor* programme for an interview. Island had been chosen by the *Book Society* for October (the UK version of the US *Book-of-the-Month Club*) for October release, a huge commercial accolade in that it would put the name Behan in tens of thousands of British households. *The Hostage*, in the meantime, had been chosen by the French Theatre Critics Association as the season's top play, a similar award having gone two years earlier to *The Quare Fellow,* the title of which translated intriguingly into *Le Client du Matin.*

The Crazy Life of Brendan Behan

Further Behan was invited to participate in a literary lunch with the *Yorkshire Post* and, though he did not yet know it, he was being sized up to take part in the British version of *This Is Your life,* hosted by one time boxing announcer Eamonn Andrews, as much a big TV name in Europe as was that of Ralph Edwards, founder of the show, in the U.S. The catch for Behan was that he was not the guest of honour, this distinction going to Stephen Behan, his father, hence the need to keep Brendan out of the picture till shortly before show time which, in any case, was filmed ahead of time rather than shown live. Behan, stung by jealousy, try to throw narrative bowling balls among the tenpins but he had not reckoned on the strong personalities of his father and the extraordinarily extrovert mother, Kathleen, who ensured that the show was the life of Stephen Behan, not Brendan. As a post-script Andrews, years after Brendan's death, did a surprise 'Life' show for Dominic Behan, a talented writer and folk singer in his own rite, and one less apt to have to prove himself by disruptive behaviour.

The run-up to the *Yorkshire Post* literary lunch turned out to be a near calamity. Behan was invited to be put up as a guest of Mr and Mrs. Max and Margaret Sylvester at their roomy home in northwest London. Several days before the lunch, rather than co-operate in the planning of the event or simply being a civil quest he sat recumbent in the lounge room barking commands at all and sundry while swigging back gin by the glassful. An informal lunch in London the following day produced more of the same but the plans firmed up. They included luncheon guests Lord Robert Boothby, a witty and mischievous peer, not above committing gross indiscretions of his own; Kenneth Allsop, Frank Swinnerton, Ursula Bloom and other members of the contemporary literati, and Kenneth Young, editor of the *Yorkshire Post*. Also invited were Valentine Iremonger, who it emerged had edited the text of *Brendan Behan's Island*. Also on board was Jeff's daughter Diana.

The lunch took place and Behan found that many of the literary crowd were as adept at toping as he was; the day passed with many close calls, much laughter and many breaches of protocol, the occasion being without disaster but propelling Behan into a week-long bout of drinking, culminating in his collapse and an emergency trip to Westminster Hospital. Jeffs once again called on David Astor to help convince Behan that a tough, abstemious regime was necessary if he was going to recover his health, But Astor, on visiting Behan, found the author unable to recognize him. Behan soon fled the hospital, having regained a degree of mobility and sought out his more wastrel companions whose friendship extended no further than their possession of flasks of spirits.

But in New York, Bernard Geis was excited by the reviews for Behan's Island and the possibility of producing something out of his Irish Rebel writings. One of these was a collection of his *Irish Press* columns, which Behan and Jeffs dubbed '*Hold Your Hour and Have Another.*' It was not the kind of book that would be a big seller ordinarily, but on the strength of Behan's name, anything bearing his imprimatur was likely to be a decent money spinner. Finally, he had once written a collection of connected fictional stories dating back a decade, and it was estimated that the writing was good enough for a prelaunch under the title of *The Scarperers,* a breezy novel that percolated with colour through its use of 1950s Dublin argot. *The Scarperers* might have come straight out of Damon Runyon, whose comical writings about Broadway low-life had brought him international fame, notably through the stage adaptation of *Guys and Dolls* and the introduction to a theatre-going public of a cast of eccentric characters not unlike Brendan Francis Behan.

CHAPTER EIGHTEEN

CHELSEA NIGHTS

"I have never ridiculed my faith, but as regards my fatherland, the first duty of a writer is to let his fatherland down, otherwise he is no writer. In the name of Jesus, how the hell can a writer attack anyone else's fatherland if he doesn't attack his own . . .?" – Brendan Behan

BRENDAN BEHAN MAY have truly believed he could become a New Yorker, but to those able to take a long view it looked as if he was sailing into ever colder and more dangerous waters. He was losing his sense of feeling in his hands, and needed rest and recuperation. But by rejecting the generous offer of David Astor, he was signing his own death warrant. The support of his wife was not enough to restore marital equilibrium and, in any case, there was little left to restore after the birth of Brendan Junior to Valerie Danby-Smith and the emotional tug of war that followed. Valerie continued to work in New York for the Hemingway literary estate and, as this gave her a base, she was able to 'hang out' with Brendan from time to time. But it was not the same as being married. Valerie, in her own memoir of those days, said that Brendan was torn between his family in Dublin and his family in New York. The way he dealt with the problem was to drink and forget, a form of cure that only deepened his health problems. Said Valerie: "When he was in Ireland, Brendan wrote heartbreaking letters about the pain of separation and missing his little son." All the more reason to hop a plane for N.Y. – when he was not already there – but this was hardly satisfactory.

Like Scobie, the tormented protagonist in Graham Greene's novel, *The Heart of the Matter,* Behan was leading a double life; he would deal with his problems by putting them in separate boxes which he could put away and retrieve when he pleased. That was the idea, at least. But this course of action proved to be flawed, for everyone knew of his internal conflicts and the frequency with which they became public. The drunken outbursts were followed inevitably by a night in the pokey, and that followed by the benefaction of one of his friends bailing him out of hospital or jail. These incidents happened with such frequency that he was ceasing to become news and the attentions once so lavishly given him by the big city's gossip columnists now began to dry up. Still, Rae Jeffs kept after him to keep up the work on the Behan's New York book, which promised to be a money spinner.

With the doors of the Algonquin, his hotel of choice, now closed to him, he gravitated towards the Chelsea on the edge of Greenwich Village. Yet, despite his rudderless behaviour, those who knew him said that he was behaving exactly as he would have wished. He was still perceived, incorrectly, as a productive and witty Irish writer with books rolling off the presses with regularity. The fact was that genuine new material was not rolling off his typewriter at the same rate. Some of his output bore the style of 'clippings jobs', quick compilations of material in some cases written long before. Bernard Geis was still hoping for progress on *Richard's Cork Leg* that would match the magnitude of *The Hostage*. Littlewood was in the same boat. Behan, in an inexplicable fit of pique, had decided to cancel his arrangements with her, implying that their partnership was at an end. With Behan, one always took it for granted that he was not serious – better wait till the morning after to determine if he meant what he had said. Littlewood and other associates visited Dublin to take a first-hand account about the state of the Behan word machine. The only reply they got was an Irish sing-song while their car careered around the streets of Dublin. It is true that Behan owed a lot to Littlewood, but he did not like to think of himself as beholden to her in any way. He said once: "Littlewood was the only producer I ever met with a spark of genius, but I also happen to remember that her theatre (in London's east end) . . . would have shut were it not for me. Eaten bread is soon forgotten." Littlewood was reaching the conclusion that his writing days were over.

After his initial transatlantic dash to New York and the bonhomie that greeted him throughout theatreland in those early days, Behan, nearly three years on, began to see his exclusive, bespoke world start to disintegrate. He had moulded it in his own image, but the centre would no longer hold and it had begun to fragment. Norman Mailer, a promising friend at the outset of Behan's hegira to Mecca-on-the-Hudson – a man who was to New York what Behan had been to Dublin -- had other preoccupations and , sometimes deliberately, saw less and less of his Irish friend. The emotional wound this caused Behan cannot be measured, but its intent to harm must have been great for some three-and-a-half decades on, the octogenarian American deflected request to comment on Behan's New York days, saying he did not believe he had anything to contribute.

From the swank, popular media-centric hotels of mid-town to more haunting accommodations further down Manhattan Island, Behan heard the call from New York's nether regions.

Chelsea nights

This meant the Hotel Chelsea, a hostelry-cum-apartment house that had long had a Bohemian clientele.

Because he was in New York rather than London or Dublin, he occasionally took note of his personal appearance – he was, after all, still in demand for photo opportunities and TV appearances, including one with Jackie Gleason, the stand-up comedian, whom he first encountered a few years before via a TV hook-up with the CBS network. With a little bit of industrious marketing, an appearance on Gleason could generate an encouraging slice of earnings; such was his popularity at the time. Gleason also won an academy award nomination for his appearance as a pool shark in *The Hustler*. When on telly Behan behaved himself and managed to overcome his stammer, but he failed to capitalise on these 'quality' associations in the absence of anything to promote.

It was now 1963 and he was virtually estranged from Beatrice. At this time, what he needed more than anything else was real friends. Luckily for him, he found them in the supportive personages of Geis, his hard-wearing publisher, and fleetingly in Katherine Dunham, famous founder of her dance troupe and discoverer of singer Eartha Kitt. With Behan having to go into hospital again, as much from diabetes and suspected hepatitis as from excessive drink, emergency measures were needed. Geis and Dunham asked Stanley Bard, then the young manager of the Chelsea, to find a room in which to park their unruly client. Bard, in the year 2007 and still at the helm, said he had been approached by Dunham, who lived at the hotel, and Geis, whom he knew well, with an appeal for help; Behan's predicament was explained to him and he said he would try and get the playwright set up. To this day, the Chelsea still attracts eccentrics, playwrights, dancers, singers, poets, the artistic and sometimes lunatic fringe of society.

The Crazy Life of Brendan Behan

"He was an interesting customer, we had heard about him from Bernard, and I was pleased to try and help. He drank himself to death but he was a good writer and he finished two of his books while here," said Bard. He did explain that the Irishman pushed those privileges to the limit. But at the time of this writing, Bard still was a bastion of discretion. He recalled:

"We agreed to take Brendan in, and it was Dunham, already living in the hotel, which looked after him at the outset. As I remember it, Rae Jeffs came over and started helping out on his writing of one of the books." This was spring 1963 and Jeffs, on the first of several quickie trips over from London set up first in the Governor Clinton hotel, close to Pennsylvania station and then in the Chelsea with tape recorder to coax Brendan along and to be on hand to help restore his health. Decades later, Jeffs still was irked at what she felt was the opportunistic way Dunham had behaved when she, Jeffs, arrived on the scene.

"I was expected to take over all responsibility for looking after Brendan, including looking after the bills but I made it clear in no uncertain terms that I was there to record the books and nothing else."

Behan's New York book was nearing publication and in the end would do respectably well. Nevertheless, it would turn out to be a tame cobbled-together commentary about New York and its street personalities many of them characters personally known to Behan as a result of his late night perambulations around Manhattan. The book was backed up by space-filling illustrations by Paul Hogarth. But since little of his time in the Big Apple was spent in a coherent state, the book's basic weakness was no surprise. It would eventually be dismissed by the author who felt ashamed at having had it ghost written. (Jeffs took a contrary view, stressing that, whatever its shortcomings, the words were his and his alone, no matter that he used a tape recorder). He would lapse into bouts of remorse that he had allowed himself to slide into such a state. Nevertheless its appearance in book shops would reassure the popular literature world that he was very much alive and well and that he would be a personality to contend with for the foreseeable future. Behan, at least, had the sense to extend a promotional 'plug' to his hosts at the Chelsea. In the book, he offers the following observation:

"John Betjeman, the English poet, who is always going round saving the most unlikely looking places such as St. Pancras Station (a huge brick built Victorian train station in North central London, now, in 2008, splendidly restored) which to me is not a thing of beauty and a joy forever, when he next comes to New York he would find it very, very impressive."

For good measure, he described the Chelsea as a marvellous institution "lovingly called by a great many people 'the Dowager of 23rd Street' because as far as I know it is the oldest building there, and is the heart and home of the street.' This was Brendan Behan, the old New York hand, speaking out. He was n his 40th year.

Thanks to Dunham, Geis, Bard and Jeffs, amongst others, Behan was showing signs of a recovery, having gained ten pounds and having recaptured some of the vigour to show that he was a man about town again. It was, of course, untrue; his emotional credit line could run just so far, and his instinct to rampage like that of an African elephant remained the bedrock of his nature.

Writer Ulick O'Connor put it another way: Behan's New Yorkers and London publics "could have no comprehension of Behan's umbilical attachment to Irish Republicanism, Socialism and Catholicism. He had allowed himself to be adopted by an international set who had not examined his credentials for admission. He was a man adrift, clinging desperately to beliefs which had supported him in the past."

To O'Connor, this was the glue holding him together, and it included belief in an after-life. In a sense, Behan might have been adrift but the ominous shadow of the Chelsea provided an umbrella for him – at least as long as the management and the regulars were prepared to tolerate Behan's antics. Like any famous hotel, the Chelsea claimed a number of odd tenants -- Tennessee Williams, Arthur Miller, William Burroughs and Arthur C. Clarke among others. No lightweights these! But then there was Behan! A case in point was the time in 1963 when Arthur Miller, creator of *Death of a Salesman* and then in residence after his divorce from Marilyn Monroe, sought to meet Behan to talk the art and craft of playwriting. Peter Arthurs set up the rendezvous for late one late spring evening, rounded up Miller and knocked on Behan's door. There they found Behan in profound flagrante with an unidentified female. Miller patiently accepted Behan's awkwardly-delivered apologies, exchanged pleasantries redolent of savoir faire and arranged to talk shop with the Irishman some other time.

Miller's own version was more discreet. In his memoirs, he explains that the two did meet up in Katherine Dunham's apartment. "He sat there, his wet hair haphazardly plastered down, his face blotched, lisping through broken teeth, laughing and eating sausages and eggs while black dancers moved in and out of the room, not knowing how to help him or whether even to try, and he said with his fixed, uneasy chuckle:

'I'm not really a playwright, you know – you would know that, of course—I'm a talker. I've got a room upstairs where I am 'talking' a book to a secretary; the publishers keep hounding me. I've done a good bit of it in the hopes they will empty another purse over me head. . . . But I did want to say hello to you, Art'r". . . .

Chelsea nights

Hello and goodbye, Miller told himself. It was clear Behan was on his way out of it. Behan, he found, was a 'rather patched-together' personality of several colours by this time, I thought, what with his desperate heedless lunging backwards towards a passing fame that required the image of the happy-go-lucky, late-rising debonair Irishman, all on a sick stomach.' Miller remembered the Irishman standing on the pavement outside the Chelsea vomit coming up and dripping on his tie as he joked and told stories while leafing through the *New York Post* to see if he had made it into any of the entertainment columns.

The American writer had a few choice words for Peter Arthurs as well. Behan's minder had had to finish fights that Behan had started and likely had got fed up with having to do so. "The man was most probably jealous of what he saw as Behan's undeserved literary fame; for he turned out to have a book of his own he was trying to get published."

To add to the poisonous atmosphere, there was the allegation that Miller said that Behan might have been suffering from syphilis, a claim that had surfaced before and which had filled Behan's closest friends with revulsion. What was a real worry was Behan's bisexuality, not such much the fact of it but of Behan's indiscretion. When on the gargle his manner of behaviour was very 'hands on' in that the playwright was incapable of keeping his wandering hands to himself, a habit which led to physical disagreements. Those who knew him well said that Behan's great fear was becoming too familiar with the wrong company and then finding himself facing a highly publicised morals charge – the kind of publicity he did not want.

Behan's stay at the Chelsea began to stimulate the literati to ponder if he wasn't going the same way as Dylan Thomas the Welsh poet who died in 1953 while resident at the self-same

Chelsea and while travelling the U. S. on a literary promotional tour. Thomas, a fellow Celt, a man of genius but also a man of excesses with whom Behan, to his frequent but not entirely justified rage, was most often associated.

The similarities were uncanny. Thomas set off on a speaking and reading tour of the U. S. Between April 21 and June 9 1953, the highlight of which was the preparation for the staging of *Under Milk Wood* at a theatre in Greenwich Village. The trip was meant to conclude with a visit by Thomas to the home of Igor Stravinsky, the Russian classical composer, in Hollywood. A proposal had been advanced that the two men work together on a libretto project. Thomas's state of health was marked by a heavy alcoholic intake and periodic blackouts, put down mainly to exhaustion. This state of affairs was amplified by a troubled marriage to his wife, Caitlin, who was feeling increasingly excluded from his personal and professional affairs. He had left Caitlin behind before setting off for the U. S. Somewhat prophetically, his abode was none other than the Chelsea, and his hangout was the White Horse tavern, near the hotel. According to John Malcolm Brinnin in his book, *Dylan Thomas in America*, the poet went on a prolonged binge which culminated in an intake of 18 shots of whisky while in the company of acquaintances and academics. Soon after he collapsed and slipped into a fatal alcoholic coma, dying in November 1953.

Although Behan was a more expansive personality, the individuality of his and Thomas's genius and both men's recklessness, not to mention their betrothal to extraordinarily patient wives, led to frequent comparisons of the Irishman and the Welshman. Mere mention of Thomas's name would have the effect of sending Behan into yet another binge, making the observation about his likeness to Thomas self-fulfilling. "He hated the comparison," Beatrice said in an interview many years later. Indeed, in that interview, she gave the impression

Chelsea nights

that she shared alloyed solidarity with her husband on the matter, despite the mountain of evidence to the contrary. "Brendan said there was no such comparison," she said.

It was at the Chelsea that Behan fell into a coma and had to be rushed to hospital where he nearly died. But his will power, bolstered by the support of friends, saved him. Behan tried sobriety once again and his health briefly recovered. But his confrontational comings and goings suggested a man addicted to being institutionalised, starting with his father, himself in Borstal and in Mountjoy and subsequently in countless hospitals in Ireland, the U.K. and finally in the U. S. and Canada. Other problems were materialising namely the effects of his diabetes and the fact that there were long periods in which he could not feel his typewriter keyboard.

Before Beatrice mounted her rescue mission in 1963 to bring her husband back to Ireland, Brendan was living a sort of bachelor's life. When it was feasible, Valerie Danby-Smith hoped to be able to stretch the relationship as the mother of the playwright's son, but this was becoming more and more impractical for the simple fact that she was not Behan's wife, a point underlined when Beatrice was on the scene. She was the working mother of a year-old son of whom Brendan was proud, and was still working for Mary Hemingway following Ernest's death. It seemed that only time was going to resolve Brendan's marital problems, certainly in the absence of any demand by either party for a divorce. It was brother Brian who would write years later that Brendan had never asked for a divorce from Beatrice . But those close to the family might have argued that he in fact did; it is just that he did not do so in so many words.

It was in April that another attempt was made to put humpty dumpty together, this time the R.M.S. Queen Elizabeth groaning up to the west side Cunard pier, there disgorging itself of transatlantic passengers, led by Beatrice Behan. No sign of Brendan to meet her but there in the customs shed were Rae Jeffs and Peter Arthurs with whom, for some reason, Beatrice got along satisfactorily. Then to the Chelsea in search of her husband. She had dramatic news. Firstly there was a tide of rumours disclosing imminent plans for a divorce, these were bluntly denied by Beatrice. She was finally shown to Brendan's room where she found him asleep. Her news for him was that after nearly a decade of marriage she was able to announce that she was pregnant. But that was spoiled by her continued differences with Brendan over Valerie. She had after all known Valerie since before *The Hostage* had ever become a success.

This spiked once and for all any lingering suggestion about a divorce. Beatrice was here to reassert the disciplines of marriage and to prepare her husband for his return to Ireland, whether he realised it or not. Meanwhile, matters were cooling between Behan, now beleaguered on many fronts, and Arthurs, with the latter slinging insults like a boxer throwing jabs. Arthurs called Behan 'a carnivorous little swine' but despite the bile he expressed the fear that he might never see Behan again.

It is difficult to imagine how deep the wells of tolerance and acceptance of the unacceptable ran within Beatrice's heart. She found herself part of a team of women (mainly) trying to resuscitate her foundering husband, rather like so many sailors trying to pull a sailing vessel off the rocks in the middle of a typhoon. No sooner is it freed than does it break its lines and head for the rocks again. Bills materialized and were not paid, at least not by him. Beatrice found some financial resources to keep on top of the costs of hotel living in New York. Beatrice, on the one hand, helped restore Behan's *physical* health while Jeffs, now having finished *Behan's New York* and working on *Confessions of an Irish Rebel*, sought to tap into what she believed was his literary potential. "I felt he still had an enormous amount to give at that time," she said years later.

Chelsea nights

No longer the grand boulevardier of 1960-61, Behan instead lurched from bar to bar and from party to party with only his memoirs to trade on. Truly imaginative projects, like *Cork Leg*, were effectively on ice and were to remain so.

Jeffs had made several trips back to London as part of the process of managing the production of the latest book. Beatrice had 'hung in' till on a summer's day, all three prepared to board the Queen Elizabeth for the return trip. Behan, perhaps having a premonition that this would be the end of his New York adventure and, thus, the end of adolescence, went on a bender a few days earlier which nearly scuppered the trip. Never easily deterred in matters bibulatory, he was prepared to do so again as the Cunarder raised anchor and set sail for the old world – the reverse of so many voyages taken by Irishmen seeking the freedom of the new world.

Transatlantic travel in those days was highly competitive and cost about $240, peak season, to cross the Atlantic, roughly in line with the cost of air travel aboard the new jetliners. The liner was running at a full load of 2,000 passengers for the five-day crossing. So, barring a heavy sea, the atmosphere on board tended to be festive as the ship mustered passengers for a lifeboat drill as it approached the Statue of Liberty. Behan, resisting the call to quarters, was in riotous form. For him it was tragedy tomorrow; comedy tonight. Decades later Jeffs was still able to laugh at Behan's antics as Manhattan disappeared from view. It was not funny at the time, she said. What happened was that, mistakenly, Cunard representatives, realizing they had a famous guest aboard, sought to capitalize on it with some on-board publicity and promotion for whatever press might also be on board. They did not take account of the volatility of their guest. Jeffs managed to get a berth in first class, putting some distance between her and the Behans who were set up in tourist class elsewhere on the ship. She admitted frankly to being relieved that she did not have to share a table with Mr. and Mrs. Behan.

"When I was told about the press reception, I told the Cunard people that this was a big mistake. Whatever you do, I instructed them, ban all alcohol at the press conference."

Her advice was ignored and she thought little more of it while taking her place at the captain's table in anticipation of a lazy, five-day midsummer crossing. "Oh, how lovely," I said to myself. Now I can relax."

Just then, she spotted a worried purser fast approaching the Captain's table. 'Are you Mrs. Jeffs? You must come quickly, there is an emergency.'

"I had to go through the kitchens to get to cabin class and when I got there I found that all hell had broken loose in the tourist class dining room. Brendan was shouting, bedlam had broken out and, in the middle of this there was Beatrice, sitting there, eating bananas and cream. I can see her now, totally unmoved or bothered while Brendan was 'effing' everybody and telling them all to go to hell."

After a short wait, the two women managed to bundle Behan out of the dining room and into a nearby cabin. The chief purser started to read the riot act, at first referring to him as 'Mister Brendan Bracken', a gross mistake as the aforementioned Mr. Bracken was Britain's wartime Information Minister, a newspaper executive and, somewhat scurrilously, rumoured to be the illegitimate son of Winston Churchill. Eventually the purser got it right. 'So, Mister Behan, we are not used to this sort of behaviour,' to which I interjected: "You're wasting your time. He hasn't the faintest idea what you are saying and he will thump you one in a minute because he knows you are being aggressive . . . I told you this was a bad thing to do, this reception. Well, you've got your publicity and now you are paying for it."

"Eventually things calmed down and the rest of the voyage went smoothly, but to this day I can see Beatrice eating that desert while this was raging around her. She was completely undisturbed."

CHAPTER NINETEEN

THE END OF SOMETHING

"I don't think Brendan was an alcoholic in the strict sense of the term. You would be a madman if you didn't agree he was addicted to drink, but what he loved most of all was the atmosphere of pubs. He didn't stash booze away in secret hiding-places at home or, indeed, evince much regard for drinking at home. Period." – Brian Behan

AFTER HIS RETURN from New York in 1963, it was not unusual to see Brendan Behan manoeuvring unsteadily around the streets of Dublin. As before, Beatrice was at his side. But her subordinated status notwithstanding, she was happy because she had finally got him out of hell and back to heaven, this time permanently. It was not a view that he shared, never mind her tactical leverage. He belonged in New York, and his latest rationale was that he had to be close to his son. But this was fast ceasing to be an option; Beatrice was pregnant and noticeably so. He felt he had been snookered, put in a position in which any attempt to escape would lead to disaster. But because of his nature, he would always be

The end of something

ready to joke and drink, and if those did not work he could resort to insult. He would often sweep up a group of strangers, frequently from the Trinity college crowd, before whom he would hold forth like a politician on the stump. If he faltered, as he often did, Beatrice would come to his rescue, promptly explaining that he was suffering from diabetes. He would just as often tell her to shut up or to stay put in the corner. She would weather these put-downs and would carry on as if nothing had happened, although habitués of the pub, perhaps unaccustomed to Behan's ways, might be put off by his bad manners.

His health was in a precarious state at this time and he was trying to stay on the wagon, at least in the morning, while he was working on tape-recordings of his New York adventures. At long last this exercise was nearing lift off. But when on a pub crawl, he was nearly always intoxicated. Beatrice remained as ever the tireless defender who regarded the protection of her marriage as a ship's carpenter would the vessel he was sailing on – any sign of a leak and she would quickly caulk the decks and and break out the block and tackle.

Typical of his pub encounters in those days was an incident recalled by Trinity student Tim Cullen who would eventually go on to be an international aid official in Washington. But at that time, the main objective was to master the art of drinking Ireland's famous national beverage.

"In my first term at Trinity . . . I spent much of my time demonstrating my inability to handle several pints of Guinness thinking that this was the right thing to do in Dublin. This was in the last months of 1963. We lived in an extraordinary lodging house in Ballsbridge presided over by a 20 stone (280 lbs) bruiser of a landlady who affected gentility. She was from the west of Ireland. Out of term time, she filled the house with actors and actresses and other odd Irish characters, some of whom were quite famous and notorious. In my first term she filled the house with actors and actresses and other odd Irish characters, some of whom were quite famous or notorious. In my first term, the appropriately named Donnybrook Garda station received a record 50 complaints about our lodging house. We all read J. P. Donleavy's *The Ginger Man,* and tried to live like him. In the atmosphere of sudden immersion in the Irishness, we went and watched Michael Macliammoir playing Oscar Wilde's *The Importance of Being Earnest* at The Gate and Sean O'Casey's *Juno and the Paycock* at The Abbey

"Against this backdrop, one evening I was in The Bailey and saw a small stocky man getting drunk on bloody marys. I blinked and realised that it was Brendan Behan. I had seen *The Hostage* at the theatre in Stratford (East) London and was excited to see the man himself two feet from me. As he launched into a very emotional rendition of Kevin Barry, I started chatting to the woman next to me and after a bit I mused on what it must be like for his wife having this cross to bear. At this point, she introduced herself as Beatrice Behan. She was very nice and was at pains to put me at ease as I was fairly embarrassed. She explained to me that he didn't actually drink an enormous amount, but as he had diabetes, the combination with the medication he was taking intensified the effect."

Investigative missions of interested parties would occasionally essay forth from London to check up on usually negative reports about his health. Joan Littlewood and Gerry Raffles, to whom he owed so much, had all but given up ever seeing a draft of *Cork Leg,* the so-called third play of the trio that started with *Quare Fellow.* Their short visit to Dublin only confirmed their worst fears.

Wrote brother Brian: "His liver was in bits as was his cerebral cortex, but he was still at the helm, three wheels on his wagon, waving at people on the street who didn't want to know. He was trying to visit old pastures imagining himself to be the man he was in New York when his plays were the property of the Sunday supplements."

The most lamentable tales were told by his wife and by Rae Jeffs, the two most battle-tested consorts. Jeffs, in an interview, remembered an earlier time sitting with him in his room at the Behan House on Anglesea Road. Jeffs was drinking a Guinness and Behan a soda water.

"I thought he was going to drink the Guinness, but he said it would be one drink too many." She recalled him saying. "No, I am not going to drink it, but I will tell you this – I would give up *Borstal Boy,* I'd give up *The Hostage* and *The Quare Fellow* to cure myself of this. . . . I'm being quite serious."

It was a peculiar situation. He still was capable of subordinating his lethal thirst to the disciplines required by Rae Jeffs to knock together the final drafts of his dictated texts. These were *Brendan Behan's New York*. (Hutchinson got it into print and on bookstands in 1964 with simultaneous publication in the US by *Little Brown*) and *Confessions of an Irish Rebel*, which *Hutchinson* wanted to get out onto the bookshelves but was only able to do so by 1965). It was Paddy O'Brien's observation, made decades before, that Behan had no capacity for drink, a few beers and he was away, shortly to be followed by disruptive behaviour then possibly a nap. Furthermore he was buoyed by the response to *Hold Your Hour and Have Another,* a compilation of light-hearted pieces written for the *Irish Press* newspaper between 1954 and 1956 in the early days of his creativity. It was amusingly illustrated by Beatrice who had demonstrated an ability to keep up her art and illustration work while chaos was breaking all round her. *Hutchinson* published the book in 1963. Its success added to the impression that Behan was as active a writer as at any other time in his career, the consuming public not being fully aware of the nearly terminal state of Behan's health. Jimmy Breslin, the New York newspaper columnist who like Behan was somewhat pugnacious and liked his drink – at least in those days – made these observations:

"Now most collections of newspaper columns are not worth the paste the author used to get them together for shipment to his editor, but this is a little big different because Behan is my set's idea of a real writer. For one thing, he thinks like a writer. The last we heard of the man he was released from the hospital where he had been taken after being found in the gutter some place with his head bashed in. Although not as bashed in as his liver must be. For another thing, Behan at least tries to write for the entertainment of a reader. He is not some outlandish homosexual trying to sound off on human destiny between paragraphs about his boyfriends, nor is Brendan a hophead of a one-shot novelist who knocks out drivel for some magazine. And he is not a two-dollar bum typewriting non-novels about such as an old friend of mine, John Stompanato. This is Himself... and when Himself takes to a writing machine it comes out right and with a little lilt running through much of it."

Breslin referred to Behan's collision with a curbstone in Dublin, perhaps inadvertently perpetuating the myth (at least held overseas) of Behan's indestructibility, the jolly, swaggering Mickser sent to the New World to amuse the expats, a man with whom one would happily hold his hour and have another. If you knew Behan in those days, it was easy to misread him, particularly if you were, like Breslin at that time, partial to a drink. The difference was that Breslin had a head for it whereas Behan did not.

Despite his return to Dublin, he began to lose what little poise he had and this included allowing himself to curse aloud before children, something he never did before. To be sure, he was possessed by more devils than one could imagine, not least the knowledge that he had a son in New York to whom open access was no longer possible. Valerie, clearly now having to look after herself and working in the publishing industry and keeping her hand in the Hemingway archives, still tried to keep an open line to Brendan and to stay up to date about his health problems, but this was becoming less and less feasible. Also like Don Quixote he would lash out at the government's censors and at its tax authorities, the former for banning publication and sale in Ireland of *Borstal Boy* and the latter for collecting taxes on the sale of the same. "They object to my tainted books but not my tainted money," he growled.

Beatrice was also in advanced pregnancy but this did not stop her from keeping track of her husband for fear that he might do himself another injury. Rae Jeffs was also spending a lot of time finishing up her projects with Brendan and they would often make up a threesome. Jeffs remembered one bizarre night at the Intercontinental Hotel with Brendan and Beatrice. They should not have been out at all, given the imminent arrival of the baby.

"There was a man there and he was most interested in what Brendan was saying and he was listening a lot. Brendan offered him a drink and he came forward and joined us, everything seemed fine. Beatrice said she did not feel well and decided to leave; I was torn, not knowing whether to go with her or to stay with Brendan. I saw Beatrice to the door and turned back to the table I don't know what happened in the intervening seconds but the man was suddenly very abusive and he asked the manager to order us to leave. I was furious, there he was , taking Brendan's drinks in the full knowledge that Brendan should not have been drinking . . . it turned out the man was writing a little synopsis of colourful Irish characters.. . . . Brendan never recovered from that drinking bout."

The Crazy Life of Brendan Behan

It was not just the encounter at the Intercontinental Hotel, but a far larger event that was to put Brendan over the top. Several days later, on November 22, he met with old friends John Ryan and Anthony Cronin for drinks at The Bailey at dusk. Someone had turned on the radio and, ashen-faced at what he heard, informed the patrons that the news bulletins out of the Washington had reported the assassination of President John F. Kennedy, a man whose very existence somehow legitimized the Irish state. It is difficult to imagine a more shocking event, particularly if one was an Irishman in Dublin. Given the personal nature of the tragedy – it was as if a close relative of the family had been slain -- there were no difficulties in finding an excuse to go drinking. The assassination was all Behan needed to abandon the ship of life; but he managed to prop himself up for a few more days, firstly visiting the U. S. Embassy to sign the book of condolences and, struggling to keep himself fit to be on hand for the birth of what would be his daughter, Blanaid Orla Mairead. The girl was born at 11:40 a.m,, a Sunday morning, two days after the Kennedy death. The baby was named for Beatrice's famous grandmother and Rae Jeffs was asked to be godmother.

It is a fact that sometimes the saga of Brendan Behan yielded to high farce. With a straight face, Beatrice recollected her account of the impact of Kennedy's death. That Friday night she decided to go to the cinema, the birth was expected the next day. She would be accompanied by her sister Celia Salkeld and Jeffs. They decided to see a much acclaimed film but one not without certain applications to her predicament. The film was *The Days of Wine and Roses,* starring Jack Lemmon and Lee Remick. The film won many awards and told the story of an alcoholic husband and his equally alcoholic wife. Even Beatrice, scarcely an ironical person, acknowledged that it wasn't the most appropriate of entertainments given the circumstances surrounding her own life. This was underlined further by the announcement in the cinema of the Kennedy

The end of something

assassination and the inevitable realisation that Brendan would once again be out on the gargle.

Despite the fact that, with Blanaid's birth, an element of joy should have barged back into the Behan household, it was increasingly obvious that Behan's life might end sooner than later. Paddy O'Brien explained that towards the end Behan took towards drinking brandy instead of porter. "The night before Brendan took really ill, he was in McDaids; we had to get him a taxi and he was taken to hospital . . . He was very sick that day, he just sat, head down, not in this world, just looking up. He was still a young man, only 40."

It emerged that he had been requested by his U. S. agent to write a short piece on President Kennedy. The request crossed the Atlantic and eventually found its way to Rae Jeffs in London. She telephoned Beatrice and was apprised of Brendan's perilous condition, but it was hoped the piece might get written. The plan then changed and Jeffs was asked to travel to Dublin to assess the true state of Brendan's condition.

Said Beatrice: "About six months before he died, he took to disappearing, which meant that I couldn't keep a check on him, which was difficult anyway for me expecting a child . . . there were endless rows in pubs, usually because no-one would serve him. I always went down to the pubs with him because I felt that, in some way, he wouldn't get into so many rows if I was there. I was there to see that people did not pick on him or that he wasn't hurt himself. He took to this thing of disappearing. I suppose it was because he was afraid of the night. Occasionally he would come home at three or four o'clock in the morning. I would have to get him some tea he would bring home anybody and everybody. The crowd of people he was with would sort out the night for him."

In January 1964, Behan landed in hospital again and again it was the Meath. "The doctor called me and said, 'Look Mrs Behan, you have been watching your husband going in and out of hospital all your life. Don't be too sure he is going to come out this time,' he said.

It was nearly St. Patrick's Day, 1964. Before flying over from London to assess his worsening health, Jeffs was telephoned and asked to postpone the trip because Brendan was back in hospital, this time in Meath hospital. This time it would be for the last time. She never saw him again; less than a week later, on March 20 1964, he was dead.

Said Beatrice, "The last time I ever spoke to him, he said to me 'I had the priest, I went to communion and confession. Now how's the Mouse (his nickname for their daughter). Would you bring her in to see me?' I said I would but told him that he would have to wait – the weather was cold and it was snowing and the Meath is an awkward distance from our place." She returned with their daughter, saw her husband slip between coherence and incoherence.

"You know, you did only one foolish t'ing, you married me."

"Well, we saw the 'two days' she said, and that was her last conversation with him.

It was just past eight o'clock at night and by then most of the family and friends had either seen Behan or were en route. Accounts differ as to who was there and who was not. John Ryan, drinking at The Bailey, was urgently called to accompany Kathleen and Stephen Behan to the hospital. "I was relieved when I heard the hospital receptionist say that only members of the family could be allowed to see him, until they countered this by telling her that I was Rory Furlong – Brendan's half-brother. Like it or not, I now had to enact the role of her surrogate offspring. Later in the day, the real Rory had trouble getting in himself due to this earlier deception" According to one account. Rory picked up the news from the car radio just a little later."

Just as deeply affected by Brendan's death as anyone present was Desmond MacNamara, who was in Rome at the time and had not seen Brendan for five months. He remembered that he was not surprised by what had happened. "I knew he was ill, I knew every phase of his life because the tom-toms beat very clearly across the Irish Sea. It was his last occasion here and it was very sad. I had arguments with him and fights with him, and he was very abusive to me and me to him. Then there were tears and apologies and recriminations and further fights. This just didn't affect me but other close friends as well. When he finally died, I was in Rome.

"It was very strange. I had walked to the Spanish Steps near where I was living. I had been drinking and had sobered up and I was walking very happily through the empty streets, the empty piazzas. They were just delivering the morning papers to the kiosque at the Piazza de Espagna. I bought a paper and opened it up, and there on the front page of *La Stampa* were the words, Behan e Morte en Dublina. This was eight o'cock, which was a shock to me, with the fountains spraying and the floodlights on and Brendan dead!"

Further eloquence in the immediate aftermath came from Ryan, who wrote: "In the moment of consummation, the intimacy and the urgency were both lost. This terrible silent event now balloons grotesquely into the banalities of the front page ... But time will take up the theme from here, will tone it down into history and, later, lovingly embroider it as legend."

But there also was anger. Brother Dominic stated simply that there was no point in conjecturing on how Brendan would have developed had he been left alone and not been eaten alive by the 'pagan' human lions into whose den he had been thrown by people who would have been terrified had he turned into a Brecht."

"For the layabouts and ponces who bled him white, I have no sympathy in knowing that they now have to go back to working for a living. For the journalists who avoided sensationalism in their death notices – and they were in the majority – I thank them for remembering The Laughing Boy as he was at other times."

It was Brian's view that Brendan and Beatrice would have been better splitting up. Sexual activity had not featured in their marriage for a long time, a point reinforced by Jeffs, barring the unexpected pregnancy of Beatrice with Blanaid, born only four months before Brendan's death. Easier said than done in Ireland, divorce would not have been possible for Brendan whose conscience would have been wracked over the stark choice between freedom and duty. Not a man to take on responsibility, he nevertheless chose the latter which, in effect, became his death sentence. Still, Brian, writing in 1998, argued that the opportunity to fulfil his dream of living out his life in New York should have been honoured. Brian believed he could have turned out plays like Niagara Falls, and took strength from the fact that *The Quare Fellow* had actually been made into a commercial movie. While it may have deviated from the original play, the film kept to the anti-death penalty spirit of Behan's original work. The implication of Brian's remark was that there were many other successes still awaiting Behan.

Brian's argument was that the relationship had become so claustrophobic that it amplified rather than lessened his inclination to drink despite Beatrice's dutiful support. The relationship was dead, he wrote, and as such people have the duty to let go.

"If he was fulfilled in a new relationship – he had already fathered two Yankee children – he might even have gone off the bottle. We have seen before how he could remain as dry as the Sahara when things were going well with his work, and America might have embraced him to its heart if he had put down roots here."

While many mourned his passing, many others were glad to see him gone. Anthony Burgess, the English-born novelist probably best known for *Clockwork Orange,* said that once in Glasnevin cemetery, he met Dominic Behan, glassy-eyed and looking for his dead brother Brendan "so he could piss on the fucker." Whether that was Dominic's true intent only he and Burgess would know, and they are both long dead. Certainly Dominic bore much resentment about his brother, notably about his being overshadowed by Brendan. He was not at the top of the popularity poll amongst the brothers. Jeffs predicted.

Dominic went on a 20-year spell of not speaking to Brian, the least antagonistic of the three writing brothers. Dominic was the first off the mark in the editorial mopping up exercise after Brendan's death. If Dominic's rendering of Brendan lacks warmth and betrays sibling tensions, it at least is honest and is no hagiography. He wisely quotes Dr. Samuel Johnson as saying to the Irish: "They are a great race who never speaks well of each other."

Dominic put it this way: "Living in Ireland, my trouble was that nobody ever spoke about me at all and, although it may be terrible to be ignored, to be ignored by somebody's brother is, I assure you, ten times worse."

Yet Dominic, like Brian, proved himself an accomplished writer, produced a west-end play, *Posterity be Damned,* and his book-cum-TV series, *Teems of Times*, was shown on Irish television. He also wrote a biography of comedian Spike Milligan and a variety of other works.

Alan Simpson, in an interview in 1980, just before his death, summed up the Behan dilemma. "The most prolific writers of our age were the two Irish ones: G. B. Shaw and Sean O'Casey, and they were both extremely abstemious gentlemen. They were both witty and good company. But Brendan had a very different outward shell. He was ultimately hail-fellow, well-met. Now this aspect of his was the real problem rather than the actual drink as such because these plays that he wrote were written in a comparatively short time.

"What he needed was a psychological rest with or without drink – it didn't matter, but he got carried away by the publicity bug and found he unable to live in a vacuum. When he wrote *Richard's Cork Leg,* his last play, that was all he wanted to write at that particular moment . . . . I have speculated that *Richard's Cork Leg* was his last will and testament, theatrically, but many people write their last wills and testaments, then hang around a bit or change them. (If only) some way had been found to cool Brendan down for a few years so he could observe the world a little bit more. . . . He really only completed a phase of his life."

CHAPTER TWENTY

CORTEGE TO GLASNEVIN

"I was so angry with Brendan for dying that I felt like kicking that coffin. Someone near to him had smuggled a bottle of brandy into the clinic where he was supposed to be protected. It put paid to him. Death by drinking. As we drove to Glasnevin through the streets lined with Dublin's poor, an old man shouted, "May he never get there." – Joan Littlewood

IT WAS A typical winter morning with some icy slush underfoot when the funeral cortege that was to bear Brendan Behan's body to Glasnevin Cemetery began to form up outside the Church of the Sacred Heart in Dublin's Donnybrook. The first stage of the trek would be somewhat indirect as the cortege made its way from southeast Dublin towards that point in the centre of Dublin where the O'Connell Bridge, named for the great 19th century patriot, crossed the Liffey. The river starts its modest voyage of 50 miles from the west out of the Dublin Hills before angling towards Dublin city and the Irish Sea. Because it cannot seem to make up its mind, many see it as a very 'Irish' river.

The Crazy Life of Brendan Behan

The cortege would straighten out and make its way directly north towards the Royal Canal and then across the Finglas Road and then a right turn into the cemetery. In all, the distance from the Behan home to Glasnevin was a little more than three miles and, as always, faster and shorter coming back. It was March 24.

Inside the packed church, Father Cyril Crean brought the requiem services to an end by calling for prayers from friends and parishioners for the repose of the soul of the lately deceased. Father Crean's sign of the cross ended the proceedings in church and served as a signal to begin the second phase of the ceremony, the procession by foot and car to Glasnevin and the orations expected to be heard once there.

There was much mingling outside the church, a few jokes were told but it was an occasion of solemnity for Behan's friends, despite his impulse, when alive, to disrupt and break out in manic laughter. There was a curiosity factor at work; too, for while there could not have been anybody in Dublin not aware that he had died, there was still a tendency to disbelieve the obvious. Besides, 41 years of age was too young to die. It couldn't be true, this news of his passing.

"I never t'ought it would happen," someone said outside the church while shuffling his feet and cupping and blowing into his mittened hands to keep warm. Paddy O'Brien, the veteran barman, concurred, but he was more inclined to take the playwright's passing in stride because he, perhaps more than anybody but members of the immediate family, had insider's knowledge of just how bad Behan's state of health was in the weeks preceding is final hospitalisation. He had been a Behan-watcher for many years and knew the story as well as anybody else.

"He was in the pub and he was drinkin' brandies. It wasn't helpin' the cause, and you could see that he was not in this world," said O'Brien, in that unmistakeable Dublin brogue of a man used to talking. That encounter in the pub marked the last time he would see the writer.

O'Brien knew Behan well, their friendship going back to Behan's teenage years. Like all good publicans, O'Brien had an acute memory, helped by the fact that he was not much of a drinker himself. He recalled Behan entering McDaids, still a teenager, laden with house painting equipment and taking a break between jobs. Behan drank several pints of porter, became jolly rather quickly, O'Brien remembered. He then retreated to the toilet and was not seen for some hours till his inert form was nudged back to consciousness. It had been found inside the McDaid's broom cupboard where extra supplies of beer were stored.

"The one t'ing I remember about t'at was how little beer it took to get to him. He really didn't have the constitution for it, but he went at it just the same."

Thus, with such memories flooding through everyone's minds, the beginning of Brendan Behan's last ride and proof, if such a thing was needed, that the Irish are as good as any people at burying their dead as well as remembering their fellows when they are alive. In Brendan's case, what started out as an interesting day turned into a day those decades later was still talked about. Not bad for a north side tenement boy of tough republican stock and with a family tree to prove it. In his cups, he sometimes made the claim that in just eight years – the span covering the time when the going was good – he had taken a drink with more Dubliners than any other man regardless of class, a word he detested.

Claims about drinking accomplishments are to be taken with a pinch of salt, but few would dispute the size of the Behan funeral in the annals of recent Irish history. Certainly, the need to fill Dublin's gossip machine would dictate that the funeral would grow in size to gargantuan proportions, certainly as large the 1922 funeral in Dublin of Michael Collins, of the 1935 funeral in Belfast of Sir Edward Carson. But if comparisons were to be made, then the real contender would come much later with the 2005 burial in Belfast of football hero George Best, a man who rivalled Behan in many ways, particularly his reckless exuberance. Like Best's funeral, Behan's grew unexpectedly, picking up stragglers as it passed through Dublin's neighbourhoods and parishes on the journey north.

He liked to teasingly claim to be the English-speaking world's most famous writer, having succeeded the late Hemingway. Of course, despite the meagreness of his output, his fame came more from his adventures than his actual writing, respectable though that was. He was certainly the most famous writer in Ireland, even if the time span was embarrassingly short. Sean O'Casey had enjoyed fame for 40 years while living most of his life in England, but that was another matter. Behan's popularity was not that universal and some of those who had helped swell the funeral cortege did so to make sure Brendan was truly gone. Brother Dominic, with whom he tilted many times, said he, Brendan, was the most arrested man in the history of the IRA.

To Paddy O'Brien, the "whole lit'r'y" world was there at the funeral, people from the theatre, government ministers, diplomats. Mattie O'Neil, an old friend, gave an oration in Irish. Leading the list of participants was, of course, the family, headed by Beatrice Behan, his wife of nine years. It was not a long union as marriages go unless you considered the evidence and the extraordinarily emotional wear and tear. There was

Brendan' father, Stephen, described by the *Irish Times'* Dermot Mulhane as a 'short, stocky manful little Dubliner' and Brendan's mother Kathleen who for all her rough edges was the heart and soul of the family.

She took care to point out that Brendan was not necessarily her favourite offspring. "I never made favourites of any of them," she recalled. "Although people think Brendan was a pet of mine, they were all the same to me. Da's mother (the Grainnie) petted him a terrible lot as I've said, but I didn't."

Emerging from the church with them in preparation for the ride to Glasnevin were the two immediate brothers, Brian and Dominic, an unusual duet. Their famous refusal to talk to each other lasted decades and only officially ended at the time of Dominic's death in 1989. Still, they successfully set out on careers as writers, essayists, commentators and playwrights themselves.

What Dominic was to remember most about that day was that it was the first time "in my company that he didn't monopolise the conversation, but then maybe he did, for all the talk was about him or his extraordinary exploits." That said, Dominic tried to dampen down forever any talk of Brendan's famous death wish. People who believed that must have been joking, he said. "Brendan wanted to live very much and I am sure he never would have allowed us to take him to the cemetery at all had it not been for the fact he was about to entertain his largest personal audience. As he said himself, 'there's no such thing as bad publicity except your own obituary'."

Many of those who helped support his success as a man of letters had made the trip to Dublin. They arrived in time for the funeral, for they, better than many of his friends knew of the state of his health. In short, while shocked at the news of his death, they were hardly surprised. Of course this meant the hurried arrival of Rae Jeffs. By now almost always known as the Lady from Sussex for giving an impression of prim Englishness, she was probably more important than anyone else for Behan's literary success. She stopped what she was doing when the news broke and flew over from London. The depth of her regard could be found in the brief Irish language inscription attached to a wreath of daffodils, tulips and carnations: "Do Brendan, Cara mo croi – Rae."

She regarded his death a waste of a good life. While much of his decline could be hung on his own self-destructiveness, accusatory fingers could and should be pointed at Behan's many thoughtless hangers-on who claimed friendship in order to get a free drink from him at a time when they had no money. "He was surrounded by too many fair-weather friends, not only in Dublin but in England. In fact everywhere he went . . . . I have seen it happen often, publicans drawing the pints the minute he came through the door knowing he would buy a round for the house."

Another friend on hand for the funeral was Joan Littlewood, a strong female figure in Behan's ambivalent life. It is easy to place her in the pantheon of those whose influence Behan, the artist, could not have done without. There were Alan Simpson and Carolyn Swift who practically broke themselves producing *The Quare Fellow* in 1954. That production brought it to the attention of a larger audience, led by Littlewood and Raffles, on the lookout for new material. Littlewood, in her memoirs, recalled how tough it could be to charge Behan's batteries when deadlines loomed. But of his death, she kept her remarks poignantly brief.

"We'd hardly recovered from the new baby's appearance (playwright Shelagh Delaney's new-born daughter Charlotte) when news reached us of Brendan Behan's death at the age of forty-one . . . . I was so angry with Brendan for dying that I felt like kicking that coffin. Someone near to him had smuggled a bottle of brandy into the clinic where he was supposed to be protected. It put paid to him. Death by drinking. As we drove to Glasnevin through the streets lined with Dublin's poor, an old man shouted, 'May he never get there'."

By the time the journey reached the river and entered north Dublin, it had begun to pick up more drifters. Rae Jeffs' abiding memory of the funeral was the sight of hundreds of old ladies with shopping baskets with chickens' heads hanging out, all chattering as the procession passed and then determinedly joining the formation. It was perhaps among Dublin's ordinary folk that one got the true measure of the playwright and why he meant what he did to his fellow citizens. Jeffs is an unusual observer in aspects of Behan's final years. She had observed that it was the IRA that had cast a protective canopy over their fallen comrade and saw to it that no harm came to him. "It was they who got him home at night," she said.

Garech Browne was sighted as was Christine Lady Longford and Christy Browne, the crippled and wheelchair-bound author of *My Left Foot,* the filmed version of which, some years later, would catapult him posthumously to fame. Mingling in the crowd were the French Sisters of Charity who the iconoclastic Behan held in special respect going back to his school days. He was not one to tolerate criticism of the clergy, particularly the sisters – unless of course he was doing it himself.

Another friend who would gain renown as one of Behan's great stage interpreters, Niall Toibin, had also found a spot in the procession; years later he would recall meeting up with Joe Dwyer in the latter's pub after the funeral was over, to be told: "Ah, sure, poor old divil, he was an awful fucking nuisance." Toibin saw the remark not as an insult but as one of the most honest epitaphs of that day "because people came out of the woodwork to pay their tributes who would not have given him the time of day when he was alive."

Valerie Danby-Smith made a deep effort to get to Dublin for the funeral, though she was careful to keep the lowest possible profile because of her status outside the Behan family as the mother of Brendan Junior. She knew there could be no room at the inn for her, and because of that she decided to keep to the sidelines. Instead, later she teamed up with Liam O'Flaherty and other members of the literati in a crowded Dublin pub where she could more easily express her feelings.

It was not likely that Eamon de Valera, president of the Republic, a man for whom many Irish had a love-hate relationship, was going to personally appear, but instead he sent Commandant R. Maclonnraic in his place. Also present were Alderman Sean Moore, and the Lord Mayor of Dublin. After the arrival of the hearse at Glasnevin, the pall-bearers again took up positions and carried the coffin to the ffrench-Salkeld's family burial plot where a grave had been prepared. The cortege made the right turn into Glasnevin and began to break formation and gather informally around the burial site.

Glasnevin is not just another cemetery, its importance to Irish history and heritage is not unlike that of Arlington Cemetery, outside of Washington, D.C., to Americans. Those who pass under its portals will find themselves inundated with the history of Ireland. The establishment of the cemetery predated the potato famine by 13 years, opening in 1832 thanks to the sponsorship of O'Connell. His presence is towering in more ways than one in that he is remembered by the impressive monument marking his burial spot. He died in 1848.

While absorbing the O'Connell monument do not be surprised if you are taken by the elbow and guided past the cemetery's many other markers. This writer well recalls one occasion when a member of the cemetery staff, her index finger shaking, pointed out that 'over there' was buried the parents of James Joyce, just maybe Ireland's most renowned – if least read – writer. Her finger now pointing in a different direction signalled the monument to Gerald Manley Hopkins, the English-born poet who died in Dublin in 1898. Nearby, she said, was the grave of Charles Stewart Parnell, a great, if tarnished, parliamentary hero in the drive for Home Rule. Of course, one could not miss the tomb of Michael Collins, the 'big fella' of the battle for independence in 1922. Roger Casement is buried in Glasnevin, too. He was buried in a traitor's grave in England, the first time round, but one country's traitor is often another country's hero. So, during the time of the Harold Wilson government in the mid-1970s, his remains were disinterred and transported to Glasnevin and reinterred with all the patriotism that could be mustered. "A suitable treat for Casement," wrote one assiduous headline writer at the time.

Maude Gonne also occupies some valuable real estate at Glasnevin, as does Constance Gore-Booth, better known as the Countess Markiewicz, the first woman member of the British House of Commons, not Nancy Astor as is commonly believed. "Ah, the one you are looking for is here," said the official, pointing to the chiselled granite free-form grave marker bearing Behan's name..

On the day itself, the burial stone was not yet there, but as many witnesses as could make it to the cemetery did so. Among those participating in these last rites was Cathal Goulding, an old IRA friendwho like Behan, was a veteran of the English prison system having been jailed in 1953 for raids on an armory in Essex. A cloud of ambiguity would hover over his memory as the years passed – while he and Brendan went back a long way, his relationship with Beatrice after her husband's death would become intimate and he would father a son, named Paudge Roger Behan, born January 1965, by her.

It now was Mattie O'Neil's turn to bring the ceremony to a close. O'Neill was an old IRA associate of Behan's going back decades and a fellow internee at the Curragh years before. The two men had nearly broken over Littlewood's production of *The Hostage* on the grounds that Littlewood had mocked the IRA. But all that was long ago, and fences had been mended. O'Neill opened with an address in the Irish language, a language Behan had learned in his youth and had polished up in Borstal prison in England, thanks to the jail's well stocked library. By his 20s, he had achieved near fluency in a language that still had a few years to go before establishing itself at the centre of Irish republicanism. In Irish O'Neill said:

"There was life throbbing in every vein of him. It is heartbreaking to see all that gaiety and all that bravery going under the soil as Glasnevin. His memory will be green as long as Dublin lies on the Liffey."

Then in English: "A great life has gone out of our lives forever and we hear the echoes of that rich inimitable baritone voice singing. Wrap up my green jacket in a brown paper parcel. I'll not need it now anymore." The closing lines were first written by Valentine Iremonger, poet, civil servant and diplomat who early on spotted Behan's talent and prodded theatrical friends to take a look at such works as *The Quare Fellow*. Iremonger long outlived Behan, dying at 78 in 1991.

John B. Keen, writer and friend, in an article published after the burial wrote: "The Dublin pubs did a roaring trade. Television cameras whirred and a Frenchman spoke over his grave. He would have enjoyed it all but he would have preferred if the 'oul wans' with their shawls and the down-and-outs with their cloth caps on the sides of their heads were up in front where they belonged, because the Dublin poor were closest to his heart. He never forgot that he was one of them. Never were so many characters gathered together in one place. It was a scene that only Brendan Behan could create."

BOOK THREE

CHAPTER TWENTY-ONE

AFTERMATH

"I often wonder if some of it happened, you know. Was that really me? I think of incidents that did happen and it is really hard to believe that they did. Was I there? Did I do this . . ?" – *Beatrice Behan, ca 1980*

AFTER IT WAS all over, the burden of putting what might euphemistically be called the Behan Estate together again fell in all directions like so many badly balanced dominoes. Beatrice, of course, was at the epicentre of the tragedy, and in proximity were Rae Jeffs, Dominic and Brian Behan, Joan Littlewood and Alan Simpson. Not all of the detritus of a misspent life was without value. There was the simple fact of Behan's renewed theatrical success which pushed Behan's reputation through to the end of the decade and into the early 1970s, particularly through the continuing sales of his autobiography and two plays.

His favourite supporters, the Irish-American community in New York, roundly applauded the Broadway success in 1970 of actor Niall Toibin's stage adaptation of *Borstal Boy*. It won Toibin a Tony Award and followed on from a 1967 debut of the adaptation at Dublin's Abbey Theatre. Toibin went on to great renown, notably in the BBC's superdrama, *Brideshead Revisited,* Toibin said he threw himself so vigorously into the role that he nearly ruined his health.

"I think I became very much imbued with his characteristics, especially when I was in New York. I tried to emulate his drinking feats on more than one occasion, and at one stage put on so much weight that when I came back from New York, I was probably 40 pounds heavier than I am now, but it was just a phase and I eventually got over it."

For Beatrice, it was too easy to say that she was long-suffering, for she had a certain equanimity of nature and stamina that provided a template for the lifestyle she was to live with Brendan. She had the ability more than most to 'not mind' what was going on around her, no matter how outrageous. But it was also certain that her nine years with Brendan were exhausting and would have provided a good example of the chaos theory in action – celestial explosions followed by periods of settlement and the brief reappearance of order, only to be followed by further explosions.

Gene Fowler, the biographer of 1930s actor John Barrymore, estimated that the great silent and early talkies movie star, famed for his classical and modern dramatic roles and an extraordinary capacity for intake of proof spirits (he was, after all, a close friend of W. C. Fields), consumed a total a total of 640 barrels of spirits in his lifetime. As time went on he found himself with a lower and lower tolerance for the drink to the extent that it would take but a few ounces to 'hit' him; he frequently was genuinely ill, only his strength of will impelling him to struggle to his feet so as to complete another day of geniality and sociability. No estimate has ever been put on Behan's consumption but there is little doubt he was in the same league. He displayed all the same symptoms, ultimately bailing himself out in a fit of energy and always being able to respond when the bell was rung for last round.

Rae Jeffs, along with Joe McGill, one of the most long-lived of close family friends and keeper of many of the Behan files and mementoes, helped Beatrice for a time to sort out the sea of paperwork, an activity startlingly reminiscent of Valerie Danby-Smith's helping sort out the Hemingway files only a few years before. Jeffs was immersed in the Behan quicksand every bit as much as Beatrice. One day she had a living author with four potentially high-selling reminiscences on the boil – the next day he was dead and buried. No matter how inevitable his demise, it was still a national shock.

It took little time for anyone in his company to realize that he had no capacity for administration (but plenty for mischief). His preferred modus operandi on such matters was akin to that of a man operating a wrecking ball in a glass skyscraper. When there was little or no money coming in, this was a self-resolving problem – no income, no envelopes to be opened or letters to be answered. But when he became famous it was another matter. He frequently signed chits, agreements, letters of intent and contracts of doubtful legality.

He made commitments that ensured that whatever royalties earned posthumously would drain away. His generosity made him his own worst enemy and an easy mark for taxi drivers and so called friends. Beatrice told the story of a taxi driver appearing at the front door weeks after her husband's death, asking for settlement of a bill for £40 that Behan apparently owed him. One invoice came from a firm of clothiers, only the clothes had all been bought not for him but by him for others. The anecdote is reminiscent of his pre-nuptial confession that his wedding clothing had been stolen. The priest hearing his confession said that the church would have helped out in the circumstances, but he was promptly interrupted, Behan replying: "No, Father, no, I mean I stole the clothing."

He made a will leaving everything to Beatrice, but she said it would have taken a hundred accountants to disentangle matters. A way was found to reimburse the income tax department, the house on Anglesea Road (now regarded as being in a posh part of town) was remortgaged and the loft, or attic, converted into flats. Beatrice began to take in lodgers and, to a small degree, became something of a curiosity, taxi and bus drivers passing slowly by the house and telling their customers that that was where Brendan Behan used to live.

Blanaid would marry and settle in England and, much later, Australia, while Paudge would eventually take over Anglesea Road and go on to develop a stage career in the family tradition. Anglesea Road's market value in 2005 was put at 1.2 million Euros, approximately £1 million.

Fifteen years after her husband's death, Beatrice was still slim and easily identifiable from photos taken years earlier. She dressed casually and had little sense of clothes consciousness in any way. She was far from outgoing but neither was she overtly shy in the face of questions about her life with Brendan. She held the view that Brendan, had he lived, would have written "something tremendous" about the renewed struggle in the North between violent republicanism and violent unionism. There is cause to doubt this in the face of the horrors and more than 3,400 murders that were to be carried out in the decades following Behan's death over the issue of the future of the Six Counties of the north

The factionalised IRA of the 1970s, 1980s and 1990s and the vicious aggressions and retaliations of Ulster terrorists were a far cry from anything Behan had been exposed to since his own troubles in Liverpool in 1939 and his own shootout, flight and arrest in 1942 at Glasnevin Cemetery. Jeffs reflected on Behan's rejection of violence as any solution to the Irish problem following a brief emotional breakdown while dictating notes for *Confessions of an Irish Rebel*. The exchange of gunfire at Irish police in Glasnevin, and the realisation that he might have killed somebody in the process, was still an emotional burden for him two decades later as he pondered on just how badly it all might have gone had he proved a more accurate marksman.

As brother Brian was to say: 'After Brendan died, Beatrice's phone stopped ringing. The constant turmoil of living in his shadow was replaced by a new problem now – loneliness." She confirmed as much herself, telling a reporter later those visitations from Brendan's friends after his death had stopped. "Not more than a half dozen have crossed this threshold, after all the glory and the parties have stopped so they see no more reason to come" said a reporter.

At some point in the late 1980s, Beatrice's own mental stamina began to weaken and although she was younger than Brendan would have been, a number of friends and acquaintances were also yielding to the finality of advancing years. Furthermore she lost her younger sister, Celia, who after a modest acting career died in 1984, aged 48 The news from the north was increasingly depressing and her husband's plays, because of their IRA content, began to lose their commercial appeal.

An enthusiastic revival of *The Hostage* was organized for the Barbican theatre in London in the mid-1990s, and Behan's irreverence and humour, plus the jingle jangle of folk music, was enough to win plaudits from the critics and help set the stage for a more substantial renewal of interest in the first part of the new century.

On March 9 1993, the Derry-born poet Robert Greacen, who was a boarder at Anglesea Road, found Beatrice dead in bed. She was buried on March 15, her remains being interred with those of her husband at Glasnevin. Foremost among the mourners were Blanaid and Paudge Behan, Conal Kearney, Niall Toibin, Cathal Goulding and labour leader Sean Garland. Brian Behan, one of Brendan's brothers, commented on speculation that Beatrice might have committed suicide. He said it was "a possibility" but he did not put much heft into such a grim suggestion. Brendan and Beatrice, despite rows, disturbances and infidelities, went the distance, said Brian. "One simple fact was that he never said he didn't love her anymore and somehow that was enough for her, even at the worst of times."

There was an innocent, pre-adolescent quality about Behan that inevitably led to blame for his death being ascribed to others. Within weeks of his death, an article published in the *Irish Democrat* (and republished in pamphlet form by a writer identifying himself as 'Feincreanach') made it onto Dublin's newsstands and demanded to know: "Who killed Brendan Behan?" Certainly he killed himself, but he was not alone for there were many accomplices. But if they assisted in Behan's long, downward ride did their participation amount to culpability, particularly in a poor country in which drink was one of the few points of departure from the daily grind.

Rae Jeffs blamed his demise on the unscrupulous barflies or genuine innocent bystanders who, too eagerly, enjoyed his generosity and goaded him into ever more heroic verbal feats while gesticulating entertainingly before the lags at this or that drinking establishment awaiting further free rounds. Conor O'Brien was specific in his condemnation of Malcolm Muggeridge on the infamous BBC programme of 1955, fuelled as it was by the British interviewer's decision to give Behan free run of the BBC's reception room drinks cabinet just before air time.

Toibin reckoned that Behan's signal accomplishment was to puncture the balloon of solemnity held by many Irish about their struggle with Britain.

"What is gone is the attitude of the self-righteous, oppressed Catholic Republican, left-wing Irishman standing alone, representing a small nation cowed by this monster (England) on his doorstep. Behan was the man who gave it the chop, really. *Borstal Boy*, its whole attitude towards the question of Irish nationalism and Catholicism is so irreverent and funny it is highly unlikely that anyone having read it could retain the same degree of sanctimonious Irish nationalism. Despite his levity and his great irreverence, it would be a mistake to say he abandoned his absolute separatism and socialist stance. I think it was the solemnity he rebelled against more than against the idealism itself."

The view was not supported in the Feincreanach article which preferred to take a Republican tack in its probing for an answer.

"Here was the dilemma. Here was the underlying frustration of all Irish writers compelled to appeal to an alien audience as well as their own. Like Shaw, he 'remained an Irishman' even at the expense of having to play Behan."

The article, in its conclusion, lashes out and blames Behan's demise on 'the false hypocritical society we live in, in which a promising writer can only develop himself at the cost of constant self-immolation, which so isolates his working life from the people that he must crash back to them with the conviviality that brings together a society, without uniting it, where the culture of a small nation lies so at the mercy of the commerce of large neighbours that both sides are poisoned by the guilt of the unnatural relationship'.

In 1967 Alan Simpson managed to stage *Richard's Cork Leg,* the play whose non-materialisation so aggravated Littlewood and Raffles and led to a break with Behan. They had to get on with other projects, such as *Oh What a Lovely War! Cork Leg* was liberally adapted from Behan's unfinished last work and was often referred to as "Alan's play". In fact, Simpson always credited Behan with having done most of the work. For Simpson, it was "Brendan's play".

Simpson moved deeper into academe in the post-Behan years, lecturing in the United States and staging plays, including those by Behan, whenever he could find a venue. *The Hostage* has become a popular play at American universities, a fact attested to by Valerie Hemingway, the mother of his only son. Simpson collapsed and died on May 8 1980 after having attended the opening performance in the Dun Laoghaire pavilion, outside Dublin, of his latest production, *McCormack.* Earlier that day he had attended a posthumous exhibition of paintings by his late daughter in the Peacock Theatre.

Alongside Simpson through this colourful period was his wife Carolyn Swift, who was credited by friends as the one member of the duopoly capable of taking executive decisions when they were needed to keep the theatre's creative momentum going. Swift separated from Simpson following his move to London in 1964. She wrote and had staged three plays, *The Millstone, Resistance* and *Lady G.* She launched herself on a successful career writing children's books. In an interview in Dublin shortly after Behan's death, she recalled the late playwright as being humble and ready to accept suggestions on how to improve the writing or the presentation of *The Quare Fellow.* She told interviewer Mary Lodge that "we saw ourselves as a revolutionary force stirring up the theatrical lethargy of post-war Ireland". She said of Behan: "He depicted in the round, no one is ever all black and white. Personal bias wasn't allowed to interfere with objectivity. He wrote composite portraits of the people he knew, in a witty, unprejudiced manner". Swift died in 2002.

While Cathal Goulding's relationship with Beatrice brought a dynamic, if posthumous, element into the saga of the Behans, one cannot leave the story without contemplating Valerie Hemingway's role as the mother of Brendan Francis Hemingway. It, too, is unknowable, and the facts of her grown up life proved enough to fill her book, *Running with the Bulls,* (published in 2004 in the U.S.). Behan's name is only cautiously mentioned by her in her book which is mainly about Hemingway. She is still closely involved with the Hemingway estate and is helping clear up matters to do with the American author's writing and correspondence.

Valerie Hemingway, in *Running with the Bulls,* sought to leave much about Behan out of the text, but conceded that such an editorial side-step was not possible and would have hurt the book's veracity. In 1966, five years after Ernest's death, she married into the Hemingway family, taking as her husband Gregory Hemingway, the estranged third son of Ernest from his marriage with Pauline Pfeiffer. It turned out to be an unhappy relationship, Gregory becoming mentally unstable and slipping into a life of cross-dressing and sexual ambiguity.

By the mid-1970s, it was clear that their marriage could not last, but Valerie still was able to keep her pledge made years before to Brendan Behan by ensuring that the boy be given an Irish education. This she did by enrolling him in Clongowes Wood College in Ireland (1974-80) and in Yale University in the U.S. (1981-84). After that, he struck out into the world of information technology, but a far different world than the names he inherited. He has worked for several decades in IT and in recent years has started up small consultancies such as C + T Consulting, and M and H Consultancy (originally Mills and Hemingway).

Aftermath

Valerie and Gregory travelled extensively at this time, but the impossibility of their relationship increased and they were divorced in 1983. During these years Valerie spent more time in Ireland working for the Guinness brewing interests and later for political leader John Hume's SDLP (Social Democratic Labour Party), which would one day become instrumental in bringing an end to violence in Northern Ireland. In 1995, Gregory then underwent a sex-change operation and in October 2001, it was learned that he had died in a woman's prison while awaiting arraignment on an indecent exposure charge. Valerie later moved to Bozeman, Montana, and became a free-lance commentator and lecturer and today is a spokeswoman for the Hemingway literary interests. Throughout these years, Valerie was careful not to trade on the Behan or Hemingway and was determined to keep her son away from unwarranted publicity, which she said she had been able to do. There is little doubt though of the emotional impact on her of her relationship with Brendan Behan and the failure to find the magic wand that would make it happen.

If Alan Simpson and Carolyn Swift were the couple who "discovered" Brendan Behan through the vehicle of their experimental theatre in Dublin, it was Joan Littlewood and her partner Gerry Raffles who gained him international fame through their groundbreaking experiments in presentation at the Stratford East theatre in east London -- now going through a revival thanks to the regeneration of the neighbourhood, more precisely Stratford le Bow, London E15, a run-down venue but one large enough to stage big league events without incurring the cost of a West-end presentation. It was Littlewood who was the creative genius and Raffles who paid the bills and generally made things run. At a meeting with Behan in Dublin in 1961, Littlewood reviewed his scattered text for the new play and found it long on colour and short on story line. Further discussions were held at a pub, but unruliness prevailed, a fist fight with the patrons ensued and Behan was taken to jail. In the end, the work was never completed.

Littlewood nevertheless admired Behan's innate talent and revived *The Hostage* in 1973, but withdrew from the theatre after the devastating loss of Raffles to diabetes in 1975. A year later she went to live in France and spent the most part of her remaining years there, virtually dropping out of theatrical productions and concentrating on her wordy autobiography, *Joan's Book, - Joan Littlewood's Peculiar History as She Tells It*. Littlewood died in London in September 2002.

Kenneth Tynan, the theatre critic, died in California in 1980, where he had gone to live for his health, after suffering for years from asthma, the soggier climes of London and New York having previously failed him. But scarcely out of his teens he went to Spain where he wrote expertly about bullfighting. His work, *Bull Fever,* became a worthy successor to Hemingway's 1930s *Death In the Afternoon,* the difference being that Hemingway saw the bullfight as a highly visual and physical art, akin to oil painting, whereas Tynan's rendering is full of theatrical comparisons. So, with his gift for words, it is not surprising that some of his coinages applied to Behan's *Quare Fellow* and *The Hostage*; his comments on these two plays rang loud and clear throughout the decade. He and Behan were scarcely natural friends and Behan, on meeting Tynan for the first time, anticipated that he would be let loose in the company of typical English "toff". That may have been how Tynan appeared to some others but it was not the way he was in real life. Littlewood, in her memoirs, recalls the two meeting in the theatre bar after a performance of *The Quare Fellow*. Tynan artlessly asked the author:

"Where were you, Brendan, when the quare feller was being topped?" Came the blunt reply:

"Wanking over a copy of *Picturegoer*."

Before Tynan's time was up, he would go on the write *Oh Calcutta* as well as find time to found the National Theatre in London. Wrote Gore Vidal shortly after Tynan's death:

"Performance was everything to him. . . . He could make one feel the excitement of an audience on a certain night; show us the sweat bubbling beneath the makeup of the actor who has managed to make bright the air within the proscenium arch."

Behan's death was both premature and overdue. That he was just 41 years old was a reminder of the diminishing options awaiting the hard drinker. Patrick Kavanagh, the poet and a man easily in conflict with Behan, did better, his life covering a span of 1904-67. For the hard-drinking Flann O'Brian, officially Brian O'Nolan of *At Swim, Two Birds* fame, his stamina gave out in 1966 when he was 55 year of age. On the other hand, a case in point was that of Sean O'Faolain, the novelist and short-story writer, who died at 91 in 1991. His claim was that he probably was Behan's first literary editor. O'Faolain, after the period of The Emergency, was editing a publication called *The Bell*. Although Behan would have many more scrapes with the law in his life, the worst of it was over and he was taking an interest in writing. O'Faolain ran the autobiographical story which turned out to be a precursor of *The Quare Fellow*.

Another of Behan's early editors was John Ryan, a beloved figure in mid-century Irish literature and in the annals of pub-crawling. Ryan, born in Dublin in 1925, founded after the war a magazine called "Envoy", which he edited for the two years of its life. Rather like The Masses in between-wars America, but for literary rather than political reasons, it exerted an influence far beyond its small circulation and was a good read in the process. Early contributors were American-born J. P. Donleavy and Brian O'Nolan, and especially Behan whose first submission to Ryan was a short story titled "A Woman of No Standing". Wrote Ryan years later: "As a piece of writing, it is as good as anything else he ever wrote; some think it was his best individual piece. It has freshness, compassion and humour."

Ryan, unlike many of his confreres, came from a comfortable background, his father owning a company called Monument Creameries. The supplemental income from this business enabled him to minimise risks on some of the publications with which he became associated (to which should be added *The Dublin Magazine* in the 1970's). Ryan would readily admit that Behan was often a boor, very hands-on in pubs, particularly when under the influence, the type of person given to pawing one's girlfriend or wife or any likely lad that crossed his bow. But said Ryan: "He was not wanting of courage, of all the writers, poets or painters of his generation, he was the only one who took up arms, literally, for the freedom of his country. If he was selfish and egotistical in other things – he was completely committed patriot." Ryan died at age 67 in 1992.

Des MacNamara, born in Dublin in 1919, met Brendan Behan in Dublin at a demonstration about the Spanish Civil War in the late 1930s. MacNamara moved to London in the early 1950's "so that I could get a divorce from my then-wife and remarry (divorce being forbidden in Ireland at the time). He settled into a flat, first in Barons Court in west London and later in West Hampstead in north-west London, where he and his wife lived out their lives. Like the Grafton Street flat in Dublin,

He saw it, too, turn into a Bohemian drop-in centre with the young Behan being a regular, and not always legal, caller given to scrapes with the law and his links with the I.R.A.

Also given to mischief, MacNamara sculpted a life-size copy of Behan's bullish, tow-head, and the two men conspired, futilely as it turned out, to steal away into a London park late at night and decapitate any statue commemorating a long-forgotten civil servant – such statues are legion in London's squares and parks – and supplant it with Behan's likeness. "Our bet was that no-one would ever have noticed," MacNamara said in an interview in 2006, alert and lively despite his advancing years and deteriorating eyesight.

In early 2004, the MacNamaras were welcomed at The Tricycle theatre in Hampstead, London, where a new rendering of *The Quare Fellow* was presented; among the cast was his son Oioean MacNamara who, at a tutorial following the play, was able to say he was the only member of the cast who knew Brendan Behan, "although I was about four at the time." Des MacNamara died in 2007.

Behan was not wanting for loyalty when it came to getting a leg up in the promotion of his writing. True, the friendships tended to show a degree of metal-fatigue as he got thrown out of more and more pubs, both in Dublin, London and New York, and the patience of those who would indulge him wore thin. Still, he found remarkable pockets of support.

One of those was Bernard Geis, the entrepreneurial publisher who thought Behan "had what it took" for an American audience and was prepared to back him, and Rae Jeffs and Hutchinson publishing in hammering out his dictated reminiscences. Geis was called on to bail Behan out of tight situations but kept the faith despite the overwhelming evidence of his final downward slide. Geis, Chicago-born in 1909, he lived to 2001.

Even greater care and support was provided by David Astor. Not only did Astor, second son of the 2nd Viscount Astor (and son of Conservative MP Lady Astor), back Behan the writer but personally met with him to discuss his state of health. Astor promised his support for whatever treatment Behan agreed to but Behan wriggled free of any commitment, no matter how generous. At age 30 in 1948, Astor took over *The Observer*. He always rated Behan's work and managed to show the common touch when dealing with the Irish playwright – it has been speculated that his easy touch might have stemmed from his own academic failures at Oxford and his own experience of a nervous breakdown. He died, much mourned, in 2001.

Another supporter vital to Behan's early success was Valentine Iremonger, a Dublin-born diplomat and man of letters. Educated by the Christian Brothers and trained in the theatre, specifically at The Abbey and The Gate, he was born in 1918. He joined Ireland's foreign affairs department and swung a little too independently for protesting the incarceration of poet Ezra Pound by the US authorities after the Second World War. For this violation of protocol, Iremonger was suspended for these efforts on Pound's behalf. After being reinstated, he was appointed to the Ministry for Local Government and was based in Dublin and London. But he spent much of his spare time involved in theatrical matters and in writing prose and poetry.

He jointly wrote *On the Barricades* in 1944 in partnership with Robert Graecen and Bruce Williamson. Significantly, it was in the 1950s that he came aware of Behan's talent, first having a chance to informally examine *The Quare Fellow* and later the autobiographical *Borstal Boy* before the publication. On his recommendation, Iremonger met with *Hutchinson's* publisher

Iain Hamilton in Dublin with the recommendation that he use the trip to find out about the "roaring young boy with real talent". The Iremonger tip-off provided *Hutchinson* with one of the planks that was to help build Behan's literary career.

A few years later, Iremonger was called again to help the publishing group complete the preparation of *Brendan Behan's Island*, one of the handful of late books dictated by Behan into a tape recorder, set up by Rae Jeffs who then prepared it for publication. "Island" was one of the author's last books and one which required the attentions of an expert on every nook and cranny of Ireland. Iremonger was impatient with the endemic conservatism in Irish letters as many books – including those of Joyce and Behan – were still banned in Ireland but were easily purchased in Great Britain. In the early 1950s, he told a seminar:

"One group of our established writers denounce you if you are not forward-moving in a sociological sense. Another group denounce you if you do not write in what they imagine to be an Irish tradition, but which in fact is nothing more than a "mode" which was evolved and popular during the period from the end of the nineteenth century to about 1930, the fraying ends of which are still simply flying. Neither group seems to be interested in the questions that present themselves to all humanity.

"The result is that whatever the vitality, communal or personal, that urges a young person to express his conceptions, he often abandons writing in despair at the lack of interest or encouragement." Iremonger's diplomatic career easily passed 40 years; he finished up in Portugal. Iremonger died in 1991.

Like Iremonger, Conor Cruise O'Brien's career in diplomacy and international and domestic politics was spectacular. He was a contemporary of Iremonger's and, in a cosy little town like Dublin; the two were close associates and friends. O'Brien, born in 1917, was far away from Behan in terms of personality. That did not stop him from playing whatever role he could in Irish letters and thanks to Iremonger, he was asked to give a free opinion on an early draft of *The Quare Fellow*. O'Brien, about 30 years of age at the time, admired the work while maintaining a traditional wariness about its author. He was at the time working in the Irish Department of Foreign Affairs. He would soon be catapulted to Paris as counsellor, assigned to the United Nations and later sent as a representative to Katanga Province, the mineral-rich province of the then-toppling Belgian Congo. In the 1970s he became a member of parliament (TD) in Ireland, which he used as a pulpit to warn of the dangers of Irish nationalism.

O'Brien, interviewed in 1980, was at that time editor-in-chief of *The Observer*. It was O'Brien's belief that Behan's main contribution to English-language literature, Irish style, "was for Dublin's spoken language, a gift which he handled as nobody had handled it since O'Casey. (O'Casey died in 1964 at the age of 84). This gift for spoken Dublin English and the huge sense of fun he had at his best was probably never fully expressed because of his life pattern, but at its best it was absolutely marvellous." O'Brien died in 2008.

In 1990, Brian Behan, born in 1926 and two years older than Dominic and three years younger than Brendan, provided a good picture of how Brendan might have turned out had he not been addicted to drink and had he used his oratorical and argumentative skills in a manner more consistent with his political views. Brian, who lived much of his life in England, was an ardent trade unionist and frequently could be seen and heard holding forth at union meetings.

He too was a playwright and essayist and a sometime-scourge of the letters-to-the-editor columns. As a young man, he spent some time as a communist but fell away from this after poignant visits to the Soviet Union and China dissuaded him from believing communism provided any answers to the world's ills, a view reinforced by the Russian invasion of Hungary in 1956.

By the time he had reached his more mature years he had all but outgrown the traditional Irishman's antipathy for the Englishman that he had held when he was a political firebrand. Brian Behan wrote on a variety of subjects, ranging from trade unionism, to plays such as *Barking Sheep*, *His Boots for the Fearless*, and *Hallelujah*. He was able to get some of his works staged in London but unable to achieve a staging in the west end.

A busy man on the speaking tour, he added to the family literary oeuvre with a colourful profile of Kathleen Behan and a profile, mainly of Brendan but sweeping himself and Dominic into *The Brothers Behan*. His works showed that there was deep conflict within the family with Dominic emerging mainly as the odd man out. He told an interviewer, in 1988: "Dominic, my youngest brother, is sexually jealous of me. I am married to a woman younger than him. He's the youngest and the shortest. The bugger actually believes he hates me, he says. "I do not speak to chaps like that. Where does he get 'chaps'?

Brian acknowledged that he and Dominic had not spoken for over thirty years, but he was prepared to agree that it was understandable given the strong personality of Brendan, with an uncle who wrote the Irish national anthem and a father who was once a guest on *This Is Your Life*. Brian spent much of his later years in the coastal town of Brighton where he died in November 2002, but his wing of the family continued to fly the creative flag when his daughter, Janet Behan, produced a play, *Brendan at the Chelsea*, which was put on in 2008 at a small arts theatre in London. Similarly, Irish filmmaker,

Peter Sheridan, in 2000, directed a short film loosely based on Behan's experiences in the Borstal reform school system.

Brendan may have seemed to be the family conundrum, but he had a close rival in brother Dominic, who wrote for nearly all types of print media and took up folk singing at the same time managing to aggravate his two well known brothers and incur the irritation of many friends of the family such as Rae Jeffs who did not get along with him. Born in 1928, he did not share the humour or resilience of the brothers nor the noisy republicanism of Brendan, as shown in the deceptive lyrics of *The Patriot Game*.

What is certain is that he disliked living in the shadow of Brendan, though he stoutly defended his brother after his death and excoriated those who exploited him. What is also certain is that he, Dominic, also was a talented writer. Dominic had his revenge with the first staging in London's west end of his own play, *Posterity be Damned,* first put on in Dublin in 1960 before moving to London just ahead of Behan's *The Hostage*. Like his brothers, he was an active trade unionist, but he left Ireland for Britain and began to write for a living. Among his works was the autobiographical *Teems of Times* in 1979, he produced *The Public World of Parable Jones,* He died in 1989.

Dominic and Brian maintained a long silence and, not long before his death, Dominic unburdened himself of the bile that had been welling up inside him. "I believe Brian has led people to believe that I didn't talk to him because he became a supporter of Leon Trotsky. Now that wouldn't be true, because even though I dislike the terrorist politics of Trotsky, when Brian went to jail for those people – the Workers' Revolutionary Party – I actually sang in a concert in Brixton (a largely West Indian neighbourhood in south London) for him when he was released . . . .

"I dislike Brian intensely, I don't hate him, I don't hate anyone, but it is true to say I don't love him. Anything but, anything but, I hate the Nazis, I hate the provisional IRA, I hate movements but I couldn't possibly hate people, I adore people. It's people that it is about. It's not about the reunification of a load of clay.

Kathleen Behan was born in 1889 at 49 Capel Street. Dublin, she was to outlive nearly all her family, dying in the 95th year in 1984. The family's Irish nationalism was deep but yielded to some basic differences. Kathleen's brother. Peadar Kearney wrote the national anthem. Nevertheless, when the children had grown up, they began migrating to England, led by Brian, Dominic, Seamus, Carmel and Sean. Brendan went to England too but his trip was on business for the IRA and the failure of his mission had the spin off effect of unintentionally producing another Irish man of letters.

One problem she could not solve was the hostility between Brendan and Dominic. All through the 1950s the two were at each other's throats. She wrote, "I couldn't bear it. . . . I told them, "Don't fight, don't beat each other, the world will beat you both long enough . . . Our Dominic and Brendan were in the same two trades – painters and then writers. Whenever their paths crossed the insults would fly, and so it went on. The press loved it, of course.

Brendan shot to fame and his star burned brightly for a decade, at most, before burning out as it plunged back towards earth. Eamon Kennedy, a career foreign service diplomat for the Irish government, recalled amusing but bumpy encounters with Behan while on post to Paris. "You will remember the parable of the talents," he once commented, "well, he wasted his."

Who can say?. The certainty is that he died in 1964; his father died in 1967 and was followed by Rory, the first born.

Kathleen enjoyed celebrity late in life, appearing on television shows and participating in interviews. She even recorded a long-play record, *When All the World was Young*, and survived long enough to see son Brian complete the ghost written text of *Mother of All the Behans,* published in 1984, the year of her death.

It may be that the person with his finger best placed on Behan's pulse was Tony Aspler who brought Behan to life in fictional form under the name of Bart Shea. Aspler's fictionalised account was based on the wreckage-strewn visit by Behan/Shea to Montreal's McGill University in the winter of 1960/61. Scarcely anyone who was there was able to get over it. Behan/Shea to Aspler:

> ". . . And all the apocryphal things they said about me I began to believe about myself. I became a victim of my own myth. I wanted to be like it. That's a terrible responsibility to have to live up to. It was as if I was looking up through my own personality; I was the shadow and the myth was the flesh . . . and all the time it got bigger and bigger, all the time feeding like some demon child on their envy. And it goaded me until my very unpredictability became predictable and I was no longer my own man. I had wrapped the chains around myself and I had denied myself the very freedom I was looking for. It was only alcohol that bridged the gap between me and the myth . . . I only wanted to write – you

must believe that – but they wanted me to perform for them."

Epilogue

JUST ABOUT ANYBODY who was anybody in Irish literature has had his books banned at one time or another, often at the behest of the Catholic Church. Brendan Behan's Borstal Boy was no exception and it was a point of anger to his supporters and particularly to his wife Beatrice, that the book was not published or legally sold in his homeland until shortly after his death in 1964. It is a strange irony that saw the book, written by Behan, an IRA troublemaker, being allowed to be sold in the UK and eventually being included as recommended literature in the British educational system.

The roll-call of those banned in the ensuing decades is truly extraordinary and in a perverse way, impressive: Samuel Beckett, Sigmund Freud, George Bernard Shaw, Kingsley Amis, Brian Moore, J. P. Donleavy, Sean O'Faolain, Frank O'Connor and James Joyce. It is popularly assumed that Joyce succumbed to the censor for the infamous Molly Bloom soliloquy in his novel *Ulysses* or for parts of *A Portrait of the Artist as a Young Man,* works deemed offensive to the church. In fact, what did for Joyce in Ireland as far as the letter of the law was concerned was the ban on his shorter novel, *Stephen Hero*.

This ran headlong into an irate church, with its own League of Decency table of morality rankings, published regularly in the Catholic press, for films and books on what or what should not be publicly available at commercial outlets. The Irish church's censorious arm, extended from the Holy See in Rome like a cascading river sending its tributaries to any place where there was a sizeable Catholic community waiting to have its wrists slapped.

Stephen Hero, an early casualty for the new nation, fell under the cosh in November 1944 after Joyce's death, the judgment being that it was "in its general tendency, indecent." The ban was revoked in April 1951. While Joyce's other books were not easily available in his home country, no other of his works was banned from publication in Ireland. This is where a catch occurs. Thanks to the British-drafted Customs Consolidation Act of 1876, which applied in Ireland (and which was partly retained by Dublin, after independence from the UK).*Ulysses* was banned in the UK. It followed then that the Irish authorities, using the British law, were able to inhibit its importation but not its publication or sale in Ireland, which in any case was a small and impoverished market.

The book was composed and written by Joyce and admired by that privy to the original text during Joyce's time in Paris where, in 1918, it was first published. The publicity generated by the US ban gave the book its renown and and enhanced the French capital's reputation as a city where, in the words of lyricist Cole Porter, 'anything goes.' Many attempts were made to circumvent the ban, notably by Sylvia Beach, the famous proprietress of Shakespeare & Co book shop and publishing house in Paris, and writs were issued. But the US was heading into the 13-year dark age of the Volsted Act which saw the virtual ban on all but medical, industrial and sacramental alcohol from 1920 to 1933. The ban on alcohol led to a crime wave in the US and its effectiveness in law enforcement collapsed spectacularly. When the act was repealed following the huge 1932 election victory of Franklin Roosevelt, correspondingly, the ban on *Ulysses* and other controversial works barred from American shores was lifted.

Specifically, *Ulysses* had been banned because it was ruled to be immoral. But by 1933 the mood had changed and federal Judge John Munro Woolsey, in his celebrated ruling, declared the book not to be immoral.

The run-up to the *Ulysses* case in the US underlined the fact that Ireland was not alone as an offender to the cause of freedom of expression in film and on stage. As recently as 1960, Henry Miller's *Tropic of Cancer* found itself before the US Supreme Court which, after the book had undergone a 13-year ban, found the work to not be obscene. The court declared that "material dealing with sex in a manner that advocates ideas or that has literary or scientific or artistic value or any other form of social importance, may not be branded as obscenity and denied the constitutional protection."

In Brendan Behan's case, Britain had no problem in publishing *Borstal Boy,* despite its Irish Republican Army themes or many other works that had been banned in Ireland. Nevertheless, in the long, struggle against censorship, international eyes in 1960 were on the UK which had authored many actions against freedom of expression over the years (only to find itself head-butted by such formidable free speech advocates as Gilbert and Sullivan).

The big case that year was Regina versus Penguin Books Limited, better known as *The Trial of Lady Chatterley,* the prosecution being brought by the Director of Public Prosecutions (DPP) of D.H. Lawrence's novel *Lady Chatterley's Lover* (32 years after its original publication). According to C.H. Rolph, who had been secretary of the Herbert Committee which had been set

Aftermath

up in the 1950s to reform and rationalise criminal law about the censorship of literature the D.P.P.

". . . .Having seen or shown advertisements about the Penguin programme (to publish the book) told the police to buy a copy of *Lady Chatterley's Lover* in the usual way. This means buying it in the Charing Cross Road (One of the world's retail centres for the sale of new and used books, located in central London), the only thoroughfare in London officially supposed to sell obscene books."

After six days of testimony, the jurors returned to court and were asked by the foreman:

"Do you find that Penguin Books Ltd is guilty or not guilty of publishing an obscene article?"

"NOT GUILTY", said the foreman loudly and firmly; and no one can ever know whether that meant "not obscene" or "obscene but justified".

Thus, midst a round of applause and cheers, the case against Lawrence's book ended, but not before a post-script from Mr Gerald Gardiner, QC, "There is one thing about which I want to be quite plain, because of my submission it is of some importance not only that you (the jury) should realise this but that everybody should realise it. It is this: that no one should think that if the use of these words for this special purpose by this particular author, in this particular book, is legitimate, it will follow that these words can be used by any scribbler writing any kind of novel."

So, a victory for freedom of expression in Ireland's former mother country. But Ireland was marching to the beat of a different drum. There arose the name of Liam O'Flaherty, a communist and for many a champion, through his writing, of the pain and drama of Ireland's civil war following the battle for independence from the UK. He is most famous for such works as *The Sniper* and *The Informer*, the latter, in its filmed version, went on to win an Academy Award in Hollywood in the 1930s. It was not the two stories that worked the censors against him. Rather, he found himself the object of the censor's red pencil with the proscription of such modern classics as *The House of God,* banned in 1930. *The Puritan,* 1932. *The Martyr,* 1933, *Shame the Devil,* 1934. *Hollywood Cemetery,* 1937 and *Land* in 1946. The reason given for banning the public dissemination of these titles on Irish soil was "a general tendency towards indecency". The embargoes remained in place till 1967 when they were all simultaneously lifted.

On February 27, 1979 a reception was given by the Allied Irish Bank in Dublin in honour of O'Flaherty, by now the Irish elder statesman of letters, then 82 years of age. The prize was accompanied by a £2,000 cheque and the creation of an annual award of £1,000 per year to candidates for excellence in Irish writing. A large crowd was gathered at the ceremony, held at the Royal Dublin Society, but a few of the guests, irked that recognition in Ireland for O'Flaherty's work had been so long in coming, thanks to censorship, were wont to describe the award as 'conscience money'. (As recently as 20 years ago I entered a Dublin book shop inquiring after O'Flaherty's works, only to be asked by the sales girl "Is he one of ours?")

Without doubt, the period from 1930s to the 1960s was grim for freedom of expression enthusiasts – there had been 1,200 books and 140 periodicals banned or censured in the 1930s alone. As Tim Pat Coogan wrote in his biography of Eamon de Valera: "In those years, outside of a very small circle, books were seldom discussed on their literary merits – the more general discussion point was: 'should it have been banned or not?' Long, tedious battles were fought, notably by writer Sean O'Faolain, as editor of the influential magazine *The Bell*.

O'Faolain had suffered as the hands of the censors with his banned novel *Bird Alone*. He edited the magazine from 1940 to 1946 when he was succeeded by Anthony Cronin.

Behan, whose voluble iconoclasm long preceded public awareness about the content of his writings, fell into the grip of the censors quite easily. With the passage of decades and with all bans rescinded, and secularisation increasingly widespread around a united Europe, it is difficult now to see why Behan was not spared the censor's cut. The difference at that time was that Ireland was then something of a clericalist democracy and guild was presumed once a complainant registered an objection to a particular work in theatrical, book or magazine form.

The shadow of the sign of the cross was omnipresent on matters involving passing a moral judgement. The censors left Behan's stage pieces, *The Quare Fellow* and *The Hostage,* alone. Much of what else he had written in Ireland had been published in the form of newspaper articles or excerpts from such longer works as his novel *The Scarperer,* or such collections as *Hold Your Hour and Have Another.* But, they took dead aim on the autobiographical classic *Borstal Boy* focused on searing confrontations between the young Behan, prison authorities and clergymen. *Borstal Boy,* thus, went far in raising the temperature of the censors with its wide use of expletives and fiery denunciations of the church following Behan's own excommunication. The ban found the work to be indecent or obscene; the prohibition order was brought down in November 1958, shortly after *Borstal's* publication in the UK (and its huge success there).

An appeal to overturn the ban was dismissed; the ban ended only in 1967 with the expiration of the prohibition order, three years after his death. There was some sweetness in the final victory, even though Behan was not around to see it, and that was the acceptance of the book on the British secondary school curriculum designating the work as recommended reading in the state's schools.

One of the more bizarre incidents of censorship occurred in 1957 when the police intervened during a presentation at Dublin's tiny Pike theatre of Tennessee William's *The Rose Tatoo, being* presented by Carolyn Swift and Alan Simpson, the theatrical pioneers who had presented to English-language audiences for the first time a few years earlier: Beckett's *Waiting for Godot* and Behan's *The Quare Fellow*. As Swift pointed out in her memoirs, the play was not actually stopped but Simpson spent a highly publicised night in jail, was brought before a tribunal and heard accusations that the play was 'indecent and profane.' This was based on the claim that one of the props portraying a central point in the story line was a sealed prophylactic – a taboo article in Catholic Ireland.

As Swift explained:"There had never been any question of using an actual contraceptive packet. These were difficult to obtain, since at that time they could only be smuggled into the country for personal use, and though it certainly would not have been impossible to obtain one, it would probably have caused embarrassment to the cast when all that was necessary was to fake one." While the play had its allotted run, despite the prolonged hearings; in the end it took more than a year for all the arguments to be heard. The charges were eventually dismissed but not before demonstrations inside the theatre and outside took place and where the voice of the noisy Brendan Behan could be heard.

What Conor O'Brien termed "the last explosion of lunacy by our censors" occurred in the 1960s when bans on indecency and obscenity were brought against the six initial works of Edna O'Brien, starting with *The Country Girls*, in 1960; *The Lonely Girl* in 1962; *The Girl With the Green Eyes* in 1964; *Girls in Their Married Bliss* in 1964; *August is a Wicked Month* in 1965 and *Casualties of Peace* in 1966. All were appealed without success, but the bans were lifted when the prohibition orders expired in 1967. The rationale for banning was that the first novel smeared Irish womanhood. O'Brien pt it differently saying the books posed a threat "because they were the first palpable voicing of the sexuality of Irish women." O'Brien's problem was that she was a woman in a male- and drink-dominated country that was even further behind many other western countries just starting to meet the challenges of creating equality under the law. In Ireland, women were not allowed on juries till 1978, and while huge changes lay ahead, O'Brien was not one to wait around, having decamped from the land of her birth for Britain where she has lived for decades.

Such was the paucity of good and challenging reading in the book stories and of listening material on domestic radio, recalled a north Dublin friend that he had no recourse in the late 1950s but to tune into Willis Conover's broadcasts under the American *Radio-Free Europe* short wave jazz feed. The mission was to deliver the good news of jazz to the millions of deprived listeners behind the Iron Curtain, not Ireland.

This is not to say that *Radio Eireann* was not doing its best to bring news, culture and the arts to its listenership, but as a state-owned radio corporation (a vest-pocket counterpart to the BBC) it fell under the government Ministry of Posts and Telegraphs and, thus, had to be careful in executing its mission statement. According to Maurice Gorham, once a Director of Broadcasting, that mission was "not merely to reflect every aspect of national activity, but to create activities that did not yet exist."

"It was expected to revive the speaking or Irish; to foster a taste for classical music; to revive Irish traditional music; to keep people on the farms; to sell goods and services of all kinds, from sausages to sweep tickets; to provide a living and a career for writers and musicians; to reunite the Irish people at home and those overseas; to end partition (of the North and South). All this in addition to broadcasting's normal duty to inform, educate and entertain. And all in a programme amounting . . . to some five-and-a-half hours a day!"

At the same time, then, it had a broadly based remit but one necessarily balancing the need for self constraint with the equally urgent requirement to make the best use of the information suitable for broadcast. As both an irritant and a guidepost, the sound waves of the BBC threaded their way across the Irish Sea and easily reached listeners in Dublin, Cork and along Ireland's east coast. So any dearth of information on current affairs and such vital social issues as divorce, birth control (and later abortion), available only in limited form through the Radio Eireann, was partly countered by the more secular and broadly based offerings emanating from the BBC's transmitters. Later it would be fired up by the creation of its partner organisation, Radio Telefis Eireann (RTE), which slowly but surely brought controversy about Ireland's more hallowed institutions, mores and customs into Irish living rooms notably through such talk show hosts as Gay Byrne. A big lift up also came in 1990 with the surprise election of Mary Robinson, an experienced professor of law at Trinity College, Dublin, as Ireland's first woman president. She later went on to become UN Commissioner for Human Rights.

It is no doubt that the Ireland of censorship would have got where it did on its own, but in issues as freedom of expression it got more than its share of help from the Westminster Parliament, firstly in the form of the Obscene Publications Act of 1857, the Indecent Advertisement Act of 1889 and the Customs Consolidation Act of 1876. Censorship laws were made in Westminster, not Dublin. This changed with the creation of the Irish Free State in 1922, and the first all-Irish censorship regulation was the Censorship of Publications

Aftermath

Act of 1929. This was followed by an amended and equally stringent, 1946 law; and in a 1967 law which yielded little to outside convention.

The big breakthrough came with the most recent legislation, the Censorship of Publications (Amendment) Act of 1998. The 1998 legislation – Ireland now had been in the European Union since 1972, and was also a signatory of the European Convention on Human Rights – was an attempt to acknowledge the obsolescence of the previous statutes which were deemed to have no place in a modern Europe. In its own language, the bill was introduced "to end an anomaly in our censorship laws as a result of which books by authors of international renown in the field of literature and medicine remain on the banned list, decades after the bans were first imposed."

The bill noted that the 1946 act provided two separate grounds for a book to be banned: that it is "indecent or obscene", or; that it "advocates the unnatural prevention of conception or the procurement of abortion or miscarriage or the use of any method, treatment or appliance for the purpose of such prevention or procurement."

The 1967 act amended the law to provide that a prohibition order imposed on a book on the grounds that it was indecent or obscene would automatically lapse after 12 years unless it was renewed by the Censorship board. The act did nothing about the second category of books – those regarded as advocating the unnatural prevention of conception or the procurement of abortion or miscarriage of the use of any method, treatment or appliance for the purpose of such prevention or procurement. This was circumvented in the 1979 Health (Family Planning) Act, which removed the unnatural prevention of conception as a ground for banning a book and the provision, with regard to abortion was significantly qualified by the Regulation of

Information (Services Outside the State for Termination of Pregnancies) Act of 1995.

Nowadays the Censorship of Publications Board exists as an independent board with reference to the Department of Justice, Equality and Law Reform. By its own admission it does not now ban books very often. In some years nothing is prohibited. The major change appears to be that of yielding the presumption of guilt to the presumption of innocence and of course the changed environment in which Ireland, as a sovereign nation within the European Union, now operates. These days the debate is about pornography and on-line access to it. But in Ireland, there are still constraints on information about such issues as abortion. According to the censorship board:

"Books are prohibited if the Censorship or Publications Board considers them to be indecent or obscene. Periodicals are prohibited if the . . . board considers them to be frequently or usually indecent or obscene. Both books and periodicals may be prohibited if the board considers that they advocate abortion or ways of carrying out abortions. Periodicals may also be prohibited if the Board is of the opinion that they have given an unduly large proportion of space to matters relating to crime. In practice, however, publications are usually only reported to the Board for obscenity. The board will measure the literary, scientific or historical merit of the publication. It will take note of its general tenor, the language in which it is written, its likely circulation and readers and anything else it feels is relevant. A prohibition order on a book comes in effect once it has been published in the official gazette, and ceases on 31 December following a period of 12 years from the date of the order first coming into effect."

INDEX

A

A Moveable Feast, 158
A Taste of Honey, 56
Act of Union, 18
After the Wake, 32
Albee, Edward, 136
Algonquin Hotel, 12, 132
Andrews, Eamonn, 166
Arthurs, Peter, 19, 154-5, 174, 180,
Astor, David, 161, 162-5, 221
Aspler, Tony, 143, 227
Avakian, George, 144

B

Baby Brendan 153, 165, 169
Bard, Stanley, 12
BBC, 74
Beckett Samuel, 60, 136
Behan, Beatrice (Beatsie), 3, 83-89, 122-3, 140, 142, 152,
    153, 160, 176-7, 191, 206, 208, 210 213
Behan, Blanaid Orla, Mairead (birth of), 189
Behan, Brendan, 2, 7, 15, 17, 38-52), 61-2, 83-9, 91-7, 109-

    17, 122-3, 141-3, 152-3, 157-60, 163-8, 181-2
Behan, Brian, 11, 183, 193, 194, 209, 223, 226
Behan, Carmel, 22
Behan, Dominic, 22, 166, 192, 194, 209, 224, 226
Behan, Janet, 224
Behan, Kathleen, 14, 19, 87, 201, 224, 226
Behan, Paudge Roger 206
Behan, Stephen, 21, 191, 201, 226
Bell, The, 60
Best, George, 200-1,
Blue Shirts 28-9
Brendan Behan's Island 58, 165
Brendan Behan's New York 118,
Brendan Behan at the Chelsea, 224
Breslin, Jimmy, 187-8
Burt, L.I., 50
Borstal Boy, 3, 39-52, 138, 140, 222
Browne, Garech, 10, 61-2, 203
Browne, Christy, 203
Brown, John Mason 121-3
Burgess, Anthony, 119, 193
Burroughs, William 174

C

Caen, Herb, 147
Canada visits, 142-5
Canadian Press, The, 144-5
Carson, Sir Edward, 200
Casement, Roger, 206
Castro, Fidel 132, 145
Catacombs, 30
Chelsea hotel, 172-6, 224
Chessman, Caryl, 69
Confessions of an Irish Rebel (A Fine Day n the Graveyard) ,
    49, 97, 151 , 180,
Collins, Michael, 200,
Cort Theatre, 131-7
Cooper, Gary, 145

Cronin, Anthony 30, 189
Cullen Tim, 184-6

D

Danby-Smith, Valerie (Hemingway), 13, 131-3, 146-9, 153-7, 158, 165, 169, 176-7, 205, 210, 216
Davis, William (Mr. and Mrs.), 148-9
Days of Wine and Roses 189
Delaney, Charlotte, 202
Delaney, Shelagh, 56-7, 202
Donleavy, J. P., 12, 16, 60-1, 220
Doyle, Jack, 125-26
Dreifus, Arthur, 155-6
Dunham, Katherine,171

E

Edwards, Hilton, 53
Edwards, Ralph, 166
English, Grainne, 21, 31-4

F

Fallon, Peter, 32
Famine, The Great, 5
Feincreanach, 214
Fianna Eireann, 37-8
Francis, Arlene, 129
Free-staters, 28-9
ffrench-Salkeld, Blained, 83
ffrench-Salkeld (Behan), Beatrice, 10, 82, 83-90
ffrench-Salkeld, Cecil 83-90
ffrench-salkeld, Celia, 83,155
Furlong, Rory, 21, 191
Furlong, Sean, 21

G

Gate, theatre, 53
Geis, Bernard, 138, 141, 165, 167, 170-74, 221

Gill, Brendan, 136
Gladstone, William Ewart, 40
Glasnevin cemetery, 48, 193,197-206
Gleason, Jackie, 121, 171
Gonne, Maude (Countess Markiewicz), 206
Goulding, Cathal, 37-8, 206, 211-12, 216
Graecen, Roert, 21-3

H

Harris, Richard, 105
Heaney, Paddy, 19,
Hemingway, Gregory, 153 217
Hemingway, Ernest 132, 145-6,177, 210, 216-7
Hemingway, Ernest (death of), 153-57
Hemingway, Mary, 132, 145, 158, 159, 175
Hogarth, Paul, 172
Hold Your Hour and Have Another, 186
Holles hospital, 2
Hollesley Bay, 40
Hostage, The, 3, 57, 89, 110, 132, 141, 165, 213
Hume, John, 217
Hutchinson's publishing 16, 43

I

Iremonger, Valentine, 166, 207, 221
Irish Republican Army (IRA), 24, 38-52, 110, 127, 203-6, 210-13
Irving, Clifford, 54
Informer, The, 11

J

Jeffs, (Sebley) Rae, 11, 16, 56-7, 80, 91-8, 131, 151-2, 165, 169, 176, 180, 202, 210, 221-2
John Bull's Other Island, 51

K

Kavanagh, Paddy, 64, 219
Keane, Fergal, 30
Keen, john B. 207
Kitt, Eartha , 171
Kee, Robert, 6
Kearney, Colbert, 34, 112
Kearney, John, 17
Kearney, Peadar, 17, 226
Kearney, Kathleen, 17
Kendrick, Alexander, 121
Kennedy, John, Fitzgerald 128, 180. 190
Knickerbocker, Paine,147

L

Laurents, Arthur, 136
Le Client du Matin (The Quare Fellow), 166
Littlewood, Joan, 12, 26-7, 73, 78, 100-6, 110-17, 125,130, 151, 170, 202, 209, 215, 218
Longford, Lady, 203
Lyons, Leonard, 127

M

Mackie, Desmond, 10, 125-26
Macliammoir, Michael, 53
MacNamara, Desmond, 11, 52-5, 64, 192, 220-1
MacNamara, Oioen, 221
McDaids pub, 85
McGill, Joe, 73, 210
McGoohan, Patrick, 155
McGuinness, Kathleen, 17, 25
Meath hospital, 2, 191
Macreamoinn, Sean, 10, 16,
Mailer, Norman, 128
Melvin Murray, 12, 100-4
Miller, Arthur 174-5
Mother of All the Behans, 226

Muggeridge, Malcolm 74, 77-80
Mulhane, Dermot, 201
Milligan, Spike, 225
Murrow, Edward R. 120-2

N

New Yorker, The, 133-37
Nixon, Richard M. 128

O

O Beachain, Brendan, 206
O'Brien, Conor Cruise, 11, 76-7, 80, 214, 222
O'Brien, Flann, 219
O'Brien, Paddy, 24, 85, 199-201,
O'Casey, Sean, 4, 115, 194 223
O'Connor, Frank, 109, 115,
O'Connor, Ulick, 84-5, 129, 173-4
O'Faolain, Sean, 60, 219-20
O'Flaherty, Liam 10
O'hetHir, Brendan (Brendan O'Hare) 10
On the Barricades, 221
Oh What a lovely War, 1 03

P

Paar, Jack 128-9
Parkinson, Michael 122-3
Patriot Game, The, 226
Parnell, Charles Stuart, 206
Pfeiffer, Pauline, 217
Pike, theatre, 66-8, 84
Plimpton, George 128
Posterity Be Damned, 194
Public World of Parable Jones, The, 225

Q

Quare Fellow, 66-70, 81, 141, 155, 207, 216, 219, 221

R

Radio Telefis Eireann (RTE), 10,
Raffles, Gerry, 12, 73, 116, 130-1, 151-2, 202,215
Richard's Cork Leg, 106, 151-2, 156, 158, 194
Running With the Bulls, 216
Runyon, Damon, 167
Ryan, John, 115, 191, 220

S

San Francisco visit, 145-8;
Scarperer, The, 141, 167
Sebley, Peter
Shaw, G. B., 194
Shea, Bart (Brendan Behan), 227
Sheridan, James, 224
Simpson, Alan, 11, 65-73, 116, 194, 209, 215-7
Soldier's Song, 20
Spinetti, Victor, 116, 130, 133-4,
Sutton, Dudley, 130
Swift, Carolyn, 11, 216
Spanish Civil War 36-8
Streets of Askelon, 143
Stearns, Marshall, 144

T

Teems of Times, 225
Theatre des Nations, 89, 113
This is Your life, 224
Thomas, Dylan 147, 175-6
Toibin, Niall, 11, 62, 113-4, 203, 209
Tony Award 209
Trevelyan, Sir Charles, 5
Twisting of Another Rope, 71
Tynan, Kenneth, 105, 218-6

V

Valera, Eamon de, 27-8, 204
Vassar college, 137
Vidal, Gore, 136

W

Waiting for Godot, 60
White Horse, 176
Williams, Tennessee, 134-5. 174
Wilson, Earl, 127
Woodham Smith, Cecil 6

Addenda

THE QUARE FELLOW
by Brendan Behan; director Joan Littlewood
Presented at the Theatre Royal, Stratford, London May 24, 1956

PRISONERS

Dunlavin:	Maxwell Shaw
Neighbour:	Gerard Dynevor
Prisoner B (A man of 30):	Brian Murphy
Lifer:	Bill Grover
Fellow:Prisoner A. (die hard):	Glynn Edwards
	Ron Brooker
Mickser:	Eric Ogle
English voice:	John Rutley
Scolara (Young prisoner):	Timothy Harley
Shaybo (Young prisoner):	George Eugeniou
Prisoner C (Boy from the isle):	Henry Livings
Prisoner D (The embezzler):	Barry Clayton
Prisoner E (the bookie):	Brian Murphy

WARDERS

Chief warder:	Maxwell Shaw

Regan: Dudley Foster
Crimmin: Brian Nunn
Donelly (Warder 1): Clive Goodwin
The new one (warder 2): Fred Cooper
The Prison governor: Robert Henderson
Holy Healey: Barry Clayton
The Hangman: Gerry Raffles
Jenkinson: Brian Murphy

THE HOSTAGE

By Brendan Behan

Directed by Joan Littlewood, Theatre Royal, Stratford, London E15

October 14, 1958

Cast

Pat, caretaker: Howard Goorney
Meg Dillon: Eileen Kennally
Monsewer: Glynn Edwards
Rio Rita: Stephen Cato
Princess Grace: Roy Barnett
Mr. Mulleady: Brian Murphy
Miss Gilchrist: Ann Beach
Colette: Yootha Joyce
Ropeen: Leila Greenwood
Leslie Williams: Alfred Lynch
Teresa: Celia Salkeld
I.R.A. officer: James Booth
Volunteer: Clive Barker
Russian sailor: Dudley Sutton
Kate: Kathleen O'Connor

Source: Methuen

THE HOSTAGE

By Brendan Behan

Performed at Cort Theatre, New York September 20 1960-January 7 1961

Produced by Leonard S. Field and Caroline Burke Swann

Directed by Joan Littlewood

Cast

Meg Dillon:	Avis Bunnnage
Miss Gilchrest:	Patience Collier
Colette:	Anita Dangler
Monsewer:	Glynn Edwards
Volunteer:	Michael Forest
Old Ropeen:	Leila Greenwood
Leslie, a soldier:	Alfred Lynch
M. Mulheady:	Aubrey Morris
Mac:	Warren O'Connell
Kate:	Kathleen O'Connnor
Jamie:	James A. Roache
Theresa:	Celia Salkeld
Pet the caretaker:	Maxwell Shaw
I.R.A. man:	Victor Spinetti
Princess Grace:	Melvin Street
Rio Rita:	Dudley Sutton
Russian Sailor:	Metro Welles

THE QUARE FELLOW (film)

By Brendan Behan

Directed by Arthur Dreifuss (1962)

Cast

Thomas Crimmin:	Patrick McGoohan
Kathleen:	Sylvia Simms
Regan:	Walter Mackeen
Donelly:	By Dermot Kelly
Chief Warder:	Jack Cunningham
Holy Healy:	Hilton Edwards
Prison Governor:	PHilip O'Flynn
Doctor Flyn:	Leo McCabe
Lavery:	Norman Rodway
Mrs O'Hara:	Marie Kean
Mickeser's wife:	Pauline Delaney
1st customs officer:	Geoff Golden
2nd customs officer:	Tom Irwin
Poet:	joseph O'Donnell
Meg:	Agnes Bernelle
Minna:	Irish Lawler
Chaplain:	Dominic Roche
Jenkinson:	Brian Hewitt-jones
Arthur O'Sullivan	Arthur O'Sullivan
Silvertop:	Aubrey Morris
Flaherty:	Eamonn Brennan
Moclser	Robert Bernall

Supporting cast

Kelly	Gerry Alexander
Old Patriot:	James Brennan
Dunlavin:	Harry Brogan
O'Connor:	James Cavery
Shamrock attendant:	Brendan Cauldwell
Publican women:	Marie Conmee

Cleary:	John Cowley
Reception warder:	Eddie Golden
Neighbour:	Eric Gorman
Food Orderly	Aiden Grennell
Charwoman:	Marissa grimes
2nd publican:	Michael C. Hennessy
Reeption clerk:	David Kelly
1st publican:	Pat Layde
Walsh:	T. P McKenna
Clancy:	Frank O'Donovan
O' Shaughnessy:	Desmond O'neill
Stretcherman:	Derry Power
Dock Worker:	Charlie Robeerts
Lavery's assistant:	Celia Salkeld
Irate citizen:	Ronnie Walsh
Carroll:	John Welsh
Ken:	Lavery
Lavery:	Michael Campion
Borstal governor:	Desmond Perry
Minister:	Ritchie Stewart
Warder O'Shea:	Patrick Layde
Italian priest:	Bill Foley
Cook:	Harry Brogan
Warders wife:	Mary O'Gorman
Immigration man:	Arthur O'Sullivan
Source:	***Four Masters***

—

BORSTAL BOY

By Brendan Behan

Adapted for stage by Frank McMahon, presented June 6

1978

The Gaiety Theatre, Dublin, director Tomas Mac Anna

Behan (in middle age):	Niall Toibin
Brendan (in his youth):	Frank Grimes
Sheila:	Maire ni Grainne
Mrs Gildea:	Katlheen Barrington
Liverpool Landlady:	Peggy Hayes
Inspector:	Desmond Perry
Sergeant:	Philip O'Flynn
Detective:	John Richardson
Policeman:	Seamus Newham
First warder	Arthur O'Sullivan
Second warder:	Clive Geraghty
Charlie:	Vincent Dowling
Callan:	Patrick Dawson
Tubby:	Ritchie Stewart
Prison chaplain:	Patrick Layde
Library warder:	Harry Brogan
Browney:	Tony Hayes
Dale:	Robert Browne
James:	John Byrne
Prison governor:	Bill Foley
Voice of judge:	Ian Priestly Mitchell
Policewoman:	Joan O'Hara
Wellsh warder:	John Richardson

Borstal boys:

Harty:	Chris O'Neill
Joe:	Robert Carlyle

Chewlips:	Eamon Morrissey
Cragg:	Pat Laffan
Jock:	Desmond Cave
Tom:	John Kavanagh Rivers
	Cive Gerghty
Shaggy:	Paddy Long
Ken:	Lavery
Lavery:	Michael Campion
Borstal governor:	Desmond Perry
Minister:	Ritchie Stewart
Warder O'Shea:	Patrick Layde
Italian priest:	Bill Foley
Cook:	Harry Brogan
Warders wife:	Mary O'Gorman
Immigration man:	Arthur O'Sullivan
Source:	Four Masters

RICHARD'S CORK LEG

By Brendan Behan

Performed at Peacock Theatre, Dublin, March 4 1972 by the Abbey Theatre Company. Director Alan Simpson; The

casts:

Bawd 1 (Maria Concepta):	Eileen Colgan
Bawd 2 (Rose of Lima):	Joan O'Hara
Blind men (Cronin):	Luke Kelly
The Hero Hogan:	Ronnie Drew

A coloured gentleman:

Bonnie Prince Charlie:	Barney McKenna
Mrs. Cronin:	Terri Donnelly
Mrs Mallarkey:	Angela Newman
Dierdre Mallarkey:	Dierdre Mallarkey

A corpse: Ciaran Bourke
Blueshirts, undertakers' men, others: John Sheehan, Ciaran Bourke, Ronnie Drew, Luke Kelly, Barney McKenna

—

THE HOSTAGE

By Brendan Behan

Barbican Theatre, London

June 14 1994

Cast:

Lardy:	Lawrence Barber
Rio Rita:	Alexi K. Campbell
Paper Boy:	Tommy Carey
Pat:	Dermot Crowley
Ropeen:	Pauline Delaney
Feargus O'Connor:	Sean Hannaway
Mr. Mulleady:	James Hayes
The Lizard:	Liz Kelter
Colete:	Miriam Kelly
Bobo:	Nick Lucas
Leslie Williams:	Damien Lyme
Princess Grace:	Sekai Matumba
I.R.A. officer:	Eoin McCarthy
Teresa:	Alison McKenna
Meg:	Dearbhla Molloy
Vicky:	Victor Power
Miss Gilchrist:	Jenny Quayle
O'Shaughnessy:	Michael Scanlon
Russian Sailor:	Peter Warnock
Monsewer:	John Woodvine

Source: Peter Michael

THE QUARE FELLOW

By Brendan Behan

Oxford Stage Company in association with Liverpool Everyman

and Playhose

directed by Kathy Burke, Music by Philip Chevron,

The Tricycle Theatre

London (Tuesday 3 April – Saturday 8 May 2004)

Cast:

Warder Donnelly:	Kieran Cunningham
Dunlavin	Ciaran Cunningham
Prisoner B:	Sean Gallagher
Prisoner A:	David Ganly
Prisoner E:	Oengus Macnamara
Scolara :	Matthew Dunphy
Shaybo:	Chistopher logan
Warder Regan:	Sean Campion
The lifer:	Gerald rooney
The Other Fellow:	Tom Vaughan Lawlor
Neighbour:	Tony Rohr
Holy Healey	Gary Liburn
Prisoner C:	Nick Danan
Prisoner D:	Pau Lloyd
Mickser:	Jason Kavanagh
The Cook	Gary Libuurn
The Chief:	Gary Liburn
Crimmin:	Patrick Lynch
Hangman:	Jay Sullivan
Jenkinson:	tom Vaughan Lawlor
New Warder:	Gerard Rooney

Prison Governor:	Oenus Macnamara
Man in Cell:	Patrick McCabe

—

THE HOSTAGE

By Brendan Behan

March 5 2008

Church Street Theatre, Washington D.C.

Director: Mark A. Rhea.

Cast: Sheri S. Herren; Timothy Hayes Lynch, Colin Smith, Sally Cusenza, Shadia Hafiz, Jim Howard, Mike Kozemchak, Rich Montgomery, Roger Pavano, Jenn Richter, Daniel Steinberg.

—

Bibliography

Selected reading for Behan, The Crazy Life

After the Wake, by Brendan Behan, Allison & Busby

As it Seemed to Me, by John Cole, Phoenix

At Swim Two Birds by Flann O'Brien, Penguin

Behan, the Complete Plays, introduction by Alan Simpson, Methuen

Brendan Behan, by Colbert Kearney, Gill Macmillan

Brendan Behan, by Ulick O'Connor, Panther Granada

Brendan Behan's Island, by Brendan Behan, Corgi

Brendan Behan's New York, by Brendan Behan, Little Brown

Brendan Behan, Man and Superman, by Rae Jeffs, Hutchinson and Co.

Brendan Behan, by Raymond Porter, Essays on Modern Writers, Columbia University Press

The Brothers Behan, by Brian Behan, Ashfield Press

Characters of Fitizrovia, by Mike Penelow and Marsha Rowe, Felix Dennis Publishers

Confession of an Irish Rebel, by Brendan Behan, Arena

Country Girls, by Edna O'Brien, Penguin

Dead as Doornails, by Anthony Cronin, Poolbeg Press

Dylan Thomas – In the Mercy of his Means, by George Tremlett, Constable and Co.

De Valera, Eamon, -- His Life, by Gus Smith

Eamon De Valera, Eamon – the Man Who Was Ireland, by Tim Pat Coogan

Eamonn Andrews – His Life, by Gus Smith, W. H. Allan

Foreign Affairs and other Stories, by Sean O'Faolain, Penguin

Hard Life,The, by Flann O'Brien, Picador

The Ginger Man, by J. P. Donleavy, Corgi

Gladstone, a Biography, by Roy Jenkins

The Great Hunger—Ireland 1845-49, by Cecil Woodham Smith, Hamish Hamilton

The History of Britain – 1668 – present, Carter and Mears

Hold Your Hour and Have Another, by Brendan Behan, Hutchinson and Co.

The Hostage, by Brendan Behan, Methuen

John Hume, by Paul Routledge, Harper Colllins

The Informer, by Liam O'Flaherty, Grossett and Dunlap

The I.R.A., by Tim Pat Coogan, Harper Collins

Ireland: a Social and Cultural History, 1922-79, by Terrence Brown, Fontana

The Irish War, by Tony Geraghty, Harper Collins

The Irish Mystique, by Max Caulfield, Prentice hall

J. P. Donleavy's Ireland, by J. P. Donleavy, Penguin

The Life of Kenneth Tynan, by Kathleen Tynan, Methuen

Paddy Kavanagh, by Antoinett, Aurora

The Making of Ireland, by James Lydon, Routledge

Michael Collins, by Rex Taylor, the New English Press

The Mad Lomasneys, by Frank O'Connor, Pan

Timebends, by Arthur Miller, Methuen

The Mother of All the Behans, by Brian Behan, Arena

My Life With Brendan, by Beatrice Behan, Leslie Frewin

Nial Toibin – Smile and Be a Villain, by Niall Toibin, Town house

My Brother Brendan, by Dominic Behan, Four Square Books

My Life with Dylan Thomas, by Caitlin Thomas, Virago Press

The Poor Mouth, by Flann O'Brien

My Oedipus Complex, by Frank O'Connor, Penguin

Prime Time, by Alexander McKendrick, Little, Brown

The Public World of Parable Jones, by Dominic Behan, Fontana

The Quare Fellow, by Brendan Behan, Methuen

The Price of My Soul, by Bernadette devlin, Pan

Remembering How we Stood, by John Ryan, Gill and Macmillan

Richard's Cork Leg, by Brendan Behan, Methuen

Running With the Bullls, by Valerie Hemingway, Ballantine Books

Sean O'Casey, by Ronald Ayling, Aurora Publishers

Taste of Honey, by Shelagh Delaney, Methuen

The Scarperer, by Brendan Behan, Arrow Books

Up Front, by Victor Spinetti, Robson Books

The Short Stories of Liam O'Flaherty, by Liam O'Flaherty, Digit

Stage by Stage, by Carolyn Swift, Poolbeg

States of Ireland by Conor Cruise O'Brien, Hutchinson and Co.

A Taste of Honey by Shelagh Delaney Methuen

Teems of Times, by Dominic Behan, Heinnemans

The Time of My Life, by Gay Byrne, Gill and Macmillan

The Time Out Quick Guide to Dublin, Penguin

Tread Softly For You Tread on My Jokes, by Malcolm Muggeridge, Collins

The Trial of Lady Chatterley, edited by C. H. Rolf, Penguin

Ulysses, by James Joyce, Penguin

The World of Jimmy Breslin, by Jimmy Breslin, Viking

Written on the Wind, edited by Louis MacRedmond, RTE Gill and Macmillan

The Wit of Brendan Behan, compiled by Sean Mccann, Leslie Frein

Writers and Politics – Essays and Criticism, by Conor Cruise O'Brien, Penguin

The World of Brendan Behan, by Sean MacCann, Four Square

Borstal Boy, by Brendan Behan, Corgi

Borstal Boy, the play, adapted by Frank McMahon, Four Masters

A Letter To the Sunday Telegraph From Borstal
Behan's True Character
(1ˢᵗ Published March 29, 1994)

"So much has been written of Brendan Behan, his genius and his addiction to alcohol in particular – but as the governor of a Borstal institution I had him in my charge and saw another side of his character that was positive and creditable. (Of course I always saw the good in criminals and tried to use that positively).

"Would you be surprised to know that he was an intensely religious boy? He came to me as a member of the IRA and as such was excommunicated. It worried him a great deal. He said to me one day: 'You must understand, sir, the freedom of Ireland is me second religion. I was bred to believe in and work for it'. But very often he would come and say: 'Governor, could you persuade the Father to let me to go Mass, for I feel all lost without its consolation?'

"I did ask the priest and he explained so I told Brendan and he was very sad. Then I said: 'Listen, said I am not a Roman Catholic but I'd like to go to mass with you . We'll sit together and I can't receive it for one reason and you for another but I shall say my prayers to the same god as you will.'

"Sometimes we would go to the R.C. chapel and I would play the organ and we'd sing – I'll Sing a Hymn to Mary' and 'Sweet Sacrament Divine,' and he would talk about his mother. Then came the day I was asked to report on his fitness for discharge. Now I wouldn't subject my countrymen to violence so I said: 'Brendan, I can't recommend your discharge unless you promise you won't go back to trying to kill my countrymen when you know they are already fighting an enemy. Do you see?

"The humour and wit of his character came up forthwith. 'Sure,' he said, 'I promise not to do anything until we are through with that Bastard Hitler, and after that I can always consider again, can't I?

"He never lost touch with me over the years – often by telephone at 1 a.m. , but never mind.. You may think of him as the (sic) drunkard but I remember him as the boy of 19 who wanted to serve god and who loved his mother and his country."

C. A. Joyce
Public Relations Officer
The Rainer Foundation
Ryde, Lo.W

Ends

About the author:

Frank Gray was born in San Francisco and grew up in the Bay Area. He got his first taste of the news business when he went to work in the early 1960s for the *Western Union Telegraph Company*. He later married and moved to Toronto, Canada, where he worked as a reporter for *The Canadian Press* news organization. He developed an interest in the aviation industry. This led to a position as public relations manager for Air Canada. Gray transferred to Montreal and then Vancouver in the 1970s and later moved his family to London where he joined *The Financial Times*. There he worked as a commissioning editor for the newspaper's fast developing foreign news department. In the late 1980s, he joined the *London Daily News*, launched by the late Robert Maxwell, as assistant business editor. Gray later returned to the FT, editing business newsletters. He has maintained an interest in the off-beat, writing on a range of 'lighter' subjects ranging from travel to boxing to cigars. Gray lives in Richmond-upon-Thames with his wife Carole.

www.ingramcontent.com/pod-product-compliance
Ingram Content Group UK Ltd.
Pitfield, Milton Keynes, MK11 3LW, UK
UKHW041533271224
3792UKWH00001B/13